THE OBERON ANTHOLOGY
OF CONTEMPORARY ARGENTINIAN PLAYS

T0347995

THE OBERON ANTHOLOGY OF CONTEMPORARY
ARGENTINIAN PLAYS

OBERON BOOKS
LONDON

WWW.OBERONBOOKS.COM

First published in 2019 by Oberon Books Ltd
521 Caledonian Road, London N7 9RH
Tel: +44 (0) 20 7607 3637 / Fax: +44 (0) 20 7607 3629
e-mail: info@oberonbooks.com
www.oberonbooks.com

Cover image: Pampas Landscape, La Pampa, Argentina by Foto 4440

Visit www.oberonbooks.com to read more about all our books and to buy them. You will
also find features, author interviews and news of any author events, and you can sign up for
e-newsletters and be the first to hear about our new releases.

10 9 8 7 6 5 4 3 2 1

Characters

The Making of an Anthology

The theatre translation project Out of the Wings was established in 2008 to make the riches of Spanish-language theatre known to the English-speaking world. We aimed to do this through creating a virtual environment that would generate new and diverse audiences. We wanted to be able to inform academic researchers, directors, actors, literary managers and students about the huge diversity of theatre making happening across the Spanish-speaking world. In order to do this we set out to produce different ways of getting the theatre known through, for example, seminars, readings, professional productions and publications. This has meant crossing bridges between academic disciplines and between academic research and theatre practice. The space between academic research and creative practice has always been a tense one, and we launched ourselves into it, aiming to use it productively to share, promote and model ways of working in theatre translation. This has meant the development of a collaborative approach to research, practice and dissemination, and this anthology of new dramatic writing from Argentina is the result of one such collaboration, between Out of the Wings, Programa Sur and the Argentine Embassy in the UK and the Instituto Nacional del Teatro (National Theatre Institute) in Argentina.

Since its inception in 2009, Programa Sur has aimed to heighten the awareness of Argentine literature and thinking through support for translation, with the aim of reaching new international audiences; more than 1300 works have been translated into 45 languages. The Instituto Nacional del Teatro was set up in 1997 as a result of a law that protected and promoted theatre as an activity because of its contribution to the consolidation of culture. The Instituto Nacional del Teatro has a duty to promote and support theatre activity in the country, which it does through fostering theatre spaces and centres, projects that address a wide range of questions about theatre production and theatre festivals beyond the metropolis of Buenos Aires. As part of its work, the Instituto Nacional del Teatro runs a competition for new dramatic writing, which has to date had 21 iterations, and the books are published by the Inteatro, the editorial of the Institute.

This model of creating an environment that brings together writing, performance, analysis and publication informed the initial Out of the Wings project. The theatre environment that we wanted to nourish was one that honoured the multiplicity of the theatre experience and that acknowledged and promoted the roles that theatre plays in the creative imagining of and reflection on the environment in which the plays are produced. Playwriting competitions remind us that not all plays are published, which has a limiting effect on their ability to reach wider audiences. The difficulty in publication also reinforces the play text as a minor form of literature, one that can only be understood in the space of performance and can have no independent reading. Here we have another and perennial tension: between the dramatic text as literary piece and as only existing in performance. In recent years this has become a productive tension, especially in the academy, where, speaking of Spanish-language theatre studies, there has been a growing understanding of the particular qualities of the dramatic text as a type of writing with quite different goals to prose and poetic texts. No longer, I think, is theatre perceived of as the literary 'Cinderella of the arts in Latin America', and this is important for its dissemination. The key point here is that there is no one space for the dramatic text. It moves along a continuum, which, in an ideal world, would go from published text to full production (or perhaps vice versa). This continuum would provide the means fully to appreciate the nature of transformation that the dramatic text undergoes as it moves from page to stage, or from stage to page. The printed text is important because it allows the reader to glimpse the potential for performance that is written into it.

The process of translation adds another dimension. It further reveals the complex multiplicity of the dramatic text as it is moved from one space and time to a new space and time, each one with its own peculiarities, challenges and demands. What is the new theatre environment? What is the audience for the work of a usually little-known writer? Who might the play speak to? How do you convince theatres to consider the play, which will inevitably hold financial risk? These are all questions that will eventually accompany the linguistic translation that has been undertaken. And if a performance takes place, the play will be submitted to many questions about its original space, about its language, about ideas or an imaginary that we have difficulty accessing from our context. The role of the translator is to move with the play. The translator has acquired deep knowledge of the text and understands the need to travel with it as it encounters new readers and theatre practitioners, whose role is to embody it and connect with new audiences.

So, the hope and aim is that what we are publishing here becomes the first step in a process that will see these plays read and performed outside Argentina. In the collaboration with the Instituto Nacional del Teatro we were guided by their selection of plays, which are by the three winners of the 18th and 19th National Playwriting Competition (Concurso Nacional de Obras de Teatro). Mariano Tenconi Blanco's *La vida extraordinaria* (*Extraordinary Life*), Fabián Miguel Díaz's *Pato verde* (*Green Duck*) and Leonel Giacometto's *Fonavi* won first, second and third prizes respectively in the 18th competition. And from the 19th competition, Franco Calluso's *Nou Fiuter (No Future)*, Juan Ignacio Fernández's *Poema ordinario (Poor Men's Poetry)* and Candelaria Sabagh's *Fuego de dragón sobre dragón de madera* (*Dragon Fire over Wood Dragon*) were the prize winners.

If one of the objectives of Programa Sur is to share the imaginary of contemporary Argentina with an international audience, then these plays take us on a quite extraordinary journey into some of the country's preoccupations. Set between Buenos Aires and Ushuaia, the most southerly town in the world, *Extraordinary Life* pays homage to one of Argentina's foundational texts, *Martin Fierro* by José Hernández, echoing a tale of lifelong friendship, trials and loyalty. *Green Duck* is a lyrical play, set in the estuaries of Northern Argentina, that gives voice to a little boy and the girl he loves. With tragic consequences, they insist on their right to delight in the natural world, despite the perilous exposure to the poison which afflicts their land and its people. *Fonavi* is a restless, claustrophobic work shot through with moments of surprising tenderness and humour. Through the oblique conversations of the characters we catch glimpses of some of Argentina's *desaparecidos* and of stories of secrecy, madness and desire. *Nou Fiuter* is set in a seemingly idyllic successful vineyard that somehow seems untouched by an earthquake that has ravaged a nearby city, leaving entire neighbourhoods destroyed. But the individual stories of the family are far from idyllic, the shockwaves from the disaster soon make themselves felt and the family's peace cannot escape the consequences. *Poor Men's Poetry* is set in 1982 in the town of San Pedro, beside the Paraná River (which runs through Brazil, Paraguay and Argentina). A family caught in a time warp of alcohol and regret carries on an uneasy existence. But with the unexpected return of a wayward son after years incommunicado, the traumas of his last visit, and of a family broken by depression and fear, rise once again to the surface. In the text of *Dragon Fire over Wood Dragon* the author reveals the play as a 'half romantic, half adolescent tale, a little bit sad, a little bit sexy, rather pathetic, very human'. It is a play about creativity, about identity and liminality.

Of course, short descriptions say almost nothing about the density of meaning and suggestion in a script. However, it's interesting to see the range of topics that arise from the reading of the plays, and the ways each of the plays takes us beyond the city into areas that are touched by global conditions, including, even when elliptically, the calamitous effects of climate change. Argentina, especially Buenos Aires, has a long history of theatre making and of being one of the main producers of theatre and of theatre publications in Latin America. It is a city with a street – Corrientes – that can match major North American and European cities for its vibrancy as a theatre centre, and it was long a major venue for touring companies, including for major opera companies. Over time the theatre in Argentina has developed from the late nineteenth and early twentieth-century gaucho performances and circuses of the River Plate cities of Buenos Aires and Montevideo. It has, at the same time, been shaped by the elite cultures of Europe. The massive immigration from Europe that started in the late nineteenth century had a transformative effect. It brought with it new voices, hybrid languages, disruption and integration, all of which were represented in the glorious Argentine grotesque, whose master was Armando Discepolo, the echoes of whose innovative theatre language can still be heard in some of the plays in this volume. And it is impossible to think of Argentine theatre without thinking of the role it played during the 1976 – 1983 dictatorship, when dramatists and theatre makers like Osvaldo Dragún, Carlos Gorostiza, Roberto Cossa and Griselda Gambaro created spaces to raise their voice against human rights abuses, and suffered repression, exile and the destruction of their theatre venues. Across these different periods there has been a continuity in the complex negotiation of the theatre space in a country that receives and transforms outside influence and where theatre writers and companies renew and insist on their place as creative and disruptive interlocutors for society.

Just as this volume was going to press the theatre company Global Voices joined with the Roundhouse Theatre to present a showcase of new Latin American writing, directed and acted primarily by Latinx artists in London. There was a sense of real shift in the representation of Latin American theatre in Britain, a sense that the stories could no longer be about them; they had to be by them. This has been one of the key strands of the work of Out of the Wings: to work to make theatre made in Latin America by Latin American writers known to an English-speaking audience, and in doing so to show the diversity of experiences and stories that emerge from that huge continent. The work of the translator is to open others to those experiences and realities and to bring to new audiences and readers the collective challenge to listen to those distant voices and not to impose ours. This volume is one way of responding to that challenge.

Catherine Boyle
London, November 2019

Translator Biographies

Catherine Boyle is Professor of Latin American Cultural Studies at King's College London. She was a co-founder of the *Journal of Latin American Cultural Studies*. She is Director of the theatre translation and performance project, Out of the Wings (www.outofthewings.org), and also of the Head for Heights Theatre Company. She is a translator of Spanish and Spanish American theatre and poetry, and her translations have been performed internationally. Since July 2016 she has been Principal Investigator on the project *Language Acts and Worldmaking* (www.languageacts.org), dedicated to regenerating and transforming approaches to teaching and research in Modern Languages.

Kate Eaton is a literary translator, theatre practitioner and researcher. She is a specialist in Cuban theatre and holds a doctorate from the University of London on the plays of Virgilio Piñera and the collaborative processes of translation for performance. She has translated a wide variety of plays across many different performance styles and genres. She has been a member of the Out of the Wings Translation Collective since 2016.

William Gregory trained as an actor at Drama Studio London and the Escuela Navarra de Teatro, and read Modern Languages at Trinity Hall, Cambridge. His translations include *B* by Guillermo Calderón (Royal Court), *Cuzco* by Víctor Sánchez Rodríguez (Theatre503), *Chamaco/Kiddo* by Abel González Melo (HOME, Manchester), *Villa* by Guillermo Calderón (Prime Cut, Belfast; PlayCo, New York), *I'd Rather Goya Robbed Me of My Sleep than Some Other Arsehole* by Rodrigo García (Gate, London), *The Concert* by Ulises Rodríguez Febles (Royal Court; BBC), *The Oberon Anthology of Contemporary Spanish Plays*, and several plays for the *Out of the Wings* Festival.

Rosalind Harvey is an award-winning literary translator. Her translation of Juan Pablo Villalobos' debut novel *Down the Rabbit Hole* was shortlisted for the 2011 Guardian First Book Award and the Oxford-Weidenfeld Prize, and her translation of his work *I'll Sell You A Dog* was longlisted for the International Dublin Literary Award and commended for the 2018 Valle-Inclán prize. She has worked on books by Guadalupe Nettel, Elvira Navarro, Enrique Vila-Matas, Héctor Abad Faciolince, and Alberto Barrera Tyszka, amongst others. She is a Fellow of the Royal Society of Literature.

Gwen MacKeith is a writer, editor and theatre translator, in particular of plays by the acclaimed Argentine dramatist Griselda Gambaro (1928-). She worked on the creation of the Out of the Wings theatre in translation project between 2008 and 2012. Her translation of *Los Siameses / Siamese Twins* by Griselda Gambaro was performed and published by Oberon books in 2011. She edits fiction for the arts quarterly, *Ambit Magazine.*

LA VIDA EXTRAORDINARIA / EXTRAORDINARY LIFE

MARIANO TENCONI BLANCO
TRANSLATED BY CATHERINE BOYLE

Mariano Tenconi Blanco

As an author and a director, Mariano Tenconi Blanco has produced *Montevideo es mi futuro eterno* (*Montevideo is My Eternal Future,* 2010), *Las lágrimas* (*The Tears,* 2014), *Futuro* (*Future,* 2015) and *Walsh Artista Contemporáneo* (*Walsh, Contemporary Author,* 2016). His works have been performed in a number of festivals and have received the prizes Premio Trinidad Guevara, Premio Hugo, Premio Teatro del Mundo de la Universidad de Buenos Aires, among others.

Tenconi Blanco was chosen in 2016 to participate in the prestigious International Writers Program, of the University of Iowa, the oldest residency for writers in the world. He also received the Germán Rozenmacher Prize for New Playwrighting in 2015 for his play *Todo tendría sentido si no existiera la muerta* (*Everything Would Make Sense if it Weren't for Death*). *La vida extraordinaria* has had extended runs in Buenos Aires in 2018 and 2019.

He was the regisseur for the operas *La libertad total* (Total Freedom) by Lucas Fagin, with a libretto by Pablo Katchadjian (2014); and *El malentendido* (*The Misunderstanding*), with a libretto by Fabián Panisello, based on the work by Camus, in the Centro de Experimentación del Teatro Colon (2016).

With the musician Ian Shifres and the producer Carolina Castro he makes up La Compañía Teatro Futuro.

Characters

AURORA
BLANCA

0.

Nothing. Absolutely nothing. There was no space. There was no time. There was nothing. It's impossible to imagine. But that's the way is it. There was absolutely nothing. It wasn't darkness. It was nothing. Or the universe started in nothing. It was by chance. An instant of glory. Or simply a caprice. A caprice out of nowhere. And all of a sudden a great explosion. An unimaginable explosion that lasted a millionth of a second. And in three minutes the universe was created. It takes longer to cook a boiled egg than it does to make the universe. A universe that has no limits, but it is nevertheless finite. We don't understand it but that's how it is. And then the universe got cold. Also like a hard-boiled egg. And the atom appeared. And then some gigantic clouds that formed stars and galaxies. One star was the Sun. And near the Sun some planets. One of those planets, the planet Earth. To explain the origin of life on Earth is even more difficult. Some think it was water. That the process could have taken millions and millions of years. But that life was chemically destined to be. Others think it was a small meteorite that brought substances that weren't found on Earth. That life was sowed on Earth by intelligent aliens. And others believe in God. Whatever it was that started life, it is the most extraordinary fact of biology. Perhaps the most extraordinary fact we know. It happened once. Only once. And since that time, it never stopped happening. Genetics. And evolution. And time. Every living being is an amplification. A reversion. A remix. What came after is easier. Or more or less so. Our ancestors are some form of bipod monkey. There are thousands of options. *Australopithecus, Homo erectus, Homo sapiens.* Whatever it was, we're still that monkey. There are more genetic differences between a zebra and a horse than between us and a monkey. One of those monkeys got its hands on a stone. And that was how industry started, Progress. Wars. In short: humanity. So many things had to happen for us to be here. What an enormous series of accidents. From the creation of the universe to the quantity of people who had to have sexual relations in the exact moment, or the number of wars, plagues, natural disasters, domestic accidents, military dictatorships, armed robberies, suicide attempts that a hundred people had to avoid for thousands and thousands of years so that we, right now, are here. Life. Life is one and the same. We are related to everything that has lived and everything that lives. To a bacterium. To an insect. To a fruit. To everything. All the same genetic thing transmitted from generation to generation for 4,000 million years. To have life is a miracle. To exist. Every transcendent moment and every insignificant moment. This second is a miracle. This second is a miracle. This second is a miracle. And so on forever.

1.

AURORA: I always hated the simulacrum of the self. But yet, here I am. Playing myself. I had forgotten that snow isn't white and made of cotton wool like my pupils draw it. Snow is frozen water that fills everything with mud. We've only walked about fifty metres and I'm caked up to the ankles. Also, Juan Carlos is holding my hand and, far from helping, is sliding along like an idiot and so the procession becomes slow and out of sync. It didn't matter how much I told my aunt that I preferred something intimate, she invited the whole of Ushuaia. Your father always owned the town bookshop, Aurora, everyone's going to want to come. But nobody reads in this town, Aunt. Me and my stupid irony. And the whole town, even the Mayor, and Juan Carlos waddling along like a penguin and me: the sad procession. And well, Blanca Fierro, my life-long best friend. And her mother too. I walk with a feeling as cold and ugly as the snow in Ushuaia. I don't cry. I'll cry later, for the rest of my life. I walk with a feeling in my chest, here, like a tightening. Like when you're a girl and you test how long you can go under water without breathing. I don't understand this. How can it be that people die? And me? What will I do with the rest of my life without my father? Death is the worst of life. These thoughts are going to make me cry and I want to look strong, so I breath, I look up, I think of something else. I think that in two days I'll be back in Buenos Aires. The priest talks very well. A friend of the town is leaving us, he says. People come up to me. I'm very sorry. You were always the light of his eyes. How grown up you are. They all know what to do. Perhaps this is what death is: a ready phrase, something practised, trivial. And Blanca comes up to me and looks me in the eye. And I look at her. And she winks at me and it's what my father always did and then all of a sudden I understand everything and what was always there right there appears, there. Everything that was always there is never going to be there again. My childhood. And then I hug her, and I gather my strength, and I don't cry. No catharsis. I'm not a girl anymore. My father is dead forever.

2.

BLANCA: The day starts in a commotion as always because my mother wakes me up shouting that it's late Blanca it's late. She's my mum and I love her very much, but the truth is I must say that sometimes I'm not very tolerant of her. Just have your coffee, it's late, she says, and then I just drink my coffee and I leave a bit out of sorts because of all the rush and because I haven't eaten anything. I need to eat something every three hours because if I don't, I feel bad and I can't get on with anyone for the rest of the day. It's snowing, it's snowing heavily, as if the sky wanted to unload itself because it too is sad. Here everyone loves Aurora's father. He's a very nice man. He was always making new friends. And well, now he's not going to be able to make any more friends because he's gone, hasn't he? That's so sad. Because it means there's going to be less friendship in the world. I'm sure that when someone dies and people say how sad and a great loss they mean things like this, something that's lost. Friendship makes the world better and then when people like that die, people who made the world better, then suddenly the world is a worse place because they've died. All the same I'm in the state of mind not to cry to help Aurora who I know prefers not to be crying in front of everyone, she's more about hiding her feelings, keeping her feelings for herself, or for me, she tells me and she cries, with me she does, but not in front of everyone else, no. As soon as we all started walking, I see her first amongst all the people and there were a lot. She's thin and beautiful like she always is, a bit serious but firm, and she's walking beside Juan Carlos, who's a good man but … Well yes he's good. And we walk on and we get to the church. And the priest speaks and says some prayers and then he says something very wise, it must be that the wisdom of God's taken over him, let's say, the priest who never was very bright, Father Esteban, all of a sudden he says something nice, he said that Don Osvaldo Cruz, a great friend of the people, has gone. Very true, I thought, Don Osvaldo was everybody's friend. And then all the women of the townspeople greet her one by one and I don't know, my mother's one of the first, as soon as someone dies, she's the first there. All the same, my mother really loves Aurora, and her father too, she always said Aurora's father was a good man, not like the monster you got, she always said that. And all of a sudden there's a type of gap and Aurora and I are looking at each other, she looks at me as if she's bereft, almost about to cry, and I don't know what I can say to her and I'm so clumsy that I feel a sort of tic, a sort of wink, that's what I do, I'm so stupid and she hugs me and I hug her and we cry our eyes out, I, really, I cry my eyes out. And in her ear very close so that she can hear me I say to her, your dad was very nice and a very good friend and you're a very good friend so as long as you're a very good friend your father will be alive in you. All the same she might not have heard me say that.

3.

AURORA: We have to leave in half an hour, Juan Carlos tells me. Before we go I want to see the sea, I say, and when I see that he's looking for his coat a bit confused (Juan Carlos's movements are always confused) I say NO, NO I prefer to go alone. This is mine, I say, I make him complicit. I put on my coat and start walking. By the last two blocks I almost can't move forward; I'm weak, I'm not used to Ushuaia anymore, I don't know. I walk on against the wind without knowing why. The wind's cutting through my face, I think. A saying. In fact the wind isn't cutting my face, it's producing a type of tachycardia; it's like bathing in frozen water. But all of a sudden, also, I smile. The strong wind sort of tickles me, makes me feel alive. Or makes me realise that I belong to nothing more than to this place. Even my father is the wind. And then I close my eyes and I imagine that I'm flying, that my father's taking me for a walk like before, like he always did. But not really. None of that. It's just the wind hitting me in the face and me smiling for no reason. Like almost everything. Just because. Being born just because. Dying just because. And in the middle everything. And everything the same. I get to the seashore. The blue sea. Blue like nothing else. No shades. Pure blue. Black it's so blue, white, grey. Or just blue. The wind stops me from hearing anything, but there's nothing to hear anyway. All of a sudden it's stopped snowing. Randomly, getting to the shore, the sea and the snow stopped, but not the wind. Is that even possible? To my left, in the distance, I see a black stain. Immediately I think, it'll be oil. Since childhood I've heard that there's oil here, that all that stuff about Las Islas is because of the oil; who knows. I walk towards it. Towards the oil. Suddenly it's as if I've understood so many wars and so much ambition, because the oil looks like a kind of magical mountain, black and gleaming. I took the pill for my nerves that Juan Carlos gave me and I ate almost nothing, perhaps I'm hallucinating. I'm a few metres away and to my surprise the first thing I make out are two enormous eyes, the size of my whole body. The eyes are open and expressive, calm. Yet, there's no life in them. I've never seen anything so dead in my life. But at the same time I've never seen anything as alive as that dead whale. I understand something. Everything. I don't know what it is. There is the whale. There am I. We're alive. Always. We're dead. Always. I touch it. I touch the dead whale. I greet it, I offer my condolences, I encourage it, hold on, I say, hello. How much life and how much death there is in everything. I'm not talking about the life cycle. I'm not emotionally ready to see it biologically. I'm talking about a mammal as large as five houses dead by the edge of the sea at the end of the world. I'm talking about this whole unfolding life. Its body as enormous as a train, soaked and with its open eyes. As if in all this death there was something that isn't yet dead, something infinite and inexplicable, something that unites us, this whale and me. All of a sudden, I feel my pain. I cry. With no other connotations. The pure verb. To cry. I cry. I want to hug that noble animal. There's something that I understand now that I couldn't explain. Everything is transitory and, nevertheless, definitive. This whale and I have lived in this country, in this time. And my father too.

4.

BLANCA: Blessed Virgin, I pray to you for Aurora's father, Don
Osvaldo, who I hope might rest in peace and is in heaven
with books just like he'd want, because he was a good man
and brought up Aurora who never wanted for anything and
all completely alone and here in the town he was much loved.
I also think Blessed Virgin something and it's a personal
thing. Maybe it's selfish but I thought about it, today it was.
That I, I thought, I'm not prepared yet, I'm not. Maybe when
I'm grown up, like forty, maybe, I don't know, maybe then I
will be. Or if I've already had children. Then yes. If I already
have children, then maybe. But not now. I can't. Although
sometimes I get very angry and it makes me cry. I don't want
my mother to die.

Thinking about death makes me feel bad. About my own
death. About death, your own. Because it's true, there are sad
moments and all that, there are, but I don't understand why
we have to die. Because everything that you live, and learn,
experiences, that you gather together, your experiences,
and sentimental things, like loves, and friends, that, and
all that, does it all go? How can that be? It's very very sad.
That everything should go. Dying. I don't understand it.
I hope that the soul exists. And heaven. And then we'll
all meet again there. Hello, how are you? Oh, you're here
too, hello, hello. Meeting everyone. Aurora's father, my
mother, everyone. Everyone we love all together. Like an
unbelievable birthday. Hopefully that's what heaven's like.

Hail Mary, full of grace, the Lord is with you, blessed are
you among all women, and blessed is the fruit of your womb,
Jesus. Holy Mary, Mother of God, pray for us sinners, now
and at the hour of our death, amen.

5

Buenos Aires, 22nd of April.

Dear Blanca,

I was only in Ushuaia for a short time, because of Juan Carlos's work and my classes, and we hardly saw each other and I left like someone whose blood was draining away. But you hugged me at the funeral, such a beautiful beautiful hug like only you could give me. And I don't know what it was, or yes I do, when I came back I remembered so many things from our childhood and adolescence. When did we stop being girls? At what precise moment? I still think that we're that age, though I don't know what age that would be, but definitely younger than we are now. More than that: I think that the age you become somebody's friend always sets the tone for that relationship. Just today I've been remembering when we were fifteen, do you remember? We used to practise how to kiss boys. Remembering us makes me feel good. Remembering you. And writing to you too.

Are you still writing? I've still got our first two poems, one I sent to you and your response. The one I sent to you, you've still got it, I hope. I'll transcribe them for you.

Mine said:

I want to send you my greeting
I'm not alone since our meeting
Nothing can part us, that is clear
Thank you, dear Blanca, for being near.

Yours said:

We reap what we sow
all year long, as you know.
Like the louse and the flea
friends for ever we will be.

I'm made of memories and books; what else, if not. I thought that maybe we could send each other our most recent poems. What do you think? I send you a big hug, and I love you for ever dear friend.

Aurora

6.

BLANCA: No, Aurora, no. You look like a drunk penguin.
Grace.
Style.

AURORA: The odyssey of style.

BLANCA: Don't lose your temper, follow me, don't be stupid, look. Clip clop clip clop. Let's see.

AURORA: I don't see why I'm going to need to walk if it's a dance.

BLANCA: Listen to the master, Aurora. Come on. Let's see.

AURORA: Let's see.

BLANCA: Do the clip clop. It helps. It has a purpose.

AURORA: Clip clop.

BLANCA: A little better. You look like my mother now.

AURORA: Thanks.

BLANCA: I was being ironic, Aurora, it was irony.

Let's do it again.

AURORA: Clip clop clip clop.

BLANCA: A definite improvement. Now you have to turn. If you only walk straight on it doesn't make much sense.

AURORA: I'm walking. Clip clop clip clop. I get to the end. I look over my shoulder slowly, as if I was going to tell it a few home truths , you see me, you see me, I blink, tic tic, I turn around, I leave.

AURORA: I've peed myself, Blanca.

BLANCA: Watch that mouth my mother'll hear, thank you.

AURORA: I can't manage all this together.

BLANCA: Okay, let's practise both things as if they were two different things, one at a time.

AURORA: Let's see.

BLANCA: Look at me, eh. Look right at me. See, see how I look. Seductive, see. Take note.

AURORA: More or less.

BLANCA: You need to concentrate, Aurora. Let's see, look at me. No, no. Look at me as if you didn't care.

No, Aurora, not like that. You look crazed.

AURORA: I don't know how to look, Blanca. If I think, I can't do it.

BLANCA: Don't think then.

Think about thinking something else. Think I'm thinking about something else I'm thinking about something else.

Now you're getting it, that's getting better.

AURORA: Thanks Blanca.

BLANCA: Now you have to practise the kissing bit.

Kissing.

The Kiss.

AURORA: Can I kiss you?

BLANCA: What?

AURORA: You've already kissed Alberto. You know how to kiss. Show me. Kiss me.

BLANCA: You mean us, you kiss me, us?

AURORA: Me kiss you. Yes.

BLANCA: On the mouth?

AURORA: Yes.

BLANCA: Tongues?

AURORA: With my tongue, yes.

BLANCA: No, I mean, you're very pretty, a very pretty girl, yes, but no, I think better not, I don't know, I think not me, do you understand, better not, Aurora, one short one, yes, a quick one maybe, yes.

AURORA: I was taking the mickey, Blanca, how are we going to kiss.

BLANCA: No, of course, I thought that too.

What an idiot.

Idiot!

You're learning far too quickly, I think.

AURORA: Good.

BLANCA: I'll show you how to kiss.

AURORA: Yes, I'm waiting.

BLANCA: Like this.

AURORA: All just like this?

BLANCA: Yes. Come on.

AURORA: No, it's fine. I'm fine with this information, I've got enough, thanks.

BLANCA: No, sir. You come here and you kiss me, did you hear.

AURORA: No.

BLANCA: Yes, yes.

No, as if you wanted to.

Again.

There, that's it, good, that's fine, that's good.

AURORA: Thanks, teacher.

BLANCA: What you need now is more attitude, Aurora. You're never going to kiss with that Virgin Mary face.

AURORA: And you, Virgin Mary, all because Alberto forced you to kiss him.

BLANCA: What do you mean a Virgin Mary, maybe now on the way to the dance, a prisoner will be on the run and he'll show us his prick.

AURORA: They must be disgusting those purple pricks like a hammered finger and there between their legs.

BLANCA: Would you suck one?

AURORA: Please, you saw those dogs when their prick comes out, it's disgusting.

BLANCA: But not a dog's, a man's. A man's prick. Look, look at this prick, look at my beautiful white prick.

AURORA: Get away, you wild dog.

BLANCA: Suck my prick, Aurora, come on.

AURORA: You suck my prick, Blanca, look, my prick's bigger.

BLANCA: Ay.

AURORA: I'm Alberto's prick, Blanca, hello, how are you.

BLANCA: I need a poo.

AURORA: Okay, you go and do what you have to do and then we'll go to the dance.

7.

AURORA:
Cucaracha
A cockroach
appeared in my lounge.
I looked at it.
It looked at me.
It was in the middle of the lounge.
Cockroaches have existed
since the time of the dinosaurs.
I suddenly felt the weight
of the whole history of biology
in the little slipper
I was holding in my hand.
I hit it hard.

Almost with rage.

As if it were a bigger beast.

I hit it twice.

Then I contemplated its dead body.

An explosion of rubber.

A big stain.

A nothing.

Or two.

BLANCA:

Heart

My heart is like a fire engine.

My heart is like the real end of the world.

My heart is like a virtuoso drummer.

My heart is like a sad autumn day.

My heart is like a capital letter.

My heart is like the heart of a man who loves my heart.

My heart is like giving a beautiful present.

My heart is like being a girl again.

My heart is like a great naked native.

My heart is like my heart, but yesterday's.

My heart is like my heart but better.

My heart is like my heart and nothing else.

8.

Ushuaia, 2ⁿᵈ of August.

Dear Aurora:

What joy what joy my God!

What beautiful news! What happiness! Do you know what? I'm beside myself with happiness.

And Juan Carlos? What does Juan Carlos say?

Know something I thought? Sorry if it's sad, but you know, Aurora, YOUR FATHER. He'd go crazy. Crazy. Your father would go crazy, Aurora. I'm going crazy too. I'm going crazy right now. A person like you, but tiny. Like you when you were a little girl. But no. Because really it's another person.

Two like you. The world's going to be a better place. If only there were ten like you. Or a hundred. A thousand! Or a whole world!

But it's not here yet, we know that. Seven more months to wait. It worries me. I can't imagine what it's like for you, your heart must be in your mouth. Because it's closer to you, inside you in fact. Let it come out, let it come out. I'm sure that's how you're feeling. But no. We have to wait seven more months, Aurora. And you have to enjoy it, I think. Enjoy that moment of being a pregnant woman, because that's what you are, Aurora. Ay, I say it and it doesn't seem true. We're still girls, I think. It feels like only yesterday that we met. We were five. I think that and I think that really, no, we're not girls anymore, Aurora. You're going to be a mother. Me and Alberto, that's not going so well, no. So … It's difficult … But you're fine. You're fine.

Do you know what I'm going to do? I've decided. I'm going to take on a few extra jobs that I'm not taking on right now (luxuries I allow myself) that way I'll save some money, I'll work some things out no matter what I need to do, but I'm going to go and meet your baby and see Buenos Aires. Think about all the outings we'll do. I've got some ideas about places I want to go to in Buenos Aires. I'm sure everything there is special. Here as you can imagine, everything's the same. Always. Winter and snow, freezing cold and the sun setting at four in the afternoon. And the people all the same as usual, always. And me always the same doing all the same things. I'm tired of all the housework. More than I am of my customers. Everything exhausts me, Aurorita. Everything except you, you've made me so happy you have no idea. Shall I tell you something else? I think it's going to a boy. It's a really strong hunch and it beats in my heart. A boy. Like your father. I love you with all my heart, and the new baby too.

Blanca

9.

AURORA: In the end nobody chooses to be born but someone
else does choose or rather chooses that yes someone chooses
for you to be born but that you're born I don't understand
why he's going so quickly because I need to get there but I
need to get there whole the two of us need to get there whole
how is it that all of a sudden someone you love and that was
with you your whole life goes wherever they go wherever
they go wherever they are wherever you are Dad I'd give
everything for you to be here with me and with Juan Manuel
Dad you were always infinite you're everything I am Dad I'M
OKAY YES CALM DOWN WE'LL GET THERE FINE
and that street which is it how strange that I've been living
in Buenos Aires for years and yet there's always a street that
I don't know or maybe this guy's taking me for a ride no no
I think that if I end up giving birth in his car it's worse for
him because then he has to stop to clean the car and he'll
lose fares for a few hours everyone's always thinking about
money and how to survive the thing is it costs so much to
live today so much it costs so much to be alive you set off
owing money and you wake up in the red and YES SIR I'M
CALM why is that man shouting with other men I'm getting
nervous and I've got a massive migraine coming on when did
these migraines start of course my head's really sore because
it never stops the brain never stops there's always some kind
of voice speaking to me and also perhaps that's why I'm
never totally happy because there's always a voice in my
head talking to me how pretty the lettering on the posters I'd
like to know how to draw those letters or draw people like
her how well that girl draws what a shame that she's stopped
there what a waste of talent but the thing is that when you're
a woman my belly's still aching and everything I hope he's
born healthy healthy healthy please let him be okay let
everything be okay how lovely the sun it's a sunny day I'm
going to tell Juan Manuel you were born on a sunny day I
hate AM radio stations so much and always politics politics
I don't understand what's so interesting about it all talking
all that talking why do they get so passionate about that if he
were born with a problem I've got a cold I can't understand
autumn I couldn't stand it I'm not so generous I don't know

18

maybe you say something and then do something else you never know what you'll do and I think and I think and I feel as if I'm shut inside my head but what nonsense I'm thinking not only am I not shut in but I have a person shut inside me or rather I have two because I have a person that's talking to me and really it's three because there will be a person inside my baby that will think things the baby already how incredible that a person grows inside you inexplicable it would be more normal to lay eggs I don't know other methods of not walking around with a human being inside you growing and all of a sudden they take it out from inside you as if we were Martians YES I'M FINE THERE'S NO NEED TO RUSH, YOU KNOW? I'm thinking nonsense or maybe it's fear could it be happiness? Could it be the happiness we're all looking for? Maybe when someone comes out from inside you that's happiness or maybe not or maybe it is but everything goes on as always only with the same happiness there that is a child of yours that's going to be yours for ever for ever because we're all afraid of being left alone and then all of a sudden there's someone who's going to love you for ever my fingers are feeling so cold especially my hands like if I had to touch something I wouldn't know how to touch it, it's as if my hands were strange to me I hope there's not long to go I can't stand it much more I can't stand my thoughts I can only think about this about the baby ay, it's coming out! I CAN'T HOLD ON SIR ARE WE NEARLY THERE YET? It hurts it hurts it hurts I'm so nervous it hurts WHEREVER YOU CAN SIR if only he were here to hold me or her and they'd give me a hug and that's the thing that at the end they give you a hug giving birth is the most real thing in the world it hurts it hurts and this head that won't stop how scary it all is everything yes.

10.

BLANCA: That bizarre creature what is it?

AURORA: I don't know what that is.

BLANCA: It's really disgusting, so it is.

AURORA: It is.

BLANCA: Why do they bring those beasts here?

AURORA: What do you want them to show in a zoo, paintings?

BLANCA: Paintings would be better than those screwed-up monsters, Aurora.

AURORA: Whose idea was it to come to the zoo?

BLANCA: No, well.

AURORA: No, well?

BLANCA: Who asked to come to the zoo?

BLANCA: I did, Aurora, I asked to come, don't ask me those pointed questions, who was it? Who was it? Like you ask your little pupils, see, I'm grown up, me, see.

AURORA: I won't, okay, but you're insufferable, Blanca.

BLANCA: You're right, okay, let's look at another animal, maybe I'll get over it.

AURORA: Okay.

BLANCA: I like giraffes.

AURORA: Giraffes?

BLANCA: Yes.

AURORA: How do you know?

BLANCA: I know.

AURORA: Oh yes? You've seen a lot of giraffes?

BLANCA: I've seen one or two, yes.

AURORA: Running around Ushuaia, in the snow, you've seen giraffes.

BLANCA: Yes.

AURORA: A giraffe.

BLANCA: Yes.

The one with the neck.

AURORA: Maybe I'm being a bit annoying, Blanca, you'll have to forgive me. Juan Manuel is out of control and I get half a night's sleep, if I'm lucky. He's a tornado, that child. All the same, take note, I don't like the cliché of the suffering mothering. But Juan Manuel, you've no idea.

BLANCA: Yes, I'm not feeling all that great either. I've finally broken up with Alberto. We broke up. It's over.

AURORA: I still remember the first time you were with Alberto.

BLANCA: Aurora!

AURORA: What? Let go of my arm, Blanca, you're crushing me.

BLANCA: Look, Aurora!

AURORA: An elephant.

BLANCA: What an incredible thing!

AURORA: What a beautiful animal!

BLANCA: It's a huge elephant, Aurora.

AURORA: *Loxodonta africano.*

That's what it says here.

The African elephant from the savannah or *Loxodonta africano* is a proboscides mammal from the family of the elephants. It is the biggest terrestrial mammal in existence at present.

BLANCA: That's clear, Aurora, of course. The biggest mammal on the planet, for sure.

AURORA: Terrestrial.

BLANCA: Look at it. It's like a universe in itself that animal. Can you imagine if each one of us was a universe in ourselves? The world would look very different, no, life, I mean, would be very different.

AURORA: It says: African elephants from the savannah are notably intelligent animals. In fact, experiments on reasoning and learning carried out on them indicate that they are the cleverest *afrotherias* that exist along with Asian apes. This is, in large measure, as a result of their large brain, home to the famous 'memory of an elephant'.

BLANCA: Memory of an elephant, yes.

AURORA: The herds are exclusively formed by the females and their daughters, and one of the female adults leads them.

BLANCA:

Anxiety

I put the rabbits in my vagina. The sheep. The goats. I put
my bed, my house. I put all my customers' clothes. I put my
Singer sewing machine. My Singer in my vagina. Working.
I put my working Singer. I put my mother in it. Yes. In
my vagina. I put all the guys I like. I put all of Ushuaia.
The church, the Town Hall, the square. I put the whole lot.
Ushuaia. All of it. I put all the wind, all the snow, everything.
All of it in my vagina. I put all of Argentina. I can't stop
putting things inside me.

AURORA:

TWO

An unremarkable mechanics.

Two dogs fornicating.

In the middle of the street,

in the full light of the day.

The dominant one bites.

It's clumsy.

It overacts.

It's anxious.

It doesn't know much.

The passive one isn't enjoying it.

It doesn't suffer.

It doesn't care.

It just lets it happen.

It does it for the sake of it.

It's incredible

that all the love in the world

depends on such a vulgar exercise.

BLANCA: You've no idea, Aurora, how strange it must be being
the masculine body of a man. And I'm not just saying that
for the sake of it, you know, although Alberto you've no idea,
looks like a fox, thick hair, and coarse to the touch, rough
hands, he's strong but medium height, as if he's compressed,
he's hard wherever you touch him he's hard hard, and me
the first thing I asked him was to grab my breasts and Alberto
grabbed them really hard like when they look for a puncture
on your bicycle tyre, like that, he grabbed really hard, I didn't
like it, it wasn't like I imagined. Then we kissed, he had that
really ugly taste of tobacco, I didn't want to kiss him any more
but I thought better of it, because I want to do it, how much
longer am I going to wait, I'm like that, see, I get anxious, ever
since I found out that it existed I don't know, at twelve, I've
wanted it to happen for once and for all so that I know what it
is and that's it, because no matter how much it was explained
to me I couldn't work out what it was really like. So, then I
said okay we'd better get on with it, let him put it in me, so
then I'll find out what this sex stuff is all about, so then I took
everything off, because he's so clumsy he'd most likely tear
my clothes. His prick was long and had a strange shape at the
end, and black, or grey, it was grey, and Alberto started to put
it in me and he couldn't and he couldn't then at some point I
thought uy don't say we're not going to do anything, I thought,
it put me in a bad mood, then I said let's see Alberto, that's
what I said to him, let's see Alberto, like saying, see, you're
hopeless, because the prick's his not mine, so, I got hold of his
prick and I sort of jumped on it, hard, a few times, and all of
a sudden it sort of started to go into me, the prick, to go into
me, and I started liking it, it hurt me, and I was shouting, and
Alberto was breathing more heavily, umm umm, he was going,
and I even liked Alberto breathing heavily, and Alberto's prick
was inside me and it was as if my organs were turning, and I
felt damp inside, like soaked with blood and oil, my oil, funny,
and as if my legs were relaxing, and as if inside in my organs
there was some type of activity, something happening inside
me that the prick must have been causing, the prick in contact
with my whole body, and all of a sudden I sort of looked at the
ceiling and I felt that the ceiling was opening and the wind

was carrying me away flying and I was flying all over Ushuaia with Alberto's grey prick inside me, that's how I felt, beautiful Aurora, you've no idea, and well, the fantasy was cut short because I see Alberto coming out of me, and he's taking out his tiny prick, half of the size it was before, and half red, or reddened, it was my blood, and Alberto looks at me and cleans himself, that's me he says, that's me?, as if he didn't want seconds of dessert, that's me. I was dirty, but I wasn't disgusted, no the absolute opposite. I felt as if we'd only just begun. As soon as I can I'm going to try again, you'll see.

13.

Ushuaia, 3rd of June.

Dear Aurora:

Mum's not well. She seems really ill. It's her stomach. Something's not working properly. It looks as if it's not minor. She's so stubborn about never wanting to go the doctor, and now when we went, she's lying on the stretcher, as white as a sheet, she had to confess that she'd been having a pain in her stomach for a while and she couldn't stand it anymore. And she looked at me with sad eyes, she never has sad eyes, and she looked at me like that, scared, and she said, it looks as if I'm in a really bad way, my girl.

I'm really worried. It seems that it's not the stomach that's the problem, it's the colon. They're doing tests. We spend our time at the hospital. I've got something to tell you: on the way back from Buenos Aires I wrote a poem about the town and sent it to a newspaper here and they're going to publish it, they said: 'it's going to be published', that's what they told me, and I thought one thing, maybe you'll work this thought out better than me, I thought about where poetry stands in relation to a medical analysis, for example, that tells you you've had it. Where does it stand? Because no matter how pretty a poem might be if there's a letter that tells you that you've had it, from a doctor, then what? That's what I was thinking. About literature. About life. About death.

Pray for us. Even though you don't believe. Pray.

A kiss,

Blanca

14.

AURORA: I don't believe it, Juan Carlos, how you can be so disrespectful of other people's wishes.

No, Juan Manuel isn't even a year old, he can't ask you for anything.

Don't make fun of me, Juan Carlos.

No, first, first, I didn't shout at you. I'm speaking to you seriously but I didn't shout. And second this has got nothing to do with your personality.

Yes. I'll let you talk.

Talk then. On you go.

Have you finished? No, no I'm not being ironic. Then you'll tell me that I don't let you talk, Juan Carlos, when I don't know if you've finished or not.

No, Juan Carlos. There's nothing to discuss. We're not getting a dog.

Yes, that is the problem, exactly. That it's already here.

I don't want to look at it.

I've got a sad face too, you look at me.

No, you know what the thing is? It's a rhetorical question, you don't have to answer. The thing is that I was teaching and writing and now I've been shut inside for a year looking after a baby and on top of that you bring me a dog. That's the thing.

I'm not a bad mother I'm a good mother. But I'm also other things, Juan Carlos, things that you don't respect. I don't want to be just a mother.

Like all our discussions, it always seems like it's about one thing when it's really about everything else.

No, it's not about the dog, but the dog isn't staying.

What liberties?

No, Juan Carlos. No.

So, let's see, what would that be like?

Do you swear you're not going to change your mind later?

Okay, I want two nights a week.

Every week.

That's my business.

Some … some meetings … literary groups, they're …

Thank you, Juan Carlos. You're an understanding man.

Well, let it in then.

It's not an ugly animal.

No, don't let it jump on me, I'm scared of it.

There were never dogs in my house. My mother didn't like them and my father respected her, even in death.

What's it called then?

It hasn't got a name?

I'll name it.

Ulysses.

15.

BLANCA:

Ushuaia

Here the wind is like a president that tells us everything we do.

Here it's day all day long or night all day long.

Here people barely speak.

Here there is a club that puts on dances and it's called the Defenders of Ushuaia.

Here the stars are like many Ushuaias hanging from heaven but with much more light than the real Ushuaia.

Here men taste of grease or of damp.

Here people mend their clothes and never buy new.

Here we're always the same people in the same places.

Here there are secrets but they're things that have no importance.

Here there's nothing to do except say what there is here.

Here I was a girl.

Here is like this and I am from here and from nowhere else.

Blanca Fierro, published in the Diario La Gaceta de Ushuaia on the 5th of June.

16.

BLANCA: Yes No Yes I don't see the necessity for this noise which is driving me crazy yes it is Mum I'm calm Mummy yes it's all going to be fine give me your hand are you cold Mummy? What cold how cold it is in here and me without a bra what an idiot I am what a brute I'm careless how idiotic worrying about me and she's blue and I'm not strong she is but not me and she's tough she keeps going and keeps going NO MUM THERE'S NOTHING WRONG NO NO YOU'RE NOT GOING TO DIE MUM NO NO NO NO DON'T CRY PLEASE DON'T CRY PLEASE DON'T CRY I can't go on like this I can't go on if she falls I'll fall she's dying of the cold of course I brought her out with only one slipper on what an idiot I am or maybe she lost it when we were getting her into the car and how strange that she didn't say anything I don't understand why this journey's taking so long if we're near the hospital IT'S OKAY we're here WE'RE HERE MUM here's her slipper how tiny she is much smaller than me YES WE'RE ALREADY HERE YES what could that house be I see through the window the pink house and that pink sky it must be seven in the evening because at this time of the year the sun sets pink and it starts disappearing at least when autumn begins I can't stop thinking pure nonsense but I mean what else do you want and also what an idiot speaking to myself as if I were two maybe it's because I feel lonely maybe HERE I AM MUM YES I'LL GET YOU WATER NOW it's solitude that turns you half mad maybe HERE WE ARE MUM WE'VE ARRIVED YES BE STRONG BE STRONG I'LL HELP YOU YES I'M SMALL BUT I'M STRONG THAT'S HOW MUM TAUGHT ME COME ON MUM COME ON I'm okay I'm okay now I'm strong that's the way it is that's how it has to be I'M HERE MUM YES IT'S ALL GOING TO BE OKAY NOW THOSE DOCTORS WILL TAKE AWAY THE BAD THING YES I hope she doesn't cry again because I can't I can't I've never seen such a pink sky as today I bet wasting time with those idiots I'll miss it maybe YES MUM I'M CALM YES I KNOW and maybe you telling me to be calm makes me more nervous because I know that you know and that I know that you're going Mum and I don't want you to and I can't I always thought about what this day would be like when we'd come to the hospital because I knew this was going to happen and yet why do some of them wear blue and others green how strange it is here that it seems as if it was always like this and this smell this smell what is it that produces this hospital smell like medicine or mash which is the smell of people dying it's what death smells like DI SANTO ROSA IS MY MOTHER'S NAME YES HERE I HAVE A TEST THAT THEY DID ALREADY I don't understand why you have to queue in hospital like wait wait wait always I don't understand YES MISS I'LL WAIT HERE I don't understand anything maybe I don't why is that woman shouting? What's happening to her? It hurts it hurts. YOU DON'T HAVE A BED? I hurt all over madam this YES THE WAITING ROOM YES if I had a lot of money I'd take a space ship to another planet where people never got ill and lived for years or all of a sudden got

bored or tired because that can happen well their lights go
out like a fridge being unplugged to defrost and when they
want to return they turn them on and there they are and
now it's colder in here than outside EXCUSE ME MADAM
PLEASE yes MUM COME HERE WE'RE GOING
TO THE WAITING ROOM SLOWLY YES calm calm
Blanquita that man's really good-looking what an idiot I'm
like a fifteen-year-old girl SLOWLY YES HELLO MISTER
BLANCA YES MY MOTHER ROSA CLAU CLAUD
CLAUS CLAUS AH KA KLAUS YES YES THANKS YES
MUM'S GOING TO THE WAITING ROOM I remember
Norway-Oslo PUT ON CLAUST'S JACKET MUM YES

17.

AURORA:
Ulysses
I have a dog.
It's called Ulysses.
It wasn't my idea,
My husband brought it home.
And now this dog is indispensable to me.
It looks sort of side-on.
Or smells the air.
It's existence in the raw.
It's a world of plenty.
This dog is my source of energy.
He is electricity,
and I am the lamp that lights up the house.
He helps me through my daily catastrophe.
Ulysses is my love this year.
He is real purity.
Everything and nothing.
The non-metaphor.
I at times am a bit melodramatic.
He simply lives.
So now I'm standing.
And I say Ulysses.

And he comes running.
We've got time.
We've got time enough.

18.

BLANCA: I say to him Hello Klaus and he says to me hello miss
my name is Klaus. And I say to him yes Klaus, the other day
you told me that you were called Klaus and that you were
from Norway. And he says to me Klaus Henriksen from
Norway. I say to him Blanca, like the colour white. He says
Blanco and I say no, Blanca, with an a. Blanca. Planca says
he. I say Blanca and he says Planca and me Blanca and him
Planca. And I say to him. How are things, Klaus? And he says
sorry but my Spanish is not good. And I say but it is, your
Spanish is outstanding. And he looks at me, it's clear that he
doesn't understand outstanding. Then he says I'm a marine
biologist, I come Yujuaiah to study species of animals from
here and compare with Norway. And I say but here in the
hospital there are people not animals, Klaus. And he says that
here in the Hospital they lend to me instruments. Instruments
he said. As he if was a musician. I laughed. But respectfully.
And he laughed too. What are you laughing about, Klaus.
And him: since you have laughed, ha, ha, ha, since you
have laughed. I was happy. I don't know why. Then he stops
himself laughing and he says how's your mother? And I say
no, Klaus, no, no, no, it's very very difficult with Mum. And
he puts his hand on mine, and I grab it, and he puts his other
hand on top, making a sandwich of my hand, and he says Be
strong, Planca. And his eyes were watering, a tear was falling
over his very very blond beard. I cried too. We'd only been
friends for five minutes and we'd already laughed and cried
together. It was a lot more than in the three years with Albert.
That's what I was thinking.

19.

AURORA: 19th de June: This is not a secret diary. This is terror.
Manifest terror. The attempt to domesticate terror through
language. I must be honest: I'm in love with a man. He's a

30

writer in the writing groups I go to. He's a tall strong man, with black hair and a black beard, a full mouth, he dresses formally – with shirt and pullovers – and at times he puts the colours together badly. His name, paradoxically, is Ulysses. I already loved a Ulysses. A dog. And now this. An aberration of a duplication. This Ulysses is not a dog. This Ulysses is the Devil. I haven't slept for three nights. My son doesn't deserve this. Neither do my students. And well, there's Juan Carlos. Love is a monster. A monster that only produces horror and sadness. Why is this happening to me? Why me?

20.

BLANCA: I want him to love me. I want him to fall in love with me. To love me madly. To say Blanca. Blanca, when he dreams. To say it properly, for once and for all. Not Planca. Blanca. Just like that. With an emphasis on the Bbb. Like the teacher. I want him to touch his prick thinking about me, to imagine me pulling my pants down and him saying Bbblanca baby come on top of me look how hard I am baby, or something like that in his own way. It's got to work out for me some time. Once, for Christ's sake. Let this guy fall in love with me. Love me. Really love me. It's not a lot to ask, damn it. For him to say how much I love her. How I love Blanca. Or say it half in Norwegian like he talks. Planca I love you so much Planca. I don't know how he'd say it. But he should say something. Something beautiful. That he loves me. He'd say to me: I want for you to speak to me. And he'd grab my wrist and say: I'm mad about you can't you see. I want him to go mad for me. Squeeze me. Touch my tits. Ask me to do dirty things. Have an endless hard-on. Look at me and say ay how I love you like fuck. Rob my pants from my drawer. Watch me pee after sex. I want us to brush our teeth together. I want him to wake up with a hard-on every morning. Look at me with pride. Cry sometimes because he loves me so much. And I say what a wimp that Norwegian is. But I say it to look good, because really I'd love him. I love him. I love you Klaus. Incredible son of a bitch. I love you. Love me too. Come on. God, just once. Once, give me it. Come on. Klaus. Fuck. Come on God. I deserve it. Yes that's it. Now. Now.

AURORA: 22nd of July: Today I told Ulysses 'I'll have a coffee with you'. He said why don't we walk, because he has the spirit of a flâneur. And I said 'no, no walking, Coffee or nothing' and so we had a coffee. The evening was short but correct. We talked about books, as always. When we were saying goodbye, Ulysses said to me, 'you know that I've fallen in love', and I said 'with what?'. He smiled and closed the door of my taxi.

3rd of August: I went out for a walk with Ulysses the dog and I realised that I'd like to walk with the other Ulysses. But I also realised something more important: the love of Ulysses the dog is the perfect love. Juan Carlos's is so calm it's boring. Ulysses's produces so much anxiety in me that it's bad for me. While Ulysses the dog is demonstrative, noble, loyal, affectionate. Why don't humans love like dogs? If we were better we'd be better.

8th of August. Today I saw Ulysses. I told him that I was going to Ushuaia for a few days because of a problem with my friend Blanca. Then we walked. For hours. He knows my situation. He also knows that we shouldn't be late but nevertheless it got late. At dinner time I announced, well, 'I'm going to get a taxi, Ulysses' and he took me by the hand, very sure, and he kissed me long and deep. I kissed him shyly, a bad kiss. I acted liked a girl. For dinner I made sausages and mash. That simple dish is Juan Carlos's favourite.

22.

BLANCA: It's as if Mum's suspended. She's hanging by a thread. I'm beside her with my head full of useless things. Yet I love being able to look after her. She's very thin. I've put a little seat in the shower and then I slowly wash her back with a sponge. She never complains about anything. She lets me bathe her slowly, wash her hair, dry her. Well, the truth is that she does complain a bit about her food. What I cook for her she eats reluctantly and what they cook for her in the hospital she leaves half-eaten and says 'it tastes of nothing'. And she's right, I've tried it and it tastes of nothing.

This is sad and maybe it's me that's trying to find the good
in all of this and maybe there's no good, there's nothing nice
about it. But the thing is that sometimes I feel as if I'm giving
her something back, I don't know, something. That somehow
I'm looking after her, bathing her, feeding her. And the circle
closes. Life. One of life's wisdoms. A bit sad but that's the
way it is. You have a baby and you look after it and you know
that in the end that baby's going to grow up and you'll be
old and that baby will look after you and won't abandon you
no matter what. It's nice. That. The loyalty between mother
and daughter. My case. And I also think that I'd like to have
a daughter. And it'll be sad that Mum won't know her. That's
going to make me sad. But that's the way life is, the cycle of
life. I'm going to be with Mum until God takes her away.

23.

AURORA: 'There is nothing more beautiful than the plane
landing in Ushuaia, my daughter', her father always said to
her. The noise of the plane is deafening. She looks through
the window. She thinks: death is the end of the metaphor.
She thinks: death can't be expressed through other concepts.
She thinks: everything is dying all the time. She thinks: death
is death. The only reality. And while she thinks things her
son wakes up. Being born is real. As real as dying, at the
very least. Or maybe more. And Juan Manuel was born.
Juan Manuel is real. Juan Manuel is more real than death.
If death and Juan Manuel were to fight, for example, and
remember Juan Manuel is just a baby, but still if death fought
Juan Manuel, Juan Manuel would be bound to win. But she
doesn't think this. Because she thinks with words. And words
don't mean anything. Nothing means anything. Except that
electricity, the electricity that comes from the eyes and the
heart. That doesn't have a word. The noise of the plane is
deafening. The plane is on its descent. It feels as if it's going
to miss. The town is in miniature. The airport tiny. The plane
seems enormous, much bigger than the town. It should be
the other way around. Ushuaia should land on the plane.
Ushuaia could fly, with all the wind there is. Fly and off.
Fly off. Somewhere else. To Buenos Aires, for example. But
Ushuaia doesn't fly. Juan Manuel does, Juan Manuel flies,

it's his first journey by plane and yet he's not nervous. The little toy plane wanting to land on the little toy runway. It'll be familiar, someone playing with little toys like he does. He doesn't know that this is real. As real as everything else. The noise of the plane is deafening. The plane descends. "There is nothing more beautiful than the plane landing in Ushuaia, my son' Aurora says to Juan Manuel. There's nothing original. The only original thing is everything.

24.

AURORA: Here I am.

BLANCA: What I needed, you know, was for you to come and give me a hug.

AURORA: How are you?

BLANCA: I don't know, she was suffering.

AURORA: Yes.

BLANCA: But I don't understand what comes now, you know? I don't understand what comes now.

I lived my whole life with her, you know? And now I say to myself: and now? That's what I'm saying. And now? No?

Yes.

That's it.

Listen, Aurora, I've got something really shocking to tell you that my mother just told me, when she was really ill.

Come, come over here.

AURORA: Here?

BLANCA: My mother said we're cursed, Blanquita. With men. We're cursed. A good man is difficult to find, she said.

AURORA: And she's right.

BLANCA: I'm going to tell you something, she says, I'm going to tell you something that you don't know, that's what she said. And she says the thing is that you weren't born in Buenos Aires because we were passing through like I told you, she says, you were born in Buenos Aires because we WERE

FROM Buenos Aires, your father and me. I thought okay, it'll just be that she's weak, poor thing, and she's talking this nonsense. But no. Listen Aurora, listen, because she tells me, she says to me, listen Blanca, and she lets it all out.

AURORA: What?

BLANCA: Well, she says, the thing is your father, well your father didn't leave you. Your father was a good father. He was a *dotor*, she says, she says *dotor*, you see, you know. And she says, he was younger than me. And she starts to tell the story. When I met him your father was studying medicine and so that he could study and not work I worked. He graduated with a good degree, she tells me, and then you were born soon after. And we were earning a lot, yes, she says, it looked as if everything was going fine. The thing is that we were doing fine, she says, because your father was doing something that wasn't allowed, she says. It seems that he was getting rid of the babies of the mothers who didn't want to have them. Aurora, I was frozen to the spot, you know, with all of this.

AURORA: And him?

BLANCA: Who?

AURORA: Blanca.

BLANCA: Come on, there's more, Aurora, there's more. Don't be impatient. Well, it was all going well for them, I've told you that.

AURORA: And he was doing something that was forbidden.

BLANCA: How do you know that?

AURORA: You told me.

BLANCA: When? I never knew, Aurora.

AURORA: Now, now, you've just told me.

BLANCA: Just now?

AURORA: That he got rid of the babies.

BLANCA: Shh. Yes. Yes. It seems that what this man who it now seems is my father, what he did was that the babies that the mothers who didn't want to have, he made it happen that they weren't born and he charged for it, he charged a lot, and well, they caught him. It seems that one mother had

35

complications, well, she wouldn't be a mother if she didn't have it, or would she?

AURORA: It doesn't matter.

BLANCA: It doesn't matter, of course. It seems that this woman suffered complications and well, she died.

AURORA: And?

BLANCA: No, well yes, he was reported and went to prison.

AURORA: Here?

BLANCA: There.

AURORA: But he came to prison here?

BLANCA: Obviously.

AURORA: It's not obvious.

BLANCA: No.

AURORA: So?

BLANCA: They sent the guy to jail here. The Church, you see, my mother told me. And then, she says, we had to sell everything in Buenos Aires, the house, everything we had, it seems she had a house and all, well, and that my mother sold everything and came here.

AURORA: And the guy? This doctor, your father.

BLANCA: You're fast, Aurora, you are, eh, fast, fast, you, yes, me, you, you got it, you got it in seconds.

But wait. It doesn't finish there. There's something else. It seems that one day, are you following me?

AURORA: Yes, yes.

BLANCA: Then one day, it seems that once my mother turns up at the prison like just out of the blue to take him food or money or something like that and that well when my mother gets there the guy's with another woman. Well, scandal, it seems that my father had been with this other woman for a while and he was going to leave my mother when the accident happened and well that this woman loved him and had managed to get money together to come and see him here in Ushuaia, it seems.

AURORA: No, no, no …

BLANCA: Yes, Aurora. Yes.

> And well, that's it. Yes. So my mother said that's the end of that bang you're dead and well but now she's dying because I know that I'm dying Blanquita I can see it in your eyes she says, that killed me, well, she says that this was the moment and that better spill the beans, that's what she said, so coarse saying spill the beans and with a doctor I thought, too, I thought all that.

AURORA: And the doctor?

BLANCA: Which one?

AURORA: Your father?

BLANCA: What father?

AURORA: The doctor, the one in prison, Blanca!

BLANCA: Don't get worked up, I didn't realise that you were talking about my new father, Aurora.

AURORA: And don't you want to meet him?

BLANCA: No, I thought not.

AURORA: Anyway there's no knowing where he was transferred when they closed the prison.

BLANCA: No.

AURORA: Do you want to meet him?

BLANCA: But I already have a father, Aurora.

25.

AURORA: When you've finished you have to say *over, over*.

BLANCA: What, Aurora?

AURORA: When you've finished you have to say over, over.

BLANCA: Are you listening, Aurora?

AURORA: Say over Blanca, for God's sake, over.

BLANCA: Over!

AURORA: And to know if you've been heard you say copy that. Over.

BLANCA: I don't understand why on this thing you say everything differently from in real life and on the telephone you say it all the same ... Over.

AURORA: Because here you press to speak, I explained it to you, don't be difficult, Blanca, eh. Over.

BLANCA: I've got nothing to say to you. Over!

AURORA: Stop shouting over, over.

BLANCA: Uh, uh, Aurora can you copy that? Aha. I surprised you, eh?

AURORA: Blanca, this sector's empty. Over.

BLANCA: I don't understand what we're talking about, over.

AURORA: I think the house is empty. Over.

BLANCA: Well, come over here where I am which is in the dining-room and there's nobody here, over.

AURORA: I'm on my way, over and out.

BLANCA: There's nobody there.

AURORA: No, there's nobody there.

BLANCA: Like a transatlantic liner.

AURORA: I don't understand.

BLANCA: It was an example.

AURORA: An example is a ghost.

AURORA: I can't see a thing, Blanca.

BLANCA: When I was a girl, I half believed that I had the gift of seeing in the dark, you know, but then I didn't, later on I didn't.

AURORA: Keep your voice down, Blanca.

BLANCA: There's supposed to be nobody here, why do we need to speak quietly, will you tell me?

AURORA: I'm terrified of bumping into something.

BLANCA: You're really clumsy, so you are, look how you're carrying that torch. You're bashing it about all over the place.

AURORA: I'm no good at this.

BLANCA: All you have to do is point the beam.

AURORA: And that's it, it's all so easy.

BLANCA: I also think you cut out your mask badly.

AURORA: Oh, she's the expert and we all do it wrong.

BLANCA: I'm already like my mother.

AURORA: I think I did cut it out badly. This eye's at the level of my nose. It's strange.

BLANCA: Maybe you cut it properly and it's your face that's strange.

AURORA: You're really wicked sometimes, eh.

BLANCA: We're in the living room, now. Let's sit down.

AURORA: Are we going to wait for this man sitting on his sofa?

BLANCA: These shoes I'm wearing pinch like hell.

AURORA: Did you come to traipse around a house in new shoes?

BLANCA: I came to see my father in new shoes.

AURORA: You're right.

BLANCA: What's wrong with you?

AURORA: I'm giving you a hug.

BLANCA: That's a lampshade, Aurora.

AURORA: I can't see anything.

BLANCA: Touch.

AURORA: If I can't see I can't feel.

BLANCA: The shoes aren't brand new. I got them from a client. A customer whose shoe size is thirty-six. But they pinch like hell.

AURORA: Don't take them off because then you'll not be able to find them in the dark.

BLANCA: He might be late.

AURORA: And …

BLANCA: If he doesn't come?

Can you imagine?

Imagine that something's happened to him and he doesn't turn up. That he died. Yes. That he got out and he fell apart and now he's breathing his last in the waiting-room of a hospital, now, at this precise moment. And me here waiting for him. Me waiting for a dead father that I never knew. Poor wretched me.

AURORA: Look, calm down, you're overcome with dark thoughts.

BLANCA: I'm a dark person, Aurora, the thing is that with you I'm a different person.

AURORA: Different? Different how?

BLANCA: Different, Aurora, different.

I BECOME STRONGER WITH YOU.

AURORA: The door, Blanca, the door!

BLANCA: No! Yes!

AURORA: Yes!

BLANCA: Hello.

You must be Emilio Fierro. A doctor. Doctor Fierro. Well Doctor Fierro I want you to stay calm. This is not an attack. No. Don't let the outfits deceive you.

I

am not a burglar.

I

am not a revolutionary.

I

am your daughter.

26.

AURORA:
Love
White pollen of worlds, sweet milk of ice

I wish to free you like a thing from the skies.
Oh to be a butterfly gigantic and divine
To plunge my head in your dust sublime!

The blood boils, a liquid of fire
It bursts from my lips and feigns desire.
Longing from the skies, yet what I would give
so that on my head that milk might drip.

Aurora Fierro, published in the *Diario La Nación* on 20th of
August

27.

BLANCA: Day 1: The place is fabulous like a fabulous dream. I
kept saying like a madwoman ayitsincredibleayitsincredible.
Klaus not a word. Looking at the icy planet like a silent lion.
I don't know why I was wearing clothes that belonged to her.
I hadn't even touched them before. And yet I brought them
for this journey. As if I was wearing them for the first time. As
if I was disguising myself as my mother for the first time now
that she's dead. Maybe I felt that the place was like heaven
and maybe that's why I wore those clothes. This place is like
a fantasy place. I said to Klaus, 'hey Klaus this place is like
a fantasy place' and he said 'no, this place is great Planca'. I
laughed but he didn't. The Antarctic is beautiful in its own way.

AURORA: 30th of August: Meeting again. It was all a mistake.
Ulysses invited me to his apartment. I said no, what was
he thinking of. He said, 'I want to fuck you', I slapped him,
turned around and left.

BLANCA: Day 5: It turns out that Klaus is wagging the tail of half
the planet, because the Norwegian Polar Institute sent him to
see if they could put a base here. Because it seems that lots of
countries have bases. We stayed at a North American base.
So Klaus spends his time speaking to the Americans and I
know hardly any English. But I watch and I learn things.
Klaus doesn't say anything to me. He only talks to me when
we get up and before we go to sleep. This morning he said
'when I small my Grandfather read me the Odyssey so I love

the world'. In reality it's always morning, because it's summer and it's daylight for 24 hours.

AURORA: 5th of September: I don't know what it is, that feeling they call Love. What I feel is a combination of some marvellous feelings and other ones that are dreadful, all together undifferentiated. I realise that I am writing all this not to write what really happened. I went to bed with Ulysses and it was unforgettable. With Juan Carlos it was always correct, I can't say that it wasn't. But well. This is what happened. I agreed to visit Ulysses's apartment. It's an old building. The apartment is small and the only things in it are books, a type-writer and a bed. Ulysses read me a book by a poet from Corrientes, a friend of his. When he finished reading he said: the future of Argentine literature is surrealism, and he started kissing me. Then he took out his penis and put it in my mouth without a word. I'd never done that. With Juan Carlos, never. I started to kiss his penis as if the penis itself was a new boyfriend and I was kissing him passionately. I liked it. Kissing his penis was like kissing his soul. 'This prick is yours, do what you want with it', he said. Prick, mine? It sounded strange to me. Belonging to a woman. Then he said to me, 'read poetry to me and don't stop', and while I was sucking his penis I was reciting ' I want to captivate your desperation, oh monkey farewell; you tremble so much in your dark islands oh monkey farewell'. Then he pushed me against one of the bookshelves and he penetrated me. It was intense, short and profound. We came together. Then we hugged, as if we'd scored a goal. Then he kissed me and looking me in the eyes he said, 'Aurora you're for real'.

28TH OF SEPTEMBER: Ulysses I thought about killing you today. Why do you exist? Then I thought about leaving my husband and son and running away with you. Then I thought about suicide.

1ST OF OCTOBER: Ulysses left me. He's an imbecile.

BLANCA: Day 12: Today was an important day. Klaus took me to see some seals. They're called Weddell seals. They're grey with little black faces. And it seems that these seals dive very deep in the sea. Then Klaus showed me his little trick, 'Come

here, put your ear here' he said. And he put his ear against
the ice, as if he was listening behind a door. I pressed my ear
against the ice and it was incredible. There was this incredible
music. It's as if robots were making music. But they weren't
robots. They were seals.

AURORA: 2nd of Ocober: I'm going to abuse my body, and know
what, it's all because of you. I'm going to take a mountain
of tranquilisers and a bottle of cheap cognac that I've just
bought at the supermarket. I'm going to turn myself inside
out. It's all over for me. It's done.

5TH OF OCTOBER: The suicide attempt cost me dear. I had
diarrhoea for three days. Juan Carlos behaved very well,
making me soup and giving me my medication. That's it.
This ridiculous end is quite enough. There are no metaphors.
I wanted to die for love and I ended up shitting all over
myself instead. I'll never fall in love again.

BLANCA: Day 18: Things that the Antarctic is not: a barren
land, a joke, a basin, a nation, a haven, a cemetery, a walk, a
charm, a certificate, a hangar, a nice thing, a copy, a nothing,
a crèche, a fashion, a museum, a tourist-site.

BLANCA: Day 23: Klaus is an underwater diver. A novelty. All
of a sudden, I saw him with an astronaut's helmet and a tube
pressed to his body. So that's how it is: Klaus plunges into
the depths to look at little animals. Not fish. Even smaller
things. It seems that there is a whole universe under the sea.
Creatures with enormous tentacles, worms with deformed
jawbones, violent and bloody and marine monsters, but the
whole horror film is a miniature that only Klaus can see with
his instruments. I like his stories. He's tired of the Americans
and he's paying me more attention. Yesterday I said to him:
and what are you looking for so much under the water,
Klaus? And he said to me: Klaus looks for the origin of life.

AURORA: 1st of December: I'm writing this diary again because
tomorrow I'm going to see Ulysses again. He left the writing
group and we've not seen each other for two months. But
there will be no sex tomorrow. Tomorrow we'll talk. We'll be
friends.

BLANCA: Day 31: Things that the Antarctic is: ice, a landscape, silence, an end, a living being, a puddle, a goal, magic, a star, a virtue, a cat, a pedestrian street, a paradise, a plan, a film, a Milanese, a beginning, a concept, a carrot, a stick, a stadium.

AURORA: 2nd of December. The train that I took to get to him left me four blocks away and I walked those blocks trying to control my nerves. I got there at ten to the hour. I sat down. I asked for a tea. I pretended to read a book but I couldn't read. Concentrate. My heart was thumping. And when it was exactly on the hour, I saw him appear in the door. At the exact time. He looked taller. Very tall. And his beard looked longer. He looked like a different man. A new man. Even more handsome than Ulysses. Yet he was still Ulysses. He sat at the table. He looked at me. I love you, Ulysses, I said. And I started to cry. Shall we go to my house? he said. He didn't even ask for his coffee. We went. We went to his house. And we made love. But this time there was nothing weird. We made that. Love. We Made Love. Now we've made it for always.

3RD OF DECEMBER: Juan Carlos: I love another man. If you ever read this diary, have the decency to: a) leave me, and leave me with my son and my life; or b) don't say a single thing.

BLANCA: Day 49: Klaus knows things about other planets. Today he told me something that caught my attention and that I want to note here. He said that in the planets closer to the earth, the ones in the solar system, it's thought that there's no life. But that in planets in other galaxies far away there could be. But the closest planet is two hundred light years away. So, if for example they had a gigantic telescope to look at Earth, what those extra-terrestrials would see wouldn't be the Earth today but the Earth two hundred years ago. I thought that for those extra-terrestrials my mother wouldn't even be born.

DAY 58: Today is the last day. In all of the time I've been here I've not had a period. I saw a group of penguins all walking together in the same waddling way and one that went the other way. Klaus told me that instead of going towards the water it was going towards the interior of the continent it was going to certain death. Let's save it, Klaus. 'No, you have to let it be', he said. And then he said: I think I am going to go back to Norway to hand in my reports in the University, then I return to Ushuaia and we get married, and then we'll go back and live in Oslo Norway. That's what he said to me. It turns out that Klaus proposed to me. But in fact he didn't propose. He told me just like that. Like telling me something that didn't have any importance. Then he said: the male penguins incubate the eggs as well as the female penguins. Did you know that, Planca?

AURORA: 5th of December. Yesterday Ulysses persuaded me to have anal sex. All the time I felt as if I was going to defecate on his penis. I don't understand the pleasure of this experience.

8TH OF DECEMBER: Why have I fallen in love with this man? Why would a woman love a man? Women are better. They've got it right those women who go with women.

Ushuaia, 9ᵗʰ of December.

Dear Aurora,

You don't know, Aurora, of course, you don't know. There's some unexpected events in my life. I'm writing with my surprising news. I'm going to have a baby. I'm going to get married. I'm going to go and live in Norway. Yes. All that. Mad, no? Or something like that. It's not one hundred absolutely one hundred percent certain. Because Klaus is like that. He doesn't say things. Or he says things but as if he's saying something else and you don't know what that other thing could be. Here he said: Planca, when I get back from Norway we'll get married and we'll go and live in Norway. Because I was in the Antarctic, Aurora. I've had a thousand adventures. And well, that's where this baby was made. Well, you know a bit about it, that I was going to the Antarctic, that I wasn't going to answer your letters. In the Antarctic Klaus would plunge beneath the ice to search for the origin of life in the world. And finally he found life. Because that's what I've got inside me. Life. Anyway, you know what, I'm going to be honest with you because if I can't talk to you I don't know who I can talk to. I'm not so happy. About being a mother I am. That news has left me over the moon I'm so happy. But not so happy with Klaus … I don't know. And it's just that I wanted love to be something else. I've become quite good friends with my father Dr Fierro. Although he's strange too. Tell me what's happening with you. I'm sending you a hug. I love you.

Blanca

29.

AURORA: Are you sure your mum won't come back, Blanquita?

BLANCA: Yes, for goodness sake, I am. She went to take measurements for a wedding dress, and that takes time.

AURORA: Okay. Shall I begin?

BLANCA: Yes, yes, begin.

AURORA: Okay. I'll start.

BLANCA: Yes.

AURORA: Okay then.

BLANCA: Come on, Aurora.

AURORA: Okay.

Okay.

Ay, I'm embarrassed.

BLANCA: Why are you embarrassed?

AURORA: Well, in case somebody catches us, I don't know,
paranoia.

BLANCA: Paranoia?

AURORA: Yes.

BLANCA: You can say 'paranoia' but you can't start?

AURORA: Well, I don't know, I don't know what's so strange
about saying the word paranoia. Now I'm paranoid that
you're taking so much notice of the word paranoia.

BLANCA: Okay, be quiet and let me. I'll go first.

AURORA: No, no. We said that today I'd start. I just have to
work up to it.

BLANCA: Okay, come, get on with it.

AURORA: No, if you get all defiant it's twice as hard.

BLANCA: 'Defiant'?

AURORA: Yes.

BLANCA: I get 'defiant'?

AURORA: Okay, I'm going to get on with it.

BLANCA: Now I'm 'defiant'?

AURORA: I'm going to start.

Bitch.

BLANCA: Bitch!

AURORA: Effing bitch!

BLANCA: Listen, Aurora, get this one. You're an effing bitch and
your mum's one too!

AURORA: Blanca, Blanca, listen. You're an effing bitch and your mum's one too!

BLANCA: AURORA: Effing twat!

AURORA: You're an effing twat bitch and your mum's one too, Blanca!

BLANCA: Twat bitch cow! Twat bitch cow!

AURORA: Wanker. Wanker! Suck my prick, you wanker!

BLANCA: Aurora: Go and fuck a donkey!

AURORA: Go and stick your head where the sun doesn't shine!

BLANCA: What, what's wrong with you, what's wrong with you?! Go back home to your twat of a mother!

AURORA: Blanquita, Blanquita. Go and fuck a clown, you effing bitch.

BLANCA: MOTHERFUCKER! MOTHERFUCKER!

AURORA: Piece of shit!

BLANCA: Pervert!

AURORA: I shit on your effing bitch mother motherfucker!

BLANCA: Aurora, Aurora, listen to this one: Son of the arsehole twat of the most holy bitch.

AURORA: The bloody fucking twat of a wanky wanker!

BLANCA: Shitty shit bitch whore bitch whore on a lorry loaded with tight twats holy load of bitch whore tight twats on a fucking twat lorry!

AURORA: I shit on your tight twat you wanker!

BLANCA: Fucking tw… oh shh shh shh …

30.

AURORA: 16th of December: I can't go on living like this. I can't. I'm a monster. I'm an egotist. I don't deserve anything from anyone. I should tear my eyes out. My son's a saint. My husband's one too. And I allow myself all sorts of perversions with this egomaniacal satyr. This has to stop.

24TH OF DECEMBER: I'm done. I can't go on. I'm worn down with nerves and desperation. I haven't had my period for months. And I even think I've lost weight. I have to put an end to this. To my life. To everything. I'm going to open the oven. I'm going to put my head in the oven. My last Christmas. I'm going to commit suicide. The way poets commit suicide. None of this makes sense.

31.

Ushuaia, 24th of December.

Dear Aurora:

What I most feared has happened. I lost my baby. The end. Now everything is sad. I don't believe in life anymore. I want to run away but I don't know where. I ring my life out like a rag, but nothing comes out. I'm all dried up. What am I going to do with myself? What am I going to do? It's sunny outside. I cry all day. Klaus had to go to Norway the day after I found out. He was supposed to be back by Christmas. My love is fading. My breasts produce milk that won't feed anyone. How sad it is when someone isn't born. I have the word unhappiness written forever on my heart. I'll talk about what I know. I'll tell you that I got your last letter. I was quite taken aback. I don't know what to say to you. How good it would be to have a normal life.

Blanca

PS: I wish you and Juan Manuel a Happy Christmas.

32.

AURORA: 24th of December. Ditto: I can't. Not in the oven. It's too cruel. Or I'm not brave enough. I'm going to set fire to myself. That's what I'm going to do. Set fire to me, my house and this diary. I can see Ulysses. Ulysses the dog. I'll die with him too. A semantic suicide. Die with the canine double of my lover. I love you too, dear animal. Let's give ourselves up. He doesn't know that he's going to die. That's what they say. I try to think like him. The mind goes blank. I'll light a paper. And the house will go up in flames. And with it my dog and my heart and my life. Let's burn, beloved hound. We'll burn in the fire of desperation. We've had enough.

33.

Ushuaia, 30ᵗʰ of December.

Dear Aurora:

Everything's the same here. The dead woman that alters dresses and writes letters. I had some tests done and my father thinks that I'm not going to be able to have children ever. On top of that, Klaus still hasn't come back. I was thinking about calling the University of Oslo to see if anyone knows anything. Could you tell me what to say? I don't speak a word of English. Write down some phrases for me and I'll pluck up the courage. I hope nothing bad's happened to him. He should have come back three months ago. Anyway. Here I am. I go to the chemist's a lot. When it's quiet. The son of Arias the pharmacist seems to quite like me so he sells me what I ask him for. I take pills for everything. Pills for the pain. Pills to sleep. Pills to get up. Pills for the sadness. Pills to eat. Pills to be dead. Pills to live. There's no psychology. I don't know how to do it. I who was two am now none. Write down some phrases in English. And tell me more about you.

I miss you a lot,

Blanca

34.

AURORA: 1ˢᵗ of January: It's a miracle I'm alive. My dog Ulysses saved my life. It seems that while the kitchen was burning and I fell unconscious because of the smoke, lying on the kitchen floor, the dog worked out how to open the front door, come back to the kitchen and drag me out through the house is if I were its baby. Or a stick like the ones he plays with. God knows what the animal was thinking. Maybe people have got it wrong, maybe dogs do know about death, and that's why Ulysses saved me. He saved me from death. He said, 'you've got to carry on living, Aurora'. The God dog. Anyway, after saving me he started to howl in the corridor with me lying there unconscious, and along came a neighbour who asked for the public telephone and called the Fire Brigade. We survived the fire my dog and I. And so did this diary that I hide because nobody must read it. This diary that I couldn't destroy. I wanted to kill myself for one Ulysses and another Ulysses saved me. Love has no metaphors. I'm going to stop all this. This time, for ever. I'm going to run away. I love you, Ulysses. Forget me if you can. I won't be able to. Now and for ever and for all eternity …

35.

BLANCA: Universitet i oslo, god morgen.

'Klaus Henriksen?'

'Brunhilde er du?'

'Inglish. Hellou, mai neim es Blanca. Aian de waif of Klaus Henriksen.'

'Klaus is not here, lady.'

'¿Cómo?'

Argentina.

Fron Argentina.

'Mr Henriksen is not in Oslo. He moves to Tromsø.'

'What?'

Klaus Henrisken plees.

'Mr Henriksen moves to Tromsø.

Beklager. Sorry.'

'¿Cómo?'

'Sorry.'

36.

AURORA: The image we have of the countryside is always slightly anachronistic. When you get as far as of Patagonia the sky is green like cement and the sea is like kerosene. I'm a fugitive on a train with a dog and one child or two. I feel undone. And yet I feel beautiful. Beautiful like Judas Iscariot. I betrayed my husband. I sat him in the dining room and I told him the whole truth. In his face: I screwed a guy for

months, Juan Carlos. I don't love you anymore. I'm going.
I'm taking your son and your dog. If you don't like it you
can kill me because I don't care anymore'. I'm a bitch. I'm
repugnant because I wanted to be. I'm not a good Argentine
woman. He cried. Juan Carlos cried. Me, nothing. I am
one holy bitch from hell. 'Don't cry, Juan Carlos, you're a
grown man. The struggle for survival: some are born again
and others fall.' And that's when he got angry. He shouted
at me. He'd never shouted at me. 'I'll destroy you, Aurora.
I'll destroy you.' He was wagging his finger at me. 'Do what
you want, Juan Carlos, what do you think you are.' Then he
took it back. He's a coward, Juan Carlos. I was taunting him.
I wanted him to do something awful, at least once, just once.
He didn't do anything. Nothing bad. He cried again. 'You're
killing me', he said. I didn't say anything else. I couldn't. I
grabbed a bag, picked up the baby and grabbed the dog's
leash. I bumped into a chair … and I left. I'm going back
to Ushuaia. That's how things grow in the wind. Twisted
but well rooted in the ground. I'm not anybody's plaything
anymore. I'm definitely pregnant. My life is a Bildungsroman
that never ends. I made myself by myself. But I'm to blame
for everything.

37.

BLANCA:

Last night

Last night

I mixed pills and alcohol again.

It's because I'm depressed.

I know it's bad.

I invited the pharmacist to my house.

He's called Victor.

He wants to look after me.

Fuck me Victor I don't need to be looked after,

I said.

I felt stupid.

I drank.

I danced.

I even cried a bit.
Victor looked on silently.
I don't know, Victor.
Sometimes I beg forgiveness.
I'd like to be stronger.
I don't know what metonymy is.
I say All and Nothing a lot.
I have problems with my self-esteem.
I always think I'm not loved.
I tend to fight with people.
I should try to fall in love.
Do you know what I mean, Victor?
It's something here in the middle of my breast that's like I
don't know what.
Why don't you try to calm down.
Fuck me Victor because if you don't I'm going to feel worse.

38.

Everything's done, God heard them tell him, and he
hadn't yet created the world. Any multiplication is still a
multiplication. And what's important is that: multiplication.
Nothing is created from nothing. For example, the word
reproduce. Produce again or produce anew. Or referring to
living beings, it is to engender and produce other beings with
the same biological characteristics.

For example, human beings. We wouldn't be here if our
parents hadn't had sex in that exact and precise second. And
if our grandparents hadn't had sex in that precise second.
And if we go back four hundred years, our existence depends
on 15,000 people having sex, on the exact day, at the exact
moment. If we go back a thousand years, luck depends on a
trillion people. We wouldn't be here without a bit of incest. In
the end we're all related.

For example, Aurora. Aurora is pregnant. 'Woman are born
to suffer', she said to Blanca. And then she said, 'I want to
have this baby and for it to be your baby'. Blanca said: 'What
are you saying, Aurora?' and Aurora said, 'I've thought hard

about it'. Blanca said again, 'What are you saying, Aurora?'
and Aurora said, 'I thought hard about it, I thought hard
about it'. She said it twice. Blanca cried. 'I don't know what
to say', she said. How strange. Saying that you don't know
what to say. But strange and all, that's what she said. It was
absolutely true. She didn't know what to say. Aurora gave
her a hug. Or just about. Aurora wasn't a friend of displays
of emotion. 'I want to ask you one thing, Blanquita. I'd
really like him to be called Ulysses'. 'Like the dog?', said
Blanca. Aurora nodded. In silence. And that's when Blanca
understood. And in that very moment, almost like a miracle,
both women thought – at the same time – about the day
they met. They were girls. They were looking at the moon.
It was as simple as that. Then came everything else. For ever.
Sometimes God appears and puts things in their place. Life is
always life, said Blanca. And Aurora answered: life is always life.

39.

BLANCA: Is your dad the man with the bookshop?

AURORA: Yes.

BLANCA: What's your name?

AURORA: Aurora.

BLANCA: Hello Aurora my name's Blanca.

AURORA: Hello.

BLANCA: I'm five, how old are you?

AURORA: Yes.

BLANCA: Yes?

AURORA: Five. Yes.

BLANCA: You're always reading books, aren't you?

AURORA: Yes.

BLANCA: Do you like reading books?

AURORA: Yes.

BLANCA: I like drawing and writing.

AURORA: Writing?

BLANCA: Yes. I write. Things. Anything.

AURORA: Ah. I've never thought about writing.

BLANCA: You can. You write and that's it, it's written down.

AURORA: Yes.

BLANCA: I want to tell you a secret.

AURORA: What?

BLANCA: The moon follows me.

AURORA: What?

BLANCA: Yes. The moon follows me.

AURORA: What are you saying?

BLANCA: It's a discovery.

AURORA: A discovery?

BLANCA: Don't be jealous, Aurora.

AURORA: Why would I be jealous?

BLANCA: You live shut up reading books and all of a sudden I
    appear and I bring you the moon.

AURORA: I don't understand what you're saying.

BLANCA: Come here. Give me your hand. Mine's clean. Give
    me yours.
    Look. Can you see it? Can you see it Aurora?
    Look now.

    Can you see it? Can you see it, Aurora?

AURORA: Yes.
    Yes.
    Yes, Blanca. Yes.

40.

BLANCA: Dad:

    I'm falling asleep and you start early tomorrow morning, so
    I'm leaving you this note.

    The plan hasn't changed. I'm leaving you your list of tasks.

ONE: Take Ulysses out. He's well trained and he doesn't do his business inside.

TWO: Buy pencils and paper for Juan Manuel and Aurora, she's going to teach him from her bed without abandoning the complete rest her doctor ordered (a wink, because you're her doctor).

THREE: If Victor turns up, don't let him in, Daddy. I have a few confessions to make to you and it's better if I do it in writing because in person I'm embarrassed, because you're my father.

I lied to Victor, and I told him I'm pregnant and that the baby's his. I don't know why I did that. Or rather I do. I do know. Because people talk. You know how it is. Then I put on a fake belly that I made myself and I went to see him and I said two words and I acted offended and I left quickly because I couldn't let him touch my belly. 'Victor I want you to know that I'm pregnant and that you're the father. I don't want us to talk, I'm VERY hurt by what you did, taking advantage of my situation, I am VERY hurt' and I left.

Four: Go to Aurora's aunt's place to get the keys to the bookshop, because she wants to go there. If you don't go, I will, now that I have a disguise. Anyway, the aunt's not too good in the head and she won't notice. Well, that's all.

I'm feeling very happy and looking positively on life, dear Father.

Kisses, Blanquita

41.

Daughter:

First of all, sorry about the writing, I never did have good handwriting: must be because I was a doctor. I'm leaving you this note for two reasons. The first is that I looked for the key to the bookshop like you asked me to and I'm leaving it on top of this note. The second, I'll be very sincere: I've left. I've run away. I don't want to die here at the end of the world. By the time you read this I'll be on my way back to Buenos Aires. I want to live, Daughter. There's still a long time to go before I die. Although I'm sure I'll be dead to you. If you saw me you'd say: you're dead to me, Dad. But no. I'm not dead. And a dead man doesn't dream, because to live you have to dream and love isn't a stone.

Aurora and you don't need me. I've seen how you looked after that woman and you fed her and gave her drinks to sip day and night through her whole pregnancy. You two don't need a man, you don't need anyone else. But remember: 'Nature does not know extinction; it only knows transformation'.

He loved you in his own way,

Dad

PS: I'm leaving you two sheets with instructions about how to help Aurora give birth, although I think it would be better to put an end to all the secrets and look for help.

42.

BLANCA: It said here, ay I don't understand.

AURORA: Come on, Blanca.

BLANCA: It's just that I can't see a thing. Didn't you know there was no electricity here?

AURORA: My aunt's senile, Blanca, what do you expect?

BLANCA: That's true, poor thing.

AURORA: And we left her in charge of a baby and a dog all night, we're mad.

BLANCA: Mad.

AURORA: There are books and dust here. And memories.

BLANCA: Yes, your dad, so many memories. We shouldn't have come to the bookshop. It was a whim of mine and look what happens.

AURORA: Come on, Blanca, it's on its way.

BLANCA: The thing is I can't understand this writing.

AURORA: Come on, let's see. It says: One, forget, forget everything you've seen in the movies: this is a real birth. He's an idiot, this man.

BLANCA: He's a disgrace.

AURORA: Ay, Blanca, son of a bitch.

BLANCA: Let's see. Two, relax and enjoy what nature is offering you: if a birth comes like this, so quickly, it's usually because the mother has dilated without complications and the birth usually goes well.

Well, that's good, it seems.

AURORA: Listen, Blanca, my heart's about to burst.

BLANCA: Hold on, hold on. Three: don't make the woman in labour, that's what it says, eh, the woman in labour, lie on her back: that only helps to complicate the birth. The ideal is to make use of the force of gravity letting the pregnant woman adopt the position that she feels best in.

AURORA: I'm dying. I'm going to die. I'm dying, Blanca, do something.

BLANCA: Four: all you have to do is observe.

AURORA: No, Blanca, help me, I'm dying.

BLANCA: When the person in attendance doesn't know what to do, the best thing is to do nothing. In fact, when the person in attendance does know what to do, if everything's going fine, the best thing is still not to do anything.

AURORA: That guy's got it all wrong, he's a monster. He wants to kill us. He wants to destroy us. All men want to destroy us. Read, Blanca, come on.

BLANCA: The thing is six says: take the newly born and put it on the naked breast of the mother as soon as it comes out.

AURORA: What newly born? I'm dying here and nothing's come out.

BLANCA: Wait.

AURORA: I've been having contractions for about an hour and my back's exploding, Blanca.

BLANCA: It doesn't say anything about that here.

AURORA: It's hard being me!

BLANCA: It's hard being me!

AURORA: Get the baby out of me, Blanca, because I'm dying, my heart's coming out my mouth.

BLANCA: Come on, we're going to do this, push.

AURORA: What?

BLANCA: Push.

AURORA: You hit me, Blanca, what's wrong with you?

BLANCA: I did. Push, for Christ's sake. Push. Push. Push.

AURORA: Uh, uh, uh.

BLANCA: Push, push.

AURORA: Uh uh that was going a bit too far, hitting me.

BLANCA: Push as if you wanted to shit, Aurora.

AURORA: Uh, uh, uh.

BLANCA: Push. Shit. Come on. Put something into it.

AURORA: Uh my heart's hurting uh uh.

BLANCA: Strength, Aurora, strength.

AURORA: I've shat myself, Blanquita. I've shat all over myself.

BLANCA: Keep going, push, push.

AURORA: Uh, uh, uh.

BLANCA: Use those abdominal muscles. It looks like it's coming.

AURORA: Uh, uh.

BLANCA: It looks like it's coming. Push.

AURORA: Uh, uh, uh.

BLANCA: The head, Aurora, the head. Push so we can get it out. Come on.

AURORA: Uh, uh, uh.

BLANCA: It's out, Aurora, it's out! It's out!

AURORA: It's out, Blanca, it's out!

BLANCA: It's out!

AURORA: A beautiful baby. Ulysses. Your baby.

BLANCA: Aurora I think it's a girl.

AURORA: It's a girl?

BLANCA: What do we do now?

AURORA: I don't know. Read.

BLANCA: Seven: cover them with warm blankets or clothes.

AURORA: What an idiot that man is.

BLANCA: Yes, better for the baby to be a girl.

AURORA: Should we cut the cord?

BLANCA: Eight: don't cut the umbilical cord or tie it. It's not necessary to do that and in fact it's better not to because that way the cord keeps on feeding blood to the baby and keeps on supplying oxygen and nutrients while the baby starts to breath for itself. After a while the cord will stop beating and it's then that you can cut it calmly.

AURORA: A contribution at last.

BLANCA: Well, we'll leave it all attached.

AURORA: Does it say anything else?

BLANCA: Nine: congratulate the mother for the beautiful baby that's just been born.

AURORA: I congratulate you, Blanca. You've given birth to a beautiful baby.

Buenos Aires, 27ᵗʰ of February.

Dear Victor Arias and Blanca Fierro:

This letter is to inform you that your daughter, Ángeles Aria, of five years of age, has scored an intelligence quotient in excess of 130. This means that Ángeles is exceptionally intellectually gifted. This will undoubtedly be a reason for joy, but we also want to advise some caution. For children it can be difficult to be different, even if that difference offers advantages. In your town there are no educational institutions for exceptionally gifted children, for which reason, we will suggest to the school that Ángeles attends that they advance her by two years, to lower third. In respect of this, we will be in touch with said institution to offer guidance.

Best wishes,

Luis Pereda

National Institute for Scientific Research into Human Intelligence

Buenos Aires, 15ᵗʰ of June.

To: Aurora Cruz, Librería Ingenieros.

From: Mario Shurukhin, Editorial Shurukhin Solo.

Dear Aurora Cruz:

We write to inform you that 'An Anthology of Women Poets from Patagonia' is of interest to us. It is important to arrange a meeting for the next time you are in Buenos Aires, so that – in your capacity as the compiler – we can discuss the terms with you. As you will know, ours is an independent editorial that does not seek economic gain, but rather artistic dissemination. The quality and variety of poetry by Patagonian woman authors you have offered made us feel obliged to take on once again the arduous adventure of independent publication. Write to us, and we will arrange a meeting.

Best wishes and congratulations,

Mario Shurukhin

45.

BLANCA: In the house there are twenty geese eating wheat
soaked in water and I'm looking at them, Victor and Ángeles
aren't there, I'm alone in the house with the geese and all of
a sudden an eagle appears and begins to break the geese's
necks one by one, get it: a psychopathic eagle. Then the eagle
looks at me and says, come on, chin up, this isn't a dream,
child, see, the eagle was talking; and then you appear, yes,
you, you're a ghost. I'm also a ghost too, but more elegant.
You're like a sleepwalker with a white dress three sizes too
big for you. I'm like an agile ghost, like a ballet ghost. Well,
you appear and all of a sudden we're flying. Both of us
flying together, in the sky. And below we can see Ushuaia,
in miniature. My house, your bookshop, the church, the
town hall, we can see it all as we fly, together. And all of a
sudden we start to throw snow. Us two. The snow is falling
from our enormous ghost arms. As if we were war planes
shooting missiles, or spaceships shooting laser beams. But we
were shooting beams of snow. And in this dream the snow is
beautiful, Beautiful like us, Aurora.

AURORA: I think this dream means something to do with death.

BLANCA: With death?

AURORA: Yes. I don't know. I don't know anything about
dreams. I never understand them, or I understand them
badly.

BLANCA: I invent any old thing.

AURORA: Here what would you say for example?

BLANCA: I'd say it's about death.

AURORA: But that's what I said.

BLANCA: Do you know what I'd say? Life is passing by, isn't it,
and people are dying and it's very sad because there's a gap,
you see. Because you go on living with those experiences and
everything you did with that person that's not here anymore.

So you feel incomplete, with those things that aren't here anymore. And you sort of talk to the dead. Hello Mum I did such and such. Aurora's dad would have said such and such if he'd seen such and such. And on it goes. You're alive but carrying all the dead. But they're not here. They're inside us. So what there is are parts inside us that are dead. They're alive because they talk, but they're dead because they're dead. The dead that talk. All the dead talk all the time. You die so much with each death. We're all going to die, Aurora. We're all going to die.

AURORA: The word death should be replaced by the word poetry.

46.

AURORA:

THE END

What will the day you'll die be like? Will it be sunny? Will it be raining? What will that last day be like? That definitive day? Will it be in your house or in a hospital? Will it be alone or accompanied? Who do you want to die with? Do you want someone to see you die? Or would it be better to be found dead? What will you think about in that last moment? Who?

BLANCA:

The End of the World

I imagine that it's the end of the world.

Two asteroids are going to crash into Planet Earth, more precisely, into the city of Ushuaia.

The fatal event is going to happen in the next 24 hours.

If an Asteroid measured around 1 kilometre, the crater that the impact would produce would be 25 kilometres, causing an earthquake in an area of 400 kilometres and generating total destruction in a radius of 200 kilometres.

But each Asteroid measures thousands of kilometres.

It's the End of the World.

Following tradition, the Asteroids were baptised with names from Greek mythology. These were called Philomela and Procne.

The news generates terror in the city of Ushuaia, which is practically empty.

The electricity has been cut, for example.

Chaos reigns.

The town priest talks on the radio. Father Esteban.

It's the will of God, he says.

And he reads a fragment of Revelation.

'And there appeared a great wonder in heaven; a woman clothed with the sun, and the moon under her feet, and upon her head a crown of twelve stars. And she being with child cried, travailing in birth, and pained to be delivered. And there appeared another wonder in heaven; and behold a great dragon, having seven heads and seven crowns upon his heads. And his tail drew the third part of the stars of heaven, and did cast them to earth: and the dragon stood before the woman which was ready to be delivered, for to devour her child as soon as it was born. And she brought forth a man child, who was to rule all nations with a rod of iron: and her child was caught up unto God, and to his throne.'

It's the End of the World.

I imagine it like that.

It's the End.

GREEN DUCK

FABIÁN DÍAZ
TRANSLATED BY GWEN MACKEITH

Fabián Díaz

Fabián has a Masters in dramaturgy and a degree in acting
from the National University of the Arts. He has written
and directed plays including *God Is In The House* (Biennial
of Young Art 2015); *Kiss, Green Duck* and *Men Return To The
Mountain* (the last two of which were awarded prizes by the
National Theatre Institute in 2012 and 2016). His works were
nominated in different categories of the Teatro del Mundo,
María Guerrero and Trinidad Guevara awards. In addition,
he has obtained distinctions and prizes for *The Runner, I
Am The One Who Wants* and *Characters*, directed by Daniel
Veronese as part of Identity X Theatre. He was selected by
the Royal Court Theatre in London to participate in the 2016-
2017 International Drama Workshop in Chile, Uruguay and
Argentina. This formed part of Panorama Sur's international
residence in dramaturgy. He is the director of the theatre
research company BESO in the city of Resistencia, Chaco.

For María

Characters

BOY IN LOVE
LONELY GIRL

BOY IN LOVE AND LONELY GIRL:
(Their voices barely a whisper.)
My father digs the earth
What does he say?
He says:
This is the siesta
this fulminant light
of the blistering sun

The bodies of the children drowned in the river
That is what I will bury

A siesta to open the earth
to dig these holes
The heat softens the earth
To dig a hole
in silence
before dusk

I see my father break the dry earth
He does not cry. He does not shout.

He says:
Do not bury the dead in the sadness of the morning
Nor in the curse of midday
Break the earth when the sun falls

...
...
...
He digs a hole
with his hands
in silence
He says:
Boy In Love
Lonely Girl

Dig a hole for them
to leave their bodies

Leave them in this earth in the middle of nowhere
Children dripping from the river
Orange over black
over blue
there is no light

Digging the earth with his hands
That's what he does
My mother brings flowers from the fields
she drops them over the dry hole

They cover us with the flowers from the river
They pray

BOY IN LOVE:

I know that I'm very little to be in love
And that I'm a holy boy, they say
That I'm a holy boy
They say it and I don't like it at all because it's a lie.
I'm not holy

You're very little to be in love, says my mother
But Mummy she's very lovely
But you're little, very little you are
Look, you don't even reach up to the table
But I want her to give me kisses
When you can work on the mountain like me and your father
shooting ducks
withstanding the sun
slaughtering the pigs, when you can do that, you can do what
you want
Slaughtering the pigs makes me feel sick
When you eat them you like them, says my mother
I don't like eating ducks or pigs or bugs
I give that meat to the dogs
it makes me feel sick
I chew it but I don't swallow
She is very lovely

You're little, very little and you can't
I don't want to see you bothering her, you know she doesn't
leave the house
How hideous, I say
How hideous, mother
And why doesn't she love me?
She doesn't even look at me
She doesn't even wave her hand

I smash all the plates
I makes holes in the sheets
Father comes from the field and gives me a smack
A smack is like this:
With this hard little bone in the finger
A smack on the head
It hurts
You want to be a little man?
I want her to give me kisses, I tell him
Brat, he shouts
I have to sweep the house
Bake the potatoes
Warm the water
It's punishment for a boy in love
A holy boy, in love
How hideous
I'm not even holy
Saints are boring and white and I'm black
Little black boy, says my mother
My darling little black boy
Little black boy in love
My father doesn't say this to me
He calls me, boy
Boy, you're going to help me to work to buy more plates
More sheets
That was my plan, to work like a man in the field
I am a man
When you can work in the mountain like your Dad and like me

you can do what you want, says my mother

She is so lovely as lovely as the rain in summer that perfumes
the earth
One day I tell her she is lovely
Or I would tell her when I see her I would say it
How lovely you are, so lovely
As lovely as ...
Boy, you're going to have to clean the whole house! Shouts
father

Punishment for not having cleaned the house like father told
me to
For doing a bad job of everything a new punishment to go to
the mountain with a machete
Yes, that's what I want
To go to the mountain
To go to the mountain
Cutting with the machete
Man's work

Look how I cut the grass with the machete
Dad!
Now I'm a man
He laughs
I stick the machete into a tree
What are you laughing for? I say
A clip round the ear which stings
A tear falls
That didn't even hurt, I say
Men don't cry over women, says father
I don't even care! I shout
A smack, with this little bone
And punishment

I have to sweep
To warm the water before the sun comes out
To go with a machete
To clean the water tank

Having the machete lets me see her close up circling her house with father
to cut the grass
I see her
She's so lovely
She wears a little headband and a white blouse that I don't even like, but that doesn't matter
She looks at me through a big window of that giant house of hers
Her house is giant
So giant that my house would fit inside hers a hundred times
When I lift the machete so that she sees me she runs inside
I'm laughing with happiness because today she looked at me
With a clipped ear
A clipped ear is like this: with the palm open so it looks like a toad
Son, do you want me to be without a job?
The house
The milk
The water
The food
The ducks
The pigs
Your house
The water in the river
This machete which you have in your hand is hers
Don't go near

I don't even know what to say
The machete being hers means that the machete isn't mine
Everything is hers
My little house which fits one hundred times into hers is also hers
The mountain
The river
It's hers, says father
Don't go near

I feel hate

How hideous, Mother, I say to her at home when she gives
me a bath

I'm not holy

I don't want to be holy

I like my hands

my feet

my scaly skin

Father and mother work all day on the mountain

I love them but one day when she loves me I'll leave them

I peer through the window, at night you can't see her distant
house well, just a light in the window

Her father gives work to my father

My father cuts their grass with a machete

feeds their pigs and their ducks

Mother cleans their house

They give us a duck

a pig

vegetables

The water we take from the rain

To work their land and live in it

To be able to be in the river

The river is a place where the ducks are reared

It's the loveliest place I know

Mummy, What's she like? Is she lovely?

Mother says nothing.

She cooks

Mother is lovely too

Mummy, what's she like? Is she lovely?

Yes

Can I come with you to her house? I'll clean with you and
see her

No

I want to come, I clean. I know how to clean. Look at me

You men can't come, says mother

The knife accidentally cuts a little bit of her finger

Ouch, she says. And she goes on cooking
Let me go one day and I'll see her
Only I can go in, she says
I touch her cut finger with my hand and it heals
It heals because I'm holy
You're a man and you don't go in, my little black boy
Men don't enter their house
Tell her to come with you one day
Let her come and see me!
She can't, she can't go out, says mother
I know she can't go out
But tell her to come, to escape!
What's her name?
Guess
Amaru
No
Eluney
No
Huilén
No, she says
Paine
Pire
Suyan
Wuayra
No
Tell me! I shout
Don't shout at me, my little black boy ... If you love her so
much one day you'll guess her name
Hideous
Hideous
Hideous
I hide in the water tank so they think I've gone forever
but father pulls me out with a rope
I climb a tree to get away
I fall from the branch and break a chair which crushes a chick

This makes me unbearably sad, to crush a chick gives me a
yellow and green and ugly sadness
Animal! Says mother. You're a wild animal like a musk hog,
poor little chick you crushed it, look!
I forgive her for what she says, because she's lovely. And
because I was a wild animal
I cry for the little chick
I can't bring it back to life
I'm not holy nor can I do magical things or even bring a little
chick back to life
Punishment of cleaning the pigsty stinking of the little dead
chick
I clean the pigs' mess which is disgusting
I have to go knee deep in the rotten mud on the girl's farm
and work there,
the mud sticks to me and I smell horrible
Behind the window I see her, she spies on me
I don't know if she laughs at my filth or if she makes fun of me
I'm filthy and I smell like a musk hog!
She thinks she's invisible with her skin all white and her dress
all smooth which I don't even like
Today I don't love her
I don't love you, I say
I put my tongue out like a snake and make the face of a rabid dog
And I spit on the back of a pig and hit it with a stick
The pig cries like a donkey
Slap from father. Like this. With his hand hard like wood
Don't hurt me, I say, but without father hearing me because
now he wants me to go and have a bath

Mother tips warm water on my scaly skin
Tell me what she's called, Mummy
You have to guess, she says
Kantyi
Malinalli
Nakawé
Sasasi

Yatzil
Susen
No
One day I'll see her, I say
Mother laughs
She puts me to bed
One day I'll see her
Go to sleep, she says
And did you see the green duck I'm rearing
I'm going to give that one away
A gift of love
She'll like it, mother
Go to sleep

I watch the dark roof
The moonlight enters
They say it has a power
That when it touches something it heals
But that's a lie
My hands are like this
But they have no power
they're just a little callused
The warm night makes me sweat
I escape through the window, I run to the river and throw
myself in
The frightened ducks clamour in the darkness
My green duck is there, among them, he's the only green one
He was born like this and he is mine
This one's yours, said father
He still doesn't fly, but he runs around very happily and he
knows me, pecks from my hands
at a few crumbs of cake and bread and herbs which I
chopped up for him
We swim together
We dive and we float
From under the water I see the moon
Like a huge pale star dancing

All my skin goes soft
I stay in the water with the green duck until I get cold
I run to the house and I sleep like this nice and cool

Father and mother go early to the mountain
So early that the sun almost hasn't yet risen
They take a little wheelbarrow
And a basket with bread for when they get hungry
That basket was mine when I was a baby. You used to sleep
in it, says mother
They go to plant seeds and to pray in the wooden church
They pray a lot
They pray for me, for my hands. That's what they say
I don't want them to pray for me
Look after the house, says father
Don't break anything, don't crush a chick and he laughs
I don't look after anything and I go to the house of the little
girl without a name
I look at her from far away

I am very little to be in love, I know
To work the mountain
I have to guess what she's called
Father and mother go to pray
That's what they do
I know
They pray for things
We pray for you, says mother
I don't want them to pray for me
We have to pray for you
And you do too. We have to pray together
We pray for you
Your father also prays
Father prays, but he punishes me with the disgusting pigs
So you learn about manly things, says mother
How disgusting, I say
How disgusting pig mess is, mother

BOY IN LOVE AND LONELY GIRL:
(Their voices barely a whisper.)
I can see my father
Tea break
Now I can see him
He bows his head
He's an enormous man
The bread on the table
The tea hot
He looks at the bread but doesn't eat it
Everything is silenced
Silence is what he wants
To roam the mountain, we roam the mountain now that we can
The last sun comes in through the window and falls on him to
shroud him
He bows his head and cries
or he seems to be crying
And this makes us sad
The last birds stop singing to open the night
I see him through the window
The mountain takes everything
What will my father do alone in his house?
He will drink tea and eat bread with pieces of meat

LONELY GIRL:
Nothing there is nothing
The house is empty and I am very lonely
Father doesn't want me to go out
I don't go out
I never go out of the house, I can never go out of the house
Father why can't I go out? Am I cursed?
The sun hurts you, daughter
But they say I am cursed
I like the sun
No, not the sun
I can go out at night, then, there's no sun at night
The mountain is dangerous for a girl

There's nothing. You can't see a thing
It's dangerous
The mountain is darkness
I want to go out, to go out of the house
Why do we have all this land if I can't go out?
Here you have all you need
Here I have nothing
Father's solemn look makes me fall silent
I remain in silence eating a piece of tortilla

Do you like it?
What?
The tortilla, says father
Yes

My mummy dies when I was born
Because of me, they say
Because I am cursed
I always knew it
That doesn't scare me
Daddy says that what's important now is that I don't go out in the sun
What's wrong with me?
Nothing's wrong with you. You just have to beware of the sun
I like the sun
The sun is strong and it's bad for you. Your skin is very white. You can't go out

I chew tortilla
I'm a lonely girl in a house in the country in the mountains lost in the middle of nowhere. There's no one, here there is no one. Not even I go out, I can't even see anything. I am all white and transparent with skin which hurts, I want to go out in the sun. So that I burn, to get a dark colour. There is nothing, no one comes
Only the little boy who spies on me

Am I lovely? Daddy, am I lovely?
You are lovely, very lovely

I am white, transparent
Whatever I touch dies, why Daddy?
That's not true
I touch a plant and it dies
I touch a butterfly and it dies
I touch a duck and it dies
One day I'll go out and I won't come back, I tell him
Silence

Father, why do the things I touch die?
Leave the cutlery on the plate
Stop eating
You have to wash all of this, he says
I want to do what you do
Daddy, I want to do country things, to go with you
One day, daughter. Maybe one day

BOY IN LOVE:

One day I hide in the long grass
The girl plays in the shade under a little blue canopy on the
terrace of her giant house
Her house is big, alone on the mountain, but big, one
hundred people could live there
I make the noise of a duck
Quaaaack quack qua quack
She lifts her head
Doesn't see me
I throw the shell of a little seed which falls on the roof
It frightens her and she freezes, she is so lovely
She's scared and runs to the house
So lovely

Mummy, take her a letter
What are you going to say to her? She asks
My things

LONELY GIRL

Before going to sleep I read the letter:

I like ducks, he says
That's why I don't eat them
Actually their meat makes me feel sick
So they don't punish me I chew it a little
But I throw it to the dog under the table
The sun is something which stings your skin, but it's lovely
when you get out of the river,
wet and cooled by the wind
The sun dries you with a little warmth
Is it true that when you touch something it dies? He asks
I'm not afraid of you
I'm telling you that you will like the sun
My house fits inside yours a hundred times
Why don't you go out?
Your name, what's it like?
Do you love me?

Father enters,
What's this? He asks
I tear up the letter

BOY IN LOVE

Did she read it? Mother, did she read it?
I didn't see her, son
What kind of face did she have?
Her eyes widened as she looked at the paper, says mother
And she didn't say anything?
She looked at me and said, is this for me? And she ran to her
room
Mummy, is it true that she can kill plants if she touches them?

LONELY GIRL:

Father picks up the little pieces of paper
Where did this come from? He asks
It's a piece of paper I found
Where?
I found it in a book
You tore it up

Because you scared me when you came in
Pick it up and go to sleep, daughter
He leaves the room
Turns out the light
I'm left with the bedside lamp and little pieces of the torn up
letter on the sheet
I gather them together
Leave them in a plant pot with a flower I cannot touch

BOY IN LOVE
I practice names
Huenu. No
Wamán. No
Siwar
Raymi
I don't like any of them
Hideous
Danaá
Ikal
If you love her so much you have to guess her name, says
mother
I'm not a witch who knows everything and can guess names
Kabil
Masawa
Rahui
Tell me Mummy what she's called
Didn't she give you a piece of paper for me?
A piece of paper with her name?
Why can't I go to her house?
Hideous
I'll cut the grass all around her house with the machete
I carry it with me all day
The sun stings me
I don't see her
She's gone
They've taken her away
She doesn't live in the mountains anymore

They must have taken her to a place for little girls who can't
see the sun
White girls don't live in the mountains
She can't touch anything
She doesn't answer letters
Is she sick?
What's wrong with her, Mummy?
Her skin is sick
She has a fever, son
Is she going to die?
You have to pray for her
I don't know how to pray, I say
Make up a prayer
I don't know how to pray!
I run through the mountainside to the river
I hug my green duck, he can almost fly
I shout like the ducks
That's my prayer
I shout like the ducks!
What's wrong with her skin?
She's weak, says mother
That's why I can't see her
Not you or anyone. She's ill, son

LONELY GIRL:
There's a river full of ducks close to the house
I want to swim in it one day
I don't care if everything I touch dies
I want to swim under the sun
Letter from the boy:
I have a duck I'm rearing
It's for you
A gift of love
A duck which has a green head
He's the only one there is
Is it true that if you touch a plant it dies?
If you touch the green duck will it die?

Don't you know how to write?

Write something to me

When you get back home can I come?

The sun is something very strong

It's true that it can burn you, but if you put yourself in the water you won't sting

or go under a tree and you won't even feel it

BOY IN LOVE:

The girl returns

I know because I see the light in her window

I escape into the night

I go barefoot so as not to make a sound and I climb the roof of the little girl's big house

I hang from my feet upside down and I spy through the window

She's under the covers

There are a few little crickets chirping, it's the only thing you can hear

everything sleeps, the ducks, the dogs, the fathers, the pigs

Only her white face appears

as lovely as the big moon in the river and the ducks which fly

With the little stick which I brought with me I tap the window

Tap-tap-tap

She opens her eyes

Tap-tap-tap

She looks at the window

Don't shout, I say

I open my mouth wide so she understands

She's frightened

Don't shout

The glow from her bedside lamp spilling out through the window lights me up

I wanted to see you, I say

It's me

I come every day with the machete, clean your house, your pigs are cared for by me

My daddy and my mummy also look after your house
She looks at me
I don't know if she hears me
Are you ill?
My mother says you have a fever
She doesn't move
I've never seen her so close up
Yesterday I ran to the river and I prayed for you calling out
with the ducks, I tell her
I thought that you had gone forever and it scared me
Her father comes in
She closes her eyes
He covers her
He doesn't see me

BOY IN LOVE AND LONELY GIRL: *(Their voices barely a whisper.)*
Mother and father go to sleep
The night
Their bodies embrace in the bed
The night of the mountain has no sound
No ducks
no dogs
A night of a moon which spreads over everything
The night has a mountain which has a house where now
mother and father sleep
alone
There is silence
A sad silence
We see all of that
Everything all at once
We can see everything all at once, the houses, the birds, the
water, the flowers ...

BOY IN LOVE
On a clear night I build a little altar by moonlight in the
shape of a duck
With branches and grasses and leaves
I paint the head and the neck green

I build it in on the mountainside for the white girl without a name
From her window she can see it
It's to make her happy

LONELY GIRL:
He leaves the letters on the window
It's a little duck altar, he writes
It's to make you get better
I get up from the bed
I look

BOY IN LOVE
I am standing by the side of the little altar
I do a dance lifting my feet and hands swivelling my head
round like a bird, I do it like a turkey, so that she believes me
that I love her
Quaaaaaaaack, quack qua quack, I sing like a bird even
though I know she can't
hear
She looks at me from her window
She laughs
I throw myself on the ground, I flap like a duck, dive into the
river, all to make her
laugh
Silly boy in love dances like a duck so the girl of colours
laughs
She lifts a hand, has my letter between her fingers, moves the
paper as if it were
a handkerchief saying hello. I like that and I look at her. She
laughs and twirls around like she's dancing, only just, she
moves slowly, it's a turn which lasts a thousand years. There
is no music, but she dances in her room. I twirl around too,
as if we were dancing together. She falls and doesn't get up. I
want to run to the window. Her father enters and puts her in
bed.

She doesn't have a fever anymore
I saw her through the window last night
But the sun kills her and she falls to the floor

Mummy, what's wrong with her?
She's ill. Very ill, son. That's what she has. Something in her skin
Is she going to die?
Hideous
And I cry
I break lots of things
I run towards the river and I throw myself in the water
Green duck flies a little, low
I made you a little altar, I say as he flies
You are a gift for the girl of colours

At home father and mother wait for me
They are sitting at the table
They're going to punish me
Sit down here, says father
You broke lots of things
That's all he says today
There's no punishment
There's nothing
A supper without sound
I look at him
Eat, says father

Quaaaaaaaak, quack qua quack
I make duck noises hidden in the long grass next to her
window
It's night and it's hot
the parents sleep
A little stone at her window
The dogs bark
Her head pops up behind the glass
I stand to come out of the grass
You don't have a fever anymore, I say with a wide mouth

She doesn't speak to me
She hears, but she doesn't see me
I'm in the grass, I say
The girl looks at me

She comes near
She sees me
I go near to her window
I stop near to her
She says nothing to me. She looks at me
We are so close, so close that if I stretch out a hand I can
touch her
I can see her near transparent skin covered in spots behind
the window
I look her in the eye and everything is in colour
She opens the window
We are so close
All her skin is in colours
I open my mouth to speak and I say
Green
Over white
From yellow
Over blue
Over red
Red girl
I look at her

She doesn't move but she hears me
You aren't white
Nor are you transparent, I tell her
Orange
Over blue
Green
Over white
Over black
She laughs
Grey, the girl is not grey
Over grey
It is not white that I see
Over black
Over black
Blue mist

Yellow
From the sun
There is no white
Over blue
Blue river
Over green
She laughs faintly, so close that if I lift my hand …
Violet
Girl of colour
Orange
No grey
Night orange
Opens green
Over blue
Blue
Bites white
Over green
All green
Black falls
A laugh comes out of her like a beam and I tell her again
Green below
Blue all alone
From fire
Green climbs
Green, the green below everything, each colour climbs over her skin
Girl a thousand colours that deep down are green
White falls
Black falls
Nothing white, there is no white in you, you are made of colours, I tell her
Fallen blue
Over white
I take a step towards her
…
My name is Tumby

Which is purple
Every colour comes from her
from orange
Red
Red are the eyes of the girl
The sun
Colour of sun
Over me
Over the water
The sun over you
All light
Soona
Is that your name?
Between her and me it's like a thousand years have passed,
standing there, face to face ... she looks at me and smiles, I
am covered in grass, sweltering with the heat of the night,
I lift my hand and I touch her forehead, only just ... I feel
like a flash of fire which sets all of me ablaze and I don't see
anything more ...

...

Run
Run
Don't stop running
Jump
Now
Jump
Don't look and jump
We are jumping into the river
Escaped from the houses
I go behind
I see her run
Run
Run
Run
I tell her
Don't stop running!

...

She runs and she laughs
Now close your eyes and jump

…

She goes ahead of me
Barefoot in the grass
Without clothes

…

Don't look when you jump
Don't look
Run and jump!

…

The river is full of ducks which start to fly and clamour
over our heads when they hear us. There are hundreds or
thousands, like a cloud which covers the sun for a moment,
they clamour and fly above us
That one there is green duck! I tell her
At this time the water is always warm from the sun of the siesta

…

She shouts and laughs
She shouts like the ducks
Don't look and jump!
What she has is not fear
It is pure shriek and laughter
The sun burns her skin
I'm not a transparent girl! She screams
There is water
wind
flowers
She runs to the edge
Close your eyes, I tell her
I hear her voice dragged by the wind, like laughter, there up
ahead
She runs as fast as she can into the middle of the ducks'
clamour and near a tree she jumps into the water of the river
for the first time

…

She stays fixed to the air

held as if she has no weight
her feet and hands float
Her arms and her hair and her back
all her skin dangling from the air like a feather caught on the
wind
all her muscles
without land
her laughter suspended in the air
I see her
only the echo of her voice clamouring in the middle of the
mountain and the siesta
...
She falls and her body smashes the surface of the water
She splashes and sinks
She does not appear
I stop running
Trapped, frozen in the light of the siesta
I watch how the river trembles in little waves
Droplets of sweat cover my eyes
The water flattens in the river and covers the transparent girl
The water is like a steely dry floor
Frozen, like me
An impenetrable surface which trapped the girl
She might appear
Now
Or not
To disappear under the water forever

There is a silence in all this land
of the wind
of the ducks
It's like a mirage of the river
without laughter
without cries
silence of eyes
of hands
of colour

Thousands of years pass one standing before the other in her
window
Imagining this

Her head appears laughing in the water

I run
Freed from the quiet
She sees me approaching the edge
I run as fast as I can
A clamour of ducks bursts out again
I close my eyes and jump

LONELY GIRL:
I love you

BOY IN LOVE:
My love

LONELY GIRL:
I love you

BOY IN LOVE:
I love you too

LONELY GIRL:
I love you
I want your hands
For them to hold me
For them to touch me
Kisses from your mouth

BOY IN LOVE:
If I could
If I could make this light
That this light of the siesta should last forever
If I could freeze this light
To make it so that a mattress of fallen feathers holds us up
floating on the water
So we do not sink
I want your hands

For them to hold me
For them to touch me
Kisses from your mouth
Or to disappear and turn into these flowers
Hardly stirred by the wind
Imperceptible
Displaced by the current towards the infinite

LONELY GIRL:

Your hands on my face
On my hair
On my mouth
Under this tree
Which is our tree, the one we're going to live in forever
I'm in love with you

BOY IN LOVE:

And I am in love with you
My hands are your hands

LONELY GIRL:

And yours are mine
On my belly
Naked
Taking refuge in the sun of the siesta
How lovely the sun is
Damp from swimming in the river
Silenced by the beating of the ducks' wings
Above my belly

BOY IN LOVE:

My naked body
Your cool hand
My hand upon your bare belly
Covered in little droplets of water
Reddened by the sun
Your skin of colours
All the colours fall

Red
over green
from yellow
and violet
and blue
My hand stained with colour goes towards your skin
All your skin in colours
And all your space

LONELY GIRL:
Kisses from your mouth
And the wetness of your tongue
Over me
Over this earth in the middle of nowhere

BOY IN LOVE:
My tongue on you
and over your arms and your neck
and over the darkness of your eyes
On your skin
All over my skin reddened by the sun
Stinging
All your skin which boils over me
Tangled
Red with heat
Open
To let us sink in the water
Forgotten by everything
…

BOY IN LOVE:
Hold me /

LONELY GIRL:
Now /

BOY IN LOVE:
Hold me /

LONELY GIRL:
I'm holding you / I bite a piece of your skin /

BOY IN LOVE:
Bite me /

LONELY GIRL:
Ah, I love you

BOY IN LOVE:
Me too, I love you

BOY IN LOVE:
My eyes are closed, there's no longer anything to see
I hear everything
The sound of the water and the wind in the tree that gives us
shade
The ducks
Your breath.
Let's go back to the water, your skin is stinging

LONELY GIRL:
Close that window daughter, says my father as he comes
through the door.
The boy disappears into the grass so that all that remains is
the touch of his finger
on my forehead
I see him leave like a shadow
Weak
Like a mountain insect
The dogs bark
My lips tremble
Daddy, I want to go to the river, I want to go swimming there
One day I want to go to the river, to throw myself into the
water with the ducks. I want to do that
If that happens, if the sun touches you once, if your skin is
reddened by the sun, daughter,
if that happens, you will die
I'm not afraid of that, I say
Close that window

BOY IN LOVE:

Father and mother put on their clean clothes very early
You get dressed too, says mother.
We're going to the church in the cart
There is a church in the middle of the mountain
God isn't there
I know
A holy boy knows that
A holy boy knows where God is and on this mountain, in this land, God isn't here
We go in the cart
I look at my trembling hands
I touched the forehead of the girl of colours
Last night
Her skin is like a bolt of electricity

The church is a farmhouse made of rotten old wood with a bent iron cross which one day will fall
A den for the pigeons and dogs dying of hunger
That is the church
We're going to hold a vigil
A boy must be buried
One more
A blind boy
From a little house. Another cursed boy
I'm not a child anymore
It's the church where mother and father pray for me
There are only a few people, people who don't look, or talk, who don't move
People who came scared
The girl of colours isn't here
Her father came, dressed in black, with a hat
I want to see her again
They bring him from his little house lost on the mountain
I don't feel scared, or sad, I feel something else
I feel heat and hate
I can heal mother's finger, but I can't bring a boy back to life

The holy boy, says an old lady and she points at me
I put on a hating face so no one comes near me
Everyone prays
And they want to touch my hands
I'm not a holy boy!
They touch me so that I heal them
The dead boy enters in a little box
They close their eyes and cover him with small stones
painted blue
I go near the box and touch him, I touch my finger with the
blind boy's finger
I feel his cold skin. Another ghost which will get lost in the
siestas of the mountain
The mountain turns silent, mute, there are no dogs, not even
ducks or crickets
Mute and deaf
The mountain can be mute and deaf and alone

They make a hole for the dead boy in the middle of the
mountain
There is no cemetery, only a hole in the earth and a cross
made of sticks
I see everything from above in a tree
Mother cries. She cries for me
Her lips wet with tears pray … they say things I can't hear
The afternoon is yellow with sadness
I stay in the tree until night falls

LONELY GIRL:
Letter
Things spin around and around after touching your forehead
I no longer think about what I need to do to win your love

BOY IN LOVE:
No reply

LONELY GIRL:
Letter
What's wrong with your skin?

BOY IN LOVE:
    No reply

LONELY GIRL:
    Letter
    Do you want to go out and about?
    To go to the river, to the mountain, to the meadow?
    I don't know what's wrong with your skin,
    nothing is so terrible
    although everyone says that it is

BOY IN LOVE:
    No reply

LONELY GIRL:
    Letter
    I'm not too little to be in love
    I like your window and your dresses and everything about you
    And all your colours and your spots

BOY IN LOVE:
    Mother and father pray
    Why do they pray?
    For the girl and for you, they say
    There is only sadness
    This I always knew
    from when my memory began,
    I knew that where we were born life is a strange thing and
    that there was sadness
    They pray because they're scared
    We pray for you
    Scared that the same thing that happened to the blind boy
    will happen to me
    My hands are like this
    My feet are like this
    My skin
    But I don't want them to pray for me, or for the girl
    We want to go to the water of the river, that's what we want

Mother cries
Father gets cross and leaves in the cart I don't know to where
Why do you cry, Mummy?
She looks at me

Mummy, what's lovely is something else, water, because
there, in the water, my body has no weight ... it's like a
feather, it has no weight, I sink and I float and I sink and I
float and it's cool and my skin stays nice and soft and there
my body is something else, I don't even see under the water
...
Mummy, under the water my body has no weight and I don't
even see it
That's what's lovely ...

Mother closes her eyes as if knowing something she'll never say
But I do know it
I'm not a holy boy

Gunshots
Like a dry blow to the back
No
I run
The river fills with dead ducks
The father of the girl of colours kills them
I climb and I see from the tree
He aims and the ducks fall in the water
Without weight
Or they disappear into the mountainside, full of holes
The dogs run and sink their teeth in
I watch how the feathers fall slowly towards the river
The father loads the gun again and again
He kills them with anger and with hate for his daughter,
he kills them because of her, because of sadness, because
everything turns sad and yellow in this land
My father brings his cart
He loads up the ducks
Ten or so arrive at our house hanging from a rope
Dead

Green duck isn't in the cart
I hate all this
I hate the smell of blood from the ducks full of holes

LONELY GIRL:

Letter from the boy.
I saw your father kill all the ducks
Green duck is injured all over by the dogs

BOY IN LOVE:

The girl replies
She says
I'm going to die as well

LONELY GIRL:

I'm like a fly trying to go through a window, I crash again
and again
I know, the fly knows that, from the other side, where all the
sunlight is, it knows that it has to go there

BOY IN LOVE:

The girl writes, at last!
Get me out of here!
That's what she writes
I creep through the grass
It prickles me, stings me, the little twigs dried out by the sun
cut me
I don't care about that and it's doesn't hurt
The girl opens the window
She comes near
I cling to her as much as I can.
Love
We are safe
Love is going to take this sadness we have in our body to hell
That's what we say
This dusk sadness
of this cold-hearted night
And alone
To hell

And our body won't go with it
I touch her forehead and everything is wiped out
Like a blow
Like a beam
Her body of colours is like a beam
Sadness which will turn to coal
May it go to hell
That's what we say

BOY IN LOVE AND LONELY GIRL:
(Their voices barely a whisper.)
This sadness will turn to coal!

BOY IN LOVE:
She opens her window
The girl doesn't speak to me
Her body burns with a fever
Her transparent skin boils
She smiles at me
She's not scared

LONELY GIRL:
I want your hands
For them to hold me
For your hands to touch me
Kisses from your mouth

BOY IN LOVE:
It's a declaration of love
We say

BOY IN LOVE AND LONELY GIRL:
(Their voices barely a whisper.)
I want your hands
For them to hold me
For your hands to touch me
Kisses from your mouth

BOY IN LOVE:
We declare it like this

Giving each other our hands
Me with my body stung by the grasses and the little twigs that scrape me
Her burning with fever
Looking into our eyes
Searching for our mouths
Searching for kisses
Our kisses are like beams
My hands covered in this coarseness tremble
Her hands like beams which leave me blind when they touch me
Will I die if you touch me?

LONELY GIRL:

I don't know

BOY IN LOVE:

Love is a gentle thing
We say I love you
My love
I love you
Her hands burn, like fire

LONELY GIRL:

Is green duck dead?

BOY IN LOVE:

No. He's injured.

LONELY GIRL:

Will you make the duck noise for me?

BOY IN LOVE:

Quaaaaaaaaaack quack qua quack
She laughs, she smiles and she's going to cry

LONELY GIRL:

Tomorrow I'm going to escape into the sun
When it's siesta time
When my father sleeps
I'm going to escape into the sun

To the river to swim with the ducks
Are you coming?

BOY IN LOVE:

She jumps out of her window and we run through the
mountainside
We wrap ourselves in a blanket I take from my bedroom
late at night in the darkness
We walk through the mountainside
The dogs look after us
They walk close by, without barking, smelling the mountain
to take care of us
The mountain insects are there, waiting
In the back of my father's cart wrapped in a blanket
our hands touch, face, eyes, arms, hair, all our skin … and it's
wonderful
No matter how holy our bodies are
Or how cursed it all is
The cart still smells of the ducks full of holes
this land's smell of yellow sadness
our body cannot see anything
less touch anything, they say
because it is holy
or because it kills
We are like sick ducks and sooner or later we'll be left full of
holes
and the whole
the whole of life like a hole
mixture of happiness and anguish and being cursed in this
cart
That's why touching our bodies is like a beam which sends it
all up in flames

LONELY GIRL:

I'm not a fly
I know I'm not a fly which rebounds against the window

BOY IN LOVE AND LONELY GIRL:
(Their voices barely a whisper.)
It's siesta time
For the girl of colours and for me
I guessed her name, Mummy
I guessed it
We're in the river

LONELY GIRL:
It's siesta time
My father's sleeping
It's the siesta when the sun burns
This siesta

BOY IN LOVE:
We escape
Us
In the middle of nowhere
Surrounded by rivers
Children deformed by the mountain's poison
We declare our love so that our sadness turns to coal
Because it is as if our body were blind
as if it were deaf and alone, surrounded by colours we can't
see
And the love our bodies have
which is not false
which passes from hand to hand
from eye to eye
from mouth to mouth
All that love comes into these words

LONELY GIRL:
I want your hands
For them to hold me
For your hands to touch me
Kisses from your mouth

BOY IN LOVE:
    We are in our tree over the river
    That is everything I want

LONELY GIRL:
    You are wild
    like each one of the ducks my father killed
    Wild boy smelling of blood
    wild blood of the green-headed duck

BOY IN LOVE:
    The sun lingers in the leaves
    Still it doesn't touch us
    The river gets warm

LONELY GIRL:
    I hate my transparent skin
    like a dead person
    All this cursed skin

BOY IN LOVE:
    She takes off her clothes
    Her red dress is a stain on the dry earth
    Her skin of a thousand colours

LONELY GIRL:
    My body is as if it had no blood

BOY IN LOVE:
    It's full of colours

LONELY GIRL:
    I don't know how much the sun will burn me
    I want the blood to go cold in my veins and for my burning
    body to sink in
    the river
    Wild boy, for your strange hands to hold me
    When the sun touches me, I will die
    That doesn't frighten me
    I am frightened of darkness

BOY IN LOVE:

I take off my clothes
These are my hands
These my feet
I am not a holy boy, girl of colours
Nor am I too little to be in love
I want all your body

LONELY GIRL:

I want your hands
For them to hold me
For your hands to touch me
Kisses from your mouth

BOY IN LOVE:

We murmur these words beneath the tree
And then we kiss

…
…
…

Now
In this siesta
Bodies stunned
Stunned by the gunshots
The father looks for us
We are blinded by the light and electricity of our bodies
We run to the river shouting
No one hears us
And no one
below this earth
from I don't know where
from the mountain
no one is a holy boy or a holy girl
and everyone is cursed
And now there is no God, or prayers, or anything
Now there is none of this for us
alone

With a sky hard with light
A sky which doesn't open

LONELY GIRL:
Red
Over white
Over red
Over green
Over blue
Over black

BOY IN LOVE:
I'm not a holy boy

LONELY GIRL:
I am no less wild
My skin stings with the sun that burns me and there is
nothing
nothing more that I want than this sun on me

BOY IN LOVE:
We stay surrounded by this light of the siesta
We jump into the river
Stunned by the shouts of the father
Our skin burns
The wetness of the water covers us
The girl laughs and shouts and sinks and surfaces to look at
the sun
And we go
We don't know where, but we go
Now
We can't see to where
We walk through the infinite river which wraps around us
We leave our bodies under the tree with our clothes
we pin them to the ground like a cross
with the same holes as the ducks
We leave our bodies in our houses
We leave them in the church

The bodies we leave in the cart, stuck together
She tickles me under the water
with her cold hand

LONELY GIRL:

Come here, go under!

BOY IN LOVE:

We leave everything
Today
Now
we go to the deepest part of the river
with the sun burning upon us
we set fire to the mountain and naked we walk through this
fire to cover ourselves in water
Our bodies cold from the deep water

LONELY GIRL:

I want your hands
For them to hold me
For your hands to touch me
Kisses from your mouth

BOY IN LOVE:

I kiss you
without sadness
it is right that
now when the water covers us
is when the green duck begins his flight

BOY IN LOVE AND LONELY GIRL:
(Their voices barely a whisper.)
We see heaven
Heaven isn't a place
Parents suspended in the light watch the water of the river
We see them from below

The mother's hands clasped over her breast
Hands soft with silence
Her body gently leaning forwards

The light of the siesta bounces off the water and bathes her
forehead
Her face

Behind her a man
Father and mother
He takes off his hat
Scarcely bows his head
The sun of the siesta burns on his back
His neck
down to his feet

The mother has a basket which now contains some flowers
Everything is luminous with the sun which spears and shatters
the water
Behind them a cart
In the sky a few clouds
Yellow
Orange
Black
The mountain is immense and deserted

Between the sky and land some birds
And over the water, skimming the skin of the river,
thousands of dragonflies
It will rain

What are the parents doing there?
They pray
What do they say?
...
They say
Perhaps they say
God
Now these children are of the water
Let's leave them there
...
The light holds over their bodies

FONAVI

LEONEL GIACOMETTO
TRANSLATED BY ROSALIND HARVEY

Leonel Giacometto

Leonel Giacometto is a writer and playwright, and occasionally works as an arts journalist and director. He lives in Rosario. He has published a novel called *Pequeñas dispersiones* (Editorial Municipal de Córdoba, 2005) and, for children, the following titles: *Náufragos y piratas* (Homo Sapiens, 2005); *Leones, osos y perdices* (Colihue, 2006); *La gata mujer* (First Prize for Puppet Theatre at the La Maison d'Amérique Latine en Rhône-Alpes, France, 2009). For the stage he has published (amongst others): *Dolor de pubis* (*Seven Authors: The New Generation*, Editorial Inteatro, Buenos Aires, 2004); *Santa Eulalia, Madagascar* (*Playwrights from Argentina's Coast*, Argentores, Buenos Aires, 2008); *Despropósito, Arritmia, Plató* (third prize in the 7th Torreperogil Playwriting Competition, Spain, 2004); *Herr Klement* (first prize for playwriting in a competition run by the local authority of Santurce, Spain, 2004); *Todos los judíos fuera de Europa; El difuntito* (Teatro x la identidad, Editorial Municipal de Rosario, 2010); *Venado tureto, Carne dulce; Bardo, vigor en la atmósfera; Pecados devorados; Hotel capricornio; La mala fe*, etc. He wrote and directed *Carne Humana* (1998), *Fingido, Real* (2007), *Latente* (2008) and *Desenmascaramiento* (2008), and his work has been performed in Argentina, Spain, El Salvador, Mexico, the United States, Poland, Costa Rica and Venezuela. In collaboration with Patricia Suárez he published *Trilogía peronista* (Teatro Vivo, Buenos Aires, 2005), and he was nominated for the ACE Prize for Best Argentine Author in both 2006 and 2007 for *Todos los judíos fuera de Europa*. He is the author and director of performance pieces such as *Lo que se pierde* (Tucumán, 2001); *Fuga* (Tandil, 2014), and *Ardida* (Tucumán, 2015). He has written for the newspapers La Capital (Rosario), El Litoral (Sante Fe) and El Ciudadano (Rosario), and currently writes for the paper Página21, as well as publishing fiction on his own blog *Putos breves, ficción jedionda* (www.putosbreves. tumblr.com). 2016 saw the premieres of the following works of his: *Hombre viajando en taxi*, performed at the San Martín Cultural Centre, directed by Ricky Pashkus, with music by Nico Cota and starring Elías Viñoles, Christian Sancho, Nahuel Mutti and Federico Coates (Buenos Aires); *Sanagasta*, directed by César Torres for the *Comedia Provincial*, La Rioja (la Rioja); *Arritmia*, in a Portuguese version (São Paulo, Brazil). In 2016, Baltasara Editora published a collection of his plays entitled '*La mala fe* and other works.'

Characters

GASTÓN MACHINEA / María Laura and
Bruno's brother

MARÍA LAURA MACHINEA / Gastón and
Bruno's sister

ELISABET VALENTINA VEGA / María Laura's
neighbour and friend

GABRIEL LUCIANO CAMAÑO / neighbour and
Gaston's friend

NEIGHBOUR'S VOICE – MALE / Between forty
and forty-five years old. Master welder by
profession. Three children.

NEIGHBOUR'S VOICE – FEMALE / Forty-five
years old. Housewife. Three children.

*Note for staging: The voices (Male and Female
Neighbours) are characters and could be actors. Or not.*

Six or seven years have passed since the year 2000. Maybe more. The country is Argentina, the province Santa Fe and the city, Rosario. We don't know the name of the neighbourhood but colloquially it is known as 'Fonavi' (Fo.Na.Vi., short for Fondo Nacional de Vivienda, or National Housing Fund): a housing complex made up of three-story apartment blocks, with twelve apartments to each building. The buildings cover an area of around eight blocks. There are several 'Fonavis' ranged around the cardinal points of the city. This one is in the north. On the third floor, in apartment 0311 of block 12, live Gastón Machinea and María Laura Machinea. We are in the living-dining room and visible in the background is a large window that looks onto the balcony which, in turn, gives onto the outside. To one side, the front door, and to the other side, almost indistinguishable from each other, three more doors that lead, respectively, to the kitchen and the bedrooms.

Gastón Machinea and María Laura Machinea's ages add up to around 60. As do those of the rest of the characters. Apart from the two neighbours.

It's night time and it's a Tuesday. Spring or autumn, it's not clear which. A little over 22 degrees. There are too many lights on. What can be seen in terms of their, shall we call it, appreciation of hygiene and order, is a question of age, and of one or two domestic oversights. There is some kind of odour in the air (it could be cigarette smoke).

Gastón Machinea and Gabriel Camaño are literally lying on a somewhat dilapidated two- or three-seater sofa. Neither very relaxed nor particularly restless, but with a certain kind of latent 'alertness' that at times is more obvious, at others, less so. Gastón's tone when he speaks is a little uneven and Gabriel occasionally responds to this. They watch TV, smoke, eat a little, drink. They get up to go to the kitchen, occasionally (Gastón gets up, Gabriel follows him), they sit down again, they stay where they are. Neither dashing nor dawdling, so to speak, despite this 'alertness' which by now is characteristic of their personalities. Gabriel has the remote control for the TV. He changes channels while Gastón asks him to do so in his slightly uneven tone which is forever tending towards an aggressive outburst. What can be seen and heard from the television and the reasons for the channel changes are a decision without any kind of stylistic aspiration, as it were. This is up to the director. They go from national channels to film channels, music, news, documentaries, cartoons, the French nun, Sister Marie Simon-Pierre, the German channel, more national ones, retro ones, even programmes that don't really exist or which are impossible to recover. Music is occasionally heard, and the languages are varied and faltering, like a flowing, guttural babble. All this with a rhythm that at times speeds up and at others eases out in Gastón and Gabriel, mainly in Gastón. They have been like this for some time.

GASTÓN: Change the channel.

GABRIEL: The Bambi effect, they call it.

GASTÓN: How do you know? Switch over.

GABRIEL: Ezequiel told me.

GASTÓN: What does Ezequiel know about that?

GABRIEL: The old man goes out hunting every couple of weeks.

GASTÓN: Where? Switch over.

GABRIEL: To the island and the for...

GASTÓN: *(Interrupting.)* Switch over.

GABRIEL: *(Interrupting.)* To the forest.

GASTÓN: What fo... *(He interrupts himself.)* No, don't switch. Leave it on that one. What forest?

GABRIEL: How d...

GASTÓN: *(Interrupting suddenly.)* Don't change it. Don't change it.

GABRIEL: How do I know, he goes to the forest, he says.

GASTÓN: Don't change over. And what does he hunt?

GABRIEL: Wild boar.

GASTÓN: And you swallowed – don't change it, I said – you swallowed the line that old man Ezequiel hunts wild boar in a forest?

GABRIEL: Yeah, why not?

GASTÓN: Because the closest forest to where we are is in Córdoba.

GABRIEL: So?

GASTÓN: I've never seen a wild boar from Córdoba round here.

GABRIEL: So?

GASTÓN: Vega's an ex-cop. No, switch over. He was fired for transporting drugs, and when you do that to the cops and you're a cop, too, you're left with nothing, no pension at all. They don't even let you do anything on the side.

GABRIEL: So?

GASTÓN: Ezequiel sells biscuits.

GABRIEL: So?

MALE NEIGHBOUR: *(Offstage and in real time. Quietly.)* 'The house is small but the heart is big.' That's what you said to Carlo. *(The female neighbour's voice murmuring away can also be heard.)*

FEMALE NEIGHBOUR: *(Offstage and in real time. Quietly.)* No, I didn't, I didn't just say that to Carlo.

MALE NEIGHBOUR: *(Offstage and in real time. Quietly.)* Be quiet.

GABRIEL: *(To GASTÓN.)* What did he say? Did you hear that?

GASTÓN: No idea. What was it?

GABRIEL: *(Quietly.)* 'The house is small but the heart is big.'

GASTÓN: He's probably pissed and the whole farce will start any minute now.

GABRIEL: Well?

Slight – and not so slight – murmurs keep coming from the neighbours' flat.

GASTÓN: Well what?

GABRIEL: Well, what about old Eze…

Slight – and not so slight – murmurs keep coming from the neighbours' flat.

GASTÓN: *(Interrupting.)* Where is Vega going to get money from to g… *(He interrupts himself.)* Hang on, let me listen. Listen to that.

GABRIEL: You can't really hear much. They must ha…

GASTÓN: *(Interrupting loudly.)* The TV, stupid.

GABRIEL suddenly gets it. They listen to a song playing on the television.

GASTÓN: You know what it says in this song?

GABRIEL: Not a clue, Cache, I don't speak English and I don't listen to thi…

119

GASTÓN: *(Cutting the other man off, brusquely.)* Shhh!!!! You hear how it goes up? Listen. I love songs that go up like that.

GABRIEL: All songs go up…

GASTÓN: *(Interrupting, as if happy at the music.)* Listen to it.

GABRIEL listens and is gradually taken in by GASTÓN's enjoyment of this song, which does just keep going up.

GASTÓN: Switch over.

A brief TV break. Slight (and not so slight) murmurs keep coming from the neighbours'.

GASTÓN: Where would Vega get money from to go hunting every couple of weeks or so?

GABRIEL: But I saw him more than once heading out in the Fiorino on a d…

GASTÓN: *(Interrupting.)* So?

GABRIEL: So you don't go out selling biscuits on Sunday mornings, or load up your pick-up with shotguns to go and sell biscuits. That's what I mean: old man Ezequiel is going somewhere with his shotgun.

GASTÓN: OK, so I was right in what I was saying to you about the Vegas family yesterday, then.

GABRIEL: I guess. Shall I change it?

GASTÓN: The fuck do you mean, I guess?

GABRIEL: Chill out.

GASTÓN: The fuck do you mean, I guess? I knew, man, I knew it, I knew it. Up here *(A brisk tap to his own forehead.)* Up here, I had it figured out up here. And I could smell it, and it just kept smelling worse and worse, man, but really bad, like something really rotten, you get me?

GABRIEL: Sure.

GASTÓN: Vega's up to something, and for some reason he's not telling Ezequiel anything and he's making the whole family swallow his little line about going out to the forest.

GABRIEL: Or he doesn't want him involved.

GASTÓN: It's like I told you: there's something else going on here.

GABRIEL: Maybe Ezequiel's the liar here too, maybe everyone in the family knows what the old guy's up to and they're all just acting dumb.

GASTÓN: Leave it. No, switch over.

Soft children's laughter from the neighbours'.

GABRIEL: His sister had another attack.

GASTÓN: Don't change it. Whose sister?

GABRIEL: Eze's sister, Cache, Elisabet.

GASTÓN: Alright, asshole, I know who she is. Why not just say Elisabet straight away, dickhead? Change over.

GABRIEL: She says she just s…

GASTÓN: *(Interrupting.)* Hang on, let me hear this. Switch over. She just what?

GABRIEL: A load of people on their own.

GASTÓN: She said that?

GABRIEL: That's what she saw.

GASTÓN: Really? Switch over.

GABRIEL: A load of people on their own. Just like that.

GASTÓN: 'I saw a load of people on their own,' that's how she said it?

GABRIEL: Yeah. I don't know why you're so surprised.

GASTÓN: I'm not, man. Change the channel.

GABRIEL: No?

GASTÓN: No.

GABRIEL: No what?

GASTÓN: It just made me…

GABRIEL: What

GASTÓN: It made me stay up all night.

GABRIEL: It's weird.

GASTÓN: The bitch is weird. I've already told you what I thought – switch over – about Elisabet, and I told you it was Churi – Pitín's brother; switch over – who gave me the dirt on all that, when that whole fuck-up happened with Norma, her son who they killed, and the house on Anchoris Street.

GABRIEL: El Chavito.

GASTÓN: Yeah, El Chavito: no way can you tell me he wasn't a super generous kid; he had something, he was loyal, a smart lad, he was, El Chavito, and nobody round here believed those three bullets in the back were for his mother, am I right?

GABRIEL: La Norma always did things properly with the cu...

GASTÓN: *(Interrupting.)* Right up until Eli barged into my life, and the rest of the Vega clan with her. Remember when I said to you that time there was something else going on here? It's still going on, I'm telling you, and Churi was right about what I told you he told me about her. Especially about her.

GABRIEL: Churi's also going around saying that stuff about antennas and h...

GASTÓN: *(Interrupting.)* And you don't believe him? Churi's mother works in Virasoro House, that's where she heard the thing about brains and antennas.

GABRIEL: But maybe the old lady heard any ol...

GASTÓN: *(Interrupting.)* But with her it's true.

GABRIEL: What is?

GASTÓN: The bitch doesn't work right.

GABRIEL: Churi's mother?

GASTÓN: No, Eli, you dickhead. Seriously, something's not quite right up here, the bitch's brain is seriously atrophied. Or worse.

GABRIEL: She's crazy.

GASTÓN: Switch over.

GABRIEL: But she's actually crazy, you get me?

GASTÓN: Yeah, man, I know, I'm the one who's been saying this to you this whole time. Right?

GABRIEL doesn't reply.

GASTÓN: Right?

GABRIEL gives a nod.

GASTÓN: And you've always been a dumb fuck, what can I say?
I never screwed her, and not because I couldn't, you know
that better than anyone. I never wanted to fuck her 'cos she's
crazy. Not even worth getting your dick sucked by crazy
women, because then they just go and spread all kinds of
bullshit about you. Like that little bitch, who told everyone in
the block I'd given her the bug. Switch over.

MALE NEIGHBOUR: *(Offstage. Quietly.)* 'The house is small but
the heart is big.' That's what you said to Carlo.

FEMALE NEIGHBOUR: *(Offstage. Quietly.)* You're still on about
that? I said it to both of them, Erika was there too, and she
was the one who s… *(Interrupting herself.)* Come here. Come
here. Come here, I s… *(Interrupting herself, loudly.)* Kids, go to
your room, come on, get out of here.

*GABRIEL looks at GASTÓN, who looks back and gives a dismissive
wave with his hand. His mind is still on the Vega family. A pause;
some TV.*

GABRIEL: And that thing with the kid, you remember?

GASTÓN looks at GABRIEL.

GASTÓN: That lot are just wicked through and through.

GABRIEL: Who?

GASTÓN: The Vegas's.

GABRIEL: I don't know what's goi…

GASTÓN: *(Interrupting.)* And you're sucking up to them, pal.
You're screwing me over there, but it's alright. You're gonna
be in with me, like I said before. And don't you forget that
not only is your friend Cache telling you this now, but he's
been saying this to you for ages.

GABRIEL: I don't get y…

GASTÓN: *(Interrupting.)* I just wanted you to wise up a bit, man.
I said you've gotta stop breaking your balls and being such

a pussy, not fucking any of those chicks who were up for it. Berenice – no; Jazmín – no; Brisa's a dog; fuck knows the list of bullshit excuses you were forever coming out with.

GABRIEL: I want something else.

GASTÓN: You want cock?

GABRIEL: Motherfucker.

GASTÓN: *(He hugs GABRIEL, or something like this.)* Don't get mad, man. I told you all of this in good faith. And I also told you that if none of that came off, Elisabet was always gonna be right there.

GABRIEL: Slutty, is what you said.

GASTÓN: I did not say she was slutty. Switch over.

GABRIEL: Slutty and easy.

GASTÓN: Easy's what I must have said. That's all. Switch over.

GABRIEL: Whatever.

GASTÓN: She's in your brain.

GABRIEL: Who is?

GASTÓN: That fucking deranged mangy cunt, that's who. And she's crazy, for fuck's sake. Crazy. Switch over.

GABRIEL: She's always going on about you.

GASTÓN: She's crazy.

GABRIEL: She drives me crazy.

GASTÓN: And what does she say about me?

GABRIEL: Mad stuff.

GASTÓN: Like what? Switch over, man. Like what?

GABRIEL: The same stuff she always says.

GASTÓN: *(Suddenly hesitant.)* Like what?

GABRIEL: She mixes you up with the people she sees, and she says that you're, I dunno.

GASTÓN: You dunno what?

GABRIEL: Well, that, that call that cries out to her and tells her this truth she says she knows about everyone who's living when she goes out to walk around the ring road.

GASTÓN: And what do you say to her?

GABRIEL: Nothing.

GASTÓN: Nothing?

GABRIEL: Nothing, nothing… Ach, what can I say, of course I don't say nothing at all; nothing's just a figure of speech.

GASTÓN: It wasn't just a figure of speech, according to you.

GABRIEL: I told you what she told me she saw.

GASTÓN: So she really did see a whole load of people alone, and she saw me there too?

GABRIEL: No.

GASTÓN: What do you mean, no?

GABRIEL: That's what she was trying to say, but there wasn't anything actually there. She sees things where there isn't anything.

GASTÓN: I don't know.

GABRIEL: Me neither.

GASTÓN: You don't know what?

GABRIEL: Nothing.

GASTÓN: Madness is catching.

GABRIEL: You reckon?

GASTÓN: Tota…

Power cut. The TV shuts itself off and all the channels go blank.

GASTÓN: What did you press?

GABRIEL: Nothing.

GASTÓN: What do you mean, nothing? What did you press?

GABRIEL: Nothing, it just went off.

GASTÓN: Change the channel, come on, let's have a look.

GABRIEL flicks quickly through the channels. They're all black.

GASTÓN: Ah, you bastard, fuck's sake, fucking motherfucking fucker...

GABRIEL: *(Interrupting.)* The plug's come out.

GASTÓN: Huh.

GABRIEL: *(By the TV.)* Nope.

GASTÓN: No?

GABRIEL: The power went.

GASTÓN: Or they cut it off.

GABRIEL: At this time?

It's not entirely clear whether GABRIEL is growing impatient because GASTÓN is growing even more impatient, but there are a few seconds of 'what shall we do?' Suddenly, GASTÓN rushes out on to the balcony. He is half-visible, or not at all, but is still audible. GABRIEL stays inside, near the window.

GASTÓN: *(Shouting.)* Vaaaaaaaaaaaaaaaampiiiiiiiiiiiiiiiiiiiiiiiiire!

GABRIEL: Can you see him?

GASTÓN: *(Shouting.)* Vaaaaaaaaaaaaaaaampiiiiiiiiiiiiiiiiiiiiiiiiiire!

A few seconds without an answer until apparently VAMPIRE shows up.

GASTÓN: *(To VAMPIRE.)* Hey, Vampire, mate, what're you up to? Have you got cable, man? *(VAMPIRE replies and points at something.)* Ah, son of a bitch. Ugh, OK, I'll have a look, but man, that son of a bitch; are we going to Norma's later on? *(VAMPIRE asks him something.)* Alright, we'll see.

GABRIEL: What is it? What are you doing?

GASTÓN is not visible – he has seemingly climbed up onto the railings on the balcony.

GASTÓN: *(Yelling.)* Apparently that son-of-a-bitch from Corrientes, Martínez, cut that connection we made with Vampi last month.

GABRIEL: Watch out.

GASTÓN: *(Offstage, balancing.)* What?

GABRIEL: Watch out you don't fall.

GASTÓN: Give me a break.

GABRIEL: I'm just saying.

GASTÓN: By the bollocks.

GABRIEL: Eh?

GASTÓN: I've got that bastard caught between one bollock and the other.

GABRIEL: He'll hear you.

GASTÓN: *(Offstage, straining somewhat from trying to reach the cable that's been cut.)* Martínez and his carpet-munching wife can suck my motherfucking dick. I hope he does hear me, the motherfucking third-floor faggot and his dykey wife who's left him. Let him hear me, let him come right out here and say it to my face.

GASTÓN grumbles. GABRIEL watches him. At the front door a key can be heard going in to the lock and opening the door. It's MARÍA LAURA getting in from work (she works at the casino). GASTÓN and GABRIEL hardly notice her; they look at each other and head out, with barely a hello. They head to the newsstand, the one that sells beers, sweets and cigarettes; and then to the other one, the one with little windows made in the breeze block walls of makeshift houses. As soon as the two men leave, MARÍA LAURA breathes for a moment or two, as if saying to herself: 'Fine, I don't care what those two are up to. I'm home now, and it's my time.' Her plan is to have a shower, sort out a few things in the apartment, and be there, just be. Once she realises the cable is out, she switches off the TV and puts on some music. Volume up high, a song plays. MARÍA LAURA, in the song and getting changed, in her room, going and turning on the shower, sorting out this, sorting out that, smoking a cigarette, relaxing to the song. Inconveniently, GASTÓN comes back, GABRIEL following after him. 'Fuck it, that motherfucking cunt,' he says as he comes in, and heads straight for the sofa. MARÍA LAURA

looks surprised for a minute, but carries on doing her own thing,
half-dressed, noticing that her brother is looking for something.

MARÍA LAURA: *(To GASTÓN.)* What's going on?

GASTÓN doesn't answer, and keeps on looking. MARÍA LAURA
looks at GABRIEL.

GABRIEL: *(To MARÍA LAURA.)* The motorbike keys.

MARÍA LAURA: Oh. *(And she makes the same expression as a few*
moments ago, says to herself: 'Fine, I don't care what those two are
up to. I'm just doing my own thing.')

GASTÓN continues to search and to curse.

GABRIEL: *(To MARÍA LAURA.)* You like Raphael?

MARÍA LAURA: A few songs. I put it on as a pick-me-up! *(She*
smiles.)

GABRIEL: Me too.

MARÍA LAURA: You listen to Raphael?

GABRIEL: Just a couple of his songs.

MARÍA LAURA: Which ones?

GABRIEL: This one, and 'The Way I Love You.'

MARÍA LAURA: *(Amused.)* I love that one. Does that not make
you a poof?

GASTÓN: *(To MARÍA LAURA, without pausing.)* How about instead
of fucking around like the two of you are doing and breaking
my fucking balls with your nonsense, you give me a fucking
hand?

GABRIEL acquiesces. MARÍA LAURA makes a face, but it's fleeting.
Her priority is the shower. Every so often GASTÓN says 'Look over
there,' to GABRIEL, who searches where the other man tells him to.
Something has happened or is happening in his body, but inside.
GASTÓN finds the keys and exits swiftly along with GABRIEL.
MARÍA LAURA has already gone to have her wash. Some time goes
by like this, with the song playing, soft shouts from the neighbours,
the sound of the shower, a few trills from MARÍA LAURA, until the
doorbell rings. MARÍA LAURA does not hear it. It rings again. Ditto.

Someone knocks from the other side with a certain amount of force so that the knock sounds, as it were, better. Ditto. Another knock. Ditto. A torrent of knocks followed by more knocks. Now MARÍA LAURA does hear, and she looks worried. She exits the bathroom soaking wet and wrapped in a towel, dripping water all over the living room. The knocking continues. From the bathroom until she finally opens the door, MARÍA LAURA, her tone rising higher and higher, says, 'I'm coming, I'm coming, who is it? I'm coming, who is it? I'm coming,' And she opens the door. It's ELISABET, a little unsettled from her own knocking, a little out of control.

MARÍA LAURA: *(Also unsettled.)* What is it? Eli?!

ELISABET: *(Unsettled, entering.)* Nothing, you just weren't answering.

MARÍA LAURA: *(Kissing her hello.)* God, Eli, why would you batter down the door like that? I was in the shower, look at me!

ELISABET: Sorry.

MARÍA LAURA: It's alright. *(She breathes.)* In two seconds I just freaked out.

ELISABET: Why?

MARÍA LAURA: That crazy knocking, Eli.

ELISABET: Yeah, you're right, that was a bit much.

Everything eases off. As they talk, one woman follows the other through the bathroom, María Laura's bedroom, the kitchen and the living room, and it is ELISABET who follows MARÍA LAURA. Every now and then, the Male and Female Neighbour can be heard arguing or speaking in loud whispers. The two women pay no attention to this. Just a few glances are exchanged, but only very occasionally. Once or twice, through the wall, during the arguing and amidst doors being slammed and other noises, you can hear, very softly, the voices of the children next door.

MARÍA LAURA: How's Eze?

ELISABET: He's OK. Things got a bit tricky at home for a while because the guy never looks after Joel.

MARÍA LAURA: What a jerk.

ELISABET: He is a jerk, and so irresponsible, don't you think?

MARÍA LAURA: Well, he's just a child, aft...

ELISABET: *(Interrupting.)* If you go and screw a prize hussy like Patricia was at the age of fourteen and get her pregnant, and then to top it all off the little bitch gets really messed up during the birth, at some point, Lali, you've got to calm the fuck down and stand on your own two feet and just get the fuck on with stuff, right?

MARÍA LAURA does not answer.

ELISABET: Right?

MARÍA LAURA nods.

ELISABET: For Joel, I mean, don't you think?

MARÍA LAURA: Yeah. Of course, but Eze's nineteen.

ELISABET: He's seventeen, actually.

MARÍA LAURA: What?

ELISABET: Well, almost eighteen. *(Playing this down.)* My folks enrolled him in school early, so the little dick wouldn't cause them any more grief.

MARÍA LAURA: That makes total sense.

ELISABET: How so?

MARÍA LAURA: Because it's hard.

ELISABET: You're right. *(Silence.)* But my mum's at the end of her rope, and so am I.

A pause. Something floats in and from ELISABET. Faintly.

MARÍA LAURA: And your old lady's alright?

ELISABET: Crazy.

MARÍA LAURA: Same as ever. Your old man?

ELISABET: He's gone hunting in the forest.

MARÍA LAURA: When?

ELISABET: Sunday.

MARÍA LAURA: Where does he hunt?

ELISABET: Some forest somewhere.

MARÍA LAURA: Which one?

ELISABET: No idea, I don't know what there is out beyond the ring road, so if he did ever tell me, I've forgotten.

MARÍA LAURA: I'm hopeless with the names of places, too.

Something floats in and from ELISABET. Faintly.

ELISABET: So where's your brother?

MARÍA LAURA: God, you know what? I'm just glad those two have gone out because I'd only just got home and they were seriously starting to do my head in.

ELISABET: Him and Gabriel, right?

MARÍA LAURA: Yep.

ELISABET: They can be so annoying.

MARÍA LAURA: Totally.

ELISABET: You know what I mean?

MARÍA LAURA: Gastón was pissed off because Martínez cut the cable.

ELISABET: Again?

MARÍA LAURA: That guy's a jerk, you know; there's a reason his wife became a dyke.

ELISABET: I saw her on Saturday in th…

MARÍA LAURA: *(Interrupting.)* And Gastón knows I get home shattered from my job, the bastard.

ELISABET: He could make more of an effort.

MARÍA LAURA: He really could.

ELISABET: Yep.

MARÍA LAURA: You know, I don't know what my brother could or couldn't do because, honestly Eli, I haven't got a fucking clue what he does with those motorbikes or how the sneaky fucker manages to sell them and always come up trumps.

ELISABET: Did they go to Norma's place?

MARÍA LAURA: I guess so. I think he owes Tata, and I don't think Gaston's got any cash.

ELISABET: Gabriel pays.

MARÍA LAURA: How do you know?

ELISABET: Recently.

MARÍA LAURA: How do you know?

ELISABET: Because he's always talking about your brother.

MARÍA LAURA: Your boyfriend had a little strop earlier.

ELISABET: He's not my boyfriend.

MARÍA LAURA: Hmmm.

ELISABET: Seriously.

MARÍA LAURA: I called him a faggot, and he kind of looked at me funny.

ELISABET: What's new?

MARÍA LAURA: How do you mean?

ELISABET: Someone calling Gabriel a faggot.

MARÍA LAURA: Why?

ELISABET: Because he is a faggot, Lali.

MARÍA LAURA: But he's going out with you, ho…

ELISABET: *(Interrupting.)* We're not going out, Lali. You know that. There's no way that that fag would want anything to do with me, even if he was completely wasted.

MARÍA LAURA: And you're OK with that?

ELISABET: Yeah, of course; he can do and say whatever the hell he wants to. He's been going around saying he's 'infatuated with me.'

MARÍA LAURA: 'Infatuated?' Is that what he says?

ELISABET: 'I'm infatuated with Elisabet.'

MARÍA LAURA: That's a fag way of saying it.

ELISABET: You see? It's not me he's after.

MARÍA LAURA: And you're not after him, either.

ELISABET: Well, duh – what would I do with a fag?

MARÍA LAURA: You could listen to Raphael.

ELISABET: Gabi doesn't listen to Raphael, but he still sucks dick.

MARÍA LAURA: He does listen to Raphael.

ELISABET: That's nothing compared to the other stuff.

MARÍA LAURA: You've got proof?

ELISABET: Yes and no.

MARÍA LAURA: So how…?

ELISABET: Like all faggots, Lali, in the ass, hard and deep.

MARÍA LAURA: How can you know and not know, is what I'm asking.

ELISABET: I just know. That's it. Gabi stinks of faggot. Half the block says he's a bender.

MARÍA LAURA: He's a bit lazy, but n…

ELISABET: *(Interrupting.)* And hanging out with your brother really isn't good for him, either.

MARÍA LAURA: What do you think?

ELISABET: About what?

MARÍA LAURA: What do you think, is Gastón a fag too?

ELISABET: Come on, Lali, your brother's the most macho guy out there.

MARÍA LAURA: That's what it seems like.

ELISABET: How do you mean?

MARÍA LAURA: Like he's having a shit time.

ELISABET: Why?

MARÍA LAURA: No idea, but I kind of get the sense the guy wants to settle down and he just can't get it together.

ELISABET: What do you mean by settle down?

MARÍA LAURA looks for a moment at ELISABET.

133

MARÍA LAURA: A girlfriend, Eli, a girlfriend, a partner, a wife, getting together, shacking up, shotgun wedding, children, kids, salaries; a wife's what he wants.

ELISABET: Cache?

MARÍA LAURA: Yep, my brother.

ELISABET looks for a moment at MARÍA LAURA.

ELISABET: Add me to the list.

MARÍA LAURA: Here we go.

ELISABET: I'm joking, girl.

MARÍA LAURA: *(Offstage. In her room.)* Look at these, do you like them?

ELISABET: They're really nice.

MARÍA LAURA: Really?

ELISABET: Yeah girl, the colour's so pretty. Do they fit?

MARÍA LAURA: Kind of.

ELISABET: What do you mean?

There is a sound that suggests MARÍA LAURA is putting on a pair of jeans and ELISABET is watching her. Shouts from the neighbours.

MARÍA LAURA: You see?

ELISABET: They fit perfectly.

MARÍA LAURA: Doesn't it make my…

ELISABET: Your bum?

MARÍA LAURA: No, Eli, here at the front, look – does it not give me cameltoe?

Laughter. Noises from the neighbours.

MARÍA LAURA: Shall I keep them on? What do you reckon?

ELISABET: You've got a great body.

MARÍA LAURA: I'm a mess.

ELISABET: I'm the one who's a mess.

MARÍA LAURA: What's up?

ELISABET: Nothing.

MARÍA LAURA: Nothing? Yeah right – come on, tell me.

ELISABET: Is it really obvious?

MARÍA LAURA: About as much as it is with me.

ELISABET: No.

MARÍA LAURA: Yeah, don't be an idiot, what you need is some love.

ELISABET: You think?

MARÍA LAURA: Me too, I'm saying.

ELISABET: Yeah, I know.

Something floats in and from ELISABET. Faintly.

MARÍA LAURA: What do you know?

ELISABET: That we both need some love.

MARÍA LAURA: So what do we do about it?

ELISABET: I don't know, but I reckon we must be doing something wrong.

MARÍA LAURA: Who, us?

ELISABET: At the very least.

MARÍA LAURA: And how do you work that one out?

ELISABET: Because you don't have any love, because I don't have any love.

MARÍA LAURA: So what do we do?

ELISABET: If you need love, if you know you do, if you already know that, then you can't let things carry on this like this. It's started.

MARÍA LAURA: What has, Eli? What ar…

ELISABET: *(Interrupting.)* Lali.

MARÍA LAURA: What?

ELISABET: I'm a bit scared.

MARÍA LAURA: Why? What's happened?

ELISABET: To me, nothing.

MARÍA LAURA: So who is it that's scared you?

ELISABET: You guys.

MARÍA LAURA: Huh?

ELISABET: I found out.

MARÍA LAURA: About what?

ELISABET: About your brother.

MARÍA LAURA: What did Gastón do?

ELISABET: Your other brother.

MARÍA LAURA: I haven't got another brother.

ELISABET: Yeah you do, Lali, I found out.

Silence.

MARÍA LAURA: About what?

Silence.

ELISABET: And it scared me.

MARÍA LAURA: Why?

Silence. The tones, the atmosphere, whatever it is that's floating in the air grows cold somehow. A bad smell, faint, but real.

ELISABET: He's called Bruno and he's the eldest.

MARÍA LAURA: I'm the eldest.

ELISABET: Your parents were guerrillas.

MARÍA LAURA: What?

ELISABET: Bombers, trouble-makers, rebels, *montoneros.*

MARÍA LAURA: They were in the People's Revolutionary Army.

ELISABET: It's the same thing.

MARÍA LAURA: No.

ELISABET: They were.

MARÍA LAURA: They weren't.

ELISABET: They were. What do you know?

MARÍA LAURA: What do *you* know?

136

ELISABET: It's all the same.

MARÍA LAURA: What do you mean, it's all the same?

ELISABET: It's all the same what they were: they were kidnapped, and you three were left with your maternal grandmother.

MARÍA LAURA: You're very confused about this, bu...

ELISABET: *(Interrupting.)* As bad as they come.

Silence.

MARÍA LAURA: Who told you all this?

ELISABET: You three were given that hundred thousand dollars payment the government gave out for being the children of disapp...

MARÍA LAURA: Stop it.

Silence.

MARÍA LAURA: Stop it.

Silence.

MARÍA LAURA: Do you know what happened? Huh? Whoever the fuck told you all this didn't te...

ELISABET: *(Interrupting.)* Bruno swiped the whole lot. The whole hundred thousand.

MARÍA LAURA: It was never a hundred thousand.

ELISABET: A thousand, then.

MARÍA LAURA: It was never that much.

ELISABET: Nearly.

MARÍA LAURA: Maybe.

Silence.

MARÍA LAURA: He made off with the whole lot to make a film.

ELISABET: They locked him up in Brazil for forty-five kilos of coke and being with a minor.

MARÍA LAURA: He left us totally broke.

ELISABET: I know.

Silence. Everything is soft, and fragile.

ELISABET: We're all totally broke.

MARÍA LAURA: So.

ELISABET: So, what?

MARÍA LAURA: So now you know all this, what now?

ELISABET: I don't know. I feel better?

MARÍA LAURA: What was it that scared you about us?

ELISABET: I was scared you were going to deny it.

MARÍA LAURA: Why would… *(She interrupts herself.)* It was your dad, wasn't it?

ELISABET: Maybe.

MARÍA LAURA: No maybe about it. How did he find out?

ELISABET: He found out. He's still go…

MARÍA LAURA: *(Interrupting.)* – What does he do in the forest, your old man?

Silence.

ELISABET: You really want to know?

MARÍA LAURA: How awful can it be?

ELISABET: It isn't awful.

MARÍA LAURA: What's out there?

ELISABET: It's not what.

MARÍA LAURA: Eh?

ELISABET: It's who. *(Silence.)* I wasn't going to say any more if you denied that stuff about Bruno.

MARÍA LAURA: What? What's that got to do with it?

ELISABET: You should know, you guys are a part of it, too. They love you.

MARÍA LAURA: What a… *(She interrupts herself.)* Who? What?

ELISABET: Shall we go to my house?

There is a moment of hesitation, but MARÍA LAURA agrees. MARÍA LAURA thinks about Bruno. The situation is a little strange for

*her. The two women leave. The neighbours argue. There is a period
of emptiness in the place, a period which gradually grows shorter
as, intermittently and from far away, a motorbike can be heard
approaching. It's GABRIEL and GASTÓN, who arrive talking,
switch off the engine talking, come up the stairs talking, and whose
talking with each other apparently makes them stop halfway up the
stairs because it takes longer than usual for the two men to enter
the living room.*

GABRIEL: She splits you up.

GASTÓN: She what?

GABRIEL: She splits you up, she separates you, she turns you
into parts.

GASTÓN: Of what?

GABRIEL: Of yourself.

GASTÓN: What are you talking about?

GABRIEL: That thing you told me she saw.

GASTÓN: Not again?

GABRIEL: What do you mean, not again?

GASTÓN: I mean, not again, not again with all that, man.

GABRIEL: It's serious.

GASTÓN: What can I say; it doesn't seem like it. There's
something going on here.

GABRIEL: Exactly.

GASTÓN: How exactly?

GABRIEL: That's why it doesn't seem like it.

GASTÓN: I'm going to fuck you up.

GABRIEL: Go ahead.

GASTÓN: You're getting involved in some shit, you idiot, and
you know it.

GABRIEL: So what?

GASTÓN: So just fucking listen to me for once, pal, I'm serious.
But you do you: I'm here for you, you know that, but don't

come running to me later with anything even weirder, you get me? I don't want any problems with these people.

GABRIEL: OK, Cache, don't freak out, man. Stop looking at me like that.

GASTÓN: I'm just saying, is all.

They go in, or have already done so.

GABRIEL: Where's your sister?

GASTÓN: Vanished, apparently.

They settle down.

GABRIEL: The thing that actually sets you off is that you're already there, as they say. And by 'already there', I don't mean like when people say, 'I'm done', I mean the opposite, actually. You're already at least getting a sense of what it's like or what it would be like, rather, if it ends up being the most specific form of all your desires, you know?

GASTÓN: Yeah, man.

GABRIEL: The ones that were slowly piling up, feeding stuff back and going around all over the place with some kind of hope or melancholy feeling that 'this' or 'that' event could, might, or will be the link in a chain that you can't even properly understand. But in any case, you're already there, like I say.

GASTÓN: That's what the bitch meant when she said she saw me there?

GABRIEL: Pretty much.

GASTÓN: And how do you remember it all?

GABRIEL: How?

GASTÓN: What do you mean, how?

GABRIEL: Why are you asking me how?

GASTÓN: You know, you idiot, how do you remember all of that, I mean.

GABRIEL: I don't get you.

GASTÓN: The words, you idiot.

GABRIEL: Ah.

GASTÓN: Melancholy sounds p...

GABRIEL: *(Interrupting.)* What does it sound like?

GASTÓN: Made up.

GABRIEL: By me?

GASTÓN: How do I know? That girl is doing something to you.

GABRIEL: She's not.

GASTÓN: No? Give it time. A few months down the line even I'm not going to understand what you're saying.

GABRIEL: No, I'm telling you, Cache, I'm just trying to understand something.

GASTÓN: What about?

GABRIEL: About me.

GASTÓN: About you?

GABRIEL: Yeah.

GASTÓN: You and that bitch?

GABRIEL: No, about myself, asshole, you get me?

Silence.

GABRIEL: Try to understand me.

GASTÓN: I am, but you're not being straight with me.

Silence.

GABRIEL: It's an urge.

GASTÓN: An urge to what?

GABRIEL: An urge.

GASTÓN: An urge to what?

GABRIEL: A urge, I don't know, an urgent urge. An urge to feel something urgently. An urge, Gastón, it's an urge.

GASTÓN: What are you talking about?

GABRIEL: Don't you have urges?

GASTÓN: Urges to do what, you idiot?

VOICE OF MALE NEIGHBOUR: *(Loudly.)* Motherfucking piece of shit. You bitch. *(It sounds as if he is knocking saucepans and plates onto the floor.)* Piece of shit, piece of shit, you worthless piece of shit. You see this, you bitch? I paid for this. I pay for all of this, you fucking whore. Let go of me.

VOICE OF FEMALE NEIGHBOUR: 'Let me go, let me go, let me go.' Stop playing the victim, you Indian faggot.

Crashes are heard against the wall. GASTÓN and GABRIEL grow worried. Cries from the male neighbour as he beats the wall.

GASTÓN: *(Quietly.)* They're always saying that.

GABRIEL: *(Dejected.)* I don't care.

GASTÓN: About what?

GABRIEL: About what you say they're always saying.

GASTÓN: Huh?

MARÍA LAURA and ELISABET arrive. Elated, together, on their way from something that now unites them. They see GASTÓN and GABRIEL listening against the wall. There is a moment with the four of them.

MARÍA LAURA: *(Quietly. About the neighbours.)* Not again?

GASTÓN: *(To MARÍA LAURA.)* Quiet.

MARÍA LAURA: *(To GABRIEL.)* Wipe that look off your face.

GASTÓN: What look?

VOICE OF MALE NEIGHBOUR: I'm serious this time. I'm serious.

VOICE OF FEMALE NEIGHBOUR: That's enough. You're pissed.

VOICE OF MALE NEIGHBOUR: You bitch. You old battle-axe. Whore, you're a whore. You're a shower of fucking witches, you are. I break my fucking balls at work and you know I do. You know it. You know it! For you and those three sons of bitches who turned out just like you.

The four exchange reactions and murmured comments. MARÍA LAURA seems slightly strange, and GASTÓN and GABRIEL notice this. ELISABET speaks very little; she does not look serious, however.

142

VOICE OF FEMALE NEIGHBOUR: Shut up shut up, just shut up, please listen to yourself, for God's sake. They're your children.

VOICE OF MALE NEIGHBOUR: I'm not going to set fire to you. I'm not going to give you the satisfaction of ending up a saint, bitch.

GABRIEL: I've got a horrible pain.

ELISABET: *(To GABRIEL.)* Me too.

GABRIEL: *(To ELISABET.)* So?

ELISABET: *(To GABRIEL.)* So what?

GASTÓN: *(To ELISABET.)* So why don't you just leave once and for all.

MARÍA LAURA: *(To all four of them.)* Let's listen. *(To ELISABET.)* Ignore him. *(A conspiratorial look.)*.

GABRIEL: *(To MARÍA LAURA.)* I admire your honesty.

MARÍA LAURA: I know you admire me.

GASTÓN: *(To ELISABET.)* I know who you are.

MARÍA LAURA: *(To GASTÓN.)* You only know what everybody else knows. Be quiet.

GASTÓN: Not you?

MARÍA LAURA: Not me.

The four are silent, but there are violent noises from the neighbours.

GASTÓN: Stop chatting shit.

MARÍA LAURA: There's something you should know, Gastón.

GABRIEL: What?

ELISABET: *(To MARÍA LAURA.)* Relax, it's your mission.

GASTÓN: *(To ELISABET.)* What are you talking about?

MARÍA LAURA: Gastón: Bruno's back.

GASTÓN: You're insane.

GABRIEL: Who?

ELISABET: *(To GASTÓN.)* I have to talk to you, as well. You can't go around with so many things left unfinished.

143

GASTÓN: *(To MARÍA LAURA.)* Tell that bitch to shut her mouth beca...

MARÍA LAURA: *(To GASTÓN. Interrupting.)* We can't go around with so many things left unfinished.

Loud, violent noises issue from the neighbours' house. Children crying, struggles, thuds, cries from the two adults. Knives, apparently. The male neighbour calls for help. So does the female neighbour. The fight continues, the shouts, the arguing. The four are rigid from the intensity of the violence coming from next door. There is a moment for everything. It is now.

GASTÓN: *(To GABRIEL.)* Shall we go round?

GABRIEL: *(To GASTÓN.)* You think?

The looks are now.

MARÍA LAURA: Let's go over.

GASTÓN: Let's go.

ELISABET: Shall we?

GABRIEL: Come on.

The four of them leave the apartment. The four of them leave, doubtfully. Slowly they walk over to the neighbours' front door. Silences and looks are shared, amongst other things. From the other side, the violent chaos continues. A family can be a battlefield, at times. Now, the four of them – GASTÓN, MARÍA LAURA, GABRIEL and ELISABET – stand like frightened children in the neighbours' doorway. The shouts and loud noises are still coming from the other side while GASTÓN, at first hesitant and looking at the others, knocks at the neighbours' door, several times, his mind made up now.

Blackout and total silence.

NOU FIUTER (NO FUTURE)
The sentimental education of the dead
La educación sentimental de los muertos

FRANCO CALLUSO
TRANSLATED BY WILLIAM GREGORY

Franco Calluso

Franco Calluso was born in Buenos Aires in 1988. He is a playwright, director and musician. He is an advanced student of Philosophy at the University of Buenos Aires. He studied playwriting at EMAD (the Metropolitan School of Dramatic Art, Buenos Aires) with Mauricio Kartun. He also trained at workshops taught by Alejandro Tantanián, Ariel Farace, Romina Paula, Mariano Tenconi Blanco and Ignacio Bartolone. His first production as a playwright and director, *Nena Dragón*, was selected for its premiere at the 2015 Opera Prima season at the Centro Cultural Ricardo Rojas. *Proyecto B21* was included in the 2016 El Porvenir (The Future) season. *Ruido Blanco* (*White Noise*), his second full-length play as a director and playwright, was selected among the projects to be developed at the 2017 Buenos Aires Young Art Biennial. He took part in the Buenos Aires Young Art Biennial in literature with his short story *Los Jabalíes* (*The Boars*), published by Eterna Cadencia in the 2017 anthology *Raros Peinados Nuevos* (*Strange New Hairstyles*). As an author he took part in the 2017 Radar Literatura festival at the Centro Cultural Recoleta. *Nou Fiuter* won first prize at the INT (National Theatre Institute) national playwriting competition of 2017.

Characters

VÍCTOR
Owner of the wine recipe. Father.

IRENE
Television's best friend. Mother.

POXI
Barely a teenager, he has no idea about
anything. Son.

OMAR
Taxi driver, signed off from work on mental
health grounds. Irene's brother.

ESPINOSA
An orphaned punk, exiled to the countryside
following the earthquake. Inexpert vineyard
assistant.

'Punk is supposedly something ugly.
I'm really ugly so I must be very punk.'

Ricardo Espinosa

'If the tomato sauce
doesn't turn the pasta
burgundy
it's disgusting'

Martín Gambarotta

EVERYONE I KNOW IS DEAD
OR, THE WINE FESTIVAL

The vineyard. The veranda of a house in the valley. Paint that has seen better days. A blueish dusk. Wine. The estate. The valley. A shed with the remains of things inside. In the shed, a drum-kit, an amplifier and an electric bass guitar. On the veranda, IRENE and VÍCTOR drink wine and watch the darkness fall.

IRENE: On the television today they tried to name all the people who'd died in the earthquake. They were reading out names for twenty minutes. Then halfway through one person's name they stopped and went silent.

VÍCTOR: And you kept listening?

IRENE: Yes. The Pope spoke as well. He said, 'Prayer will save us from sadness.' No, he said 'anguish'. He said that, and he also said, 'The real tremor is within us.'

VÍCTOR: They went silent.

IRENE: They went silent, yes.

Silence.

VÍCTOR: The other day, Ángel. I bump into him in town and he offers to bring me to the estate. I get in the truck and when he reaches the roundabout he drives into the petrol station and asks me to wait; he had something to do. I was in the passenger seat. Sun on my side. I get out of the truck to wait outside. Ángel was talking to the attendant and showing him photos of what the earthquake had done to the city. He was obsessed with those photos. I turn 'round and I see the long-distance bus pulling into the roundabout. I didn't think much; I ran, held out my hand and stopped it.

IRENE: Was he offended?

VÍCTOR: Who?

IRENE: Ángel.

VÍCTOR: I should be offended by the wine he made me drink at the festival last year.

IRENE: It was his; it wasn't that bad.

VÍCTOR: Please; no one knows if he's ever seen a real grape in his life. All shrivelled fox grapes, wine from a chemical sachet. Shall I tell you something?

IRENE: What?

VÍCTOR: He told me he's making arrangements for the wine road to reach all the way to here.

IRENE: But after the earthquake –

VÍCTOR: He can make all the arrangements he likes, but the wine road –

IRENE: I don't know if –

VÍCTOR: – if it does come this far they'll choose our wine, which is frankly superior.

IRENE: – what with the earthquake.

VÍCTOR: That's got nothing to do with it; we're talking about the wine road.

IRENE: There was a bald man talking on the television; he said, 'The wine road: an experience that shakes.'

VÍCTOR: There'll still be a wine road; there'll still be a festival; all this business about the earthquake will last for a while and then it'll stop. That's how things are. No one says a thing. And the wine remains.

Silence.

IRENE: This afternoon. My brother called and asked about the back room.

VÍCTOR: Omar?

IRENE: Omar.

VÍCTOR: What for?

IRENE: He didn't want to say very much. He said, 'Irenita, is there anyone in the back room?'

VÍCTOR: There's never anyone in the back room.

IRENE: 'I've been told I've got to leave here, even if it's just for a while.'

VÍCTOR: Why?

IRENE: I don't know.

VÍCTOR: You didn't ask?

IRENE: I didn't think to.

VÍCTOR: What about the taxi?

IRENE: I didn't ask him. On the television they said, 'Exodus: people flee the city, fearing another quake.'

Feedback from the shed. A monotone, distorted note from the bass guitar. The valley grows bluer in the night. The drum-kit tuning up. VÍCTOR stands and leans on a column on the veranda, glass of wine in hand.

VÍCTOR: I told you the drum-kit wasn't a good present.

IRENE: Is that the new assistant in there with him?

VÍCTOR: Right, I'm going inside.

IRENE: That poor boy…

VÍCTOR enters the house. In the shed, ESPINOSA, the new vineyard assistant, plays the bass. On the drums, POXI, the son of the family, approaching adolescence and banging the drums loudly and badly. A free, unbearable concert. Hardcore viticulture punk. IRENE enters the house.

ESPINOSA: Everyone I know
Is dead
The only thing I want
Doesn't exist
All my family
Are dead
I'm gonna start
My own earthquake
Everyone who loves me
Is dead
Richter! Richter!
There's no future there's no future
Richter! Richter!
There's no future for you and me!

POXI: Really good.

ESPINOSA: We should get a bit more wine.

POXI: I've done a list of potential names for the band.

ESPINOSA: Let's see.

POXI: Shall I read them out? *(Opens an exercise book.)*

ESPINOSA: Go on.

POXI: Anthrax.

ESPINOSA: Already exists.

POXI: Mud, Dead Ponies, Badaboom, The Same Thing, Bad Habits, Domestic Fires, The Bull-Heads, Wine Mutants, no, that's really bad, Totem.

ESPINOSA: Already exists.

POXI: The Corpses.

ESPINOSA: Corpses of Children already exists.

POXI: The Evil Twin? That's all I've got.

ESPINOSA: The Dead of the Earthquake.

POXI: I don't know.

ESPINOSA: I don't know.

POXI: That's it. *(Closes the exercise book.)*

ESPINOSA: It got dark.

POXI: Good; I like the valley more at night.

ESPINOSA: In the city I preferred the night. But here at six a.m. I have to be checking the must, the temperatures. I don't feel like doing anything. Why don't you get a bottle from the cellar in the house? I'm not allowed inside, but they won't say anything to you. Go on.

POXI: Mum says I can't drink wine.

ESPINOSA: Seriously, Poxi?

POXI: Seriously, she doesn't let me.

ESPINOSA: But they know you're gonna start drinking wine some time. Better sooner than later. Plus if you do it right they won't even notice.

POXI: Erm… Well.

ESPINOSA: I'll go in if you want; I don't care.

POXI: No, no… I'll go.

ESPINOSA: It's true, though: the night's impossible tonight. I'll wait for you on the roof.

ESPINOSA climbs drunkenly onto the shed roof with a bottle that has very little wine left in it. He sits on the metal rooftop and takes a swig from what is left in the bottle. POXI walks to the house and looks through the window on the veranda. He opens the window and climbs in. At the same time, IRENE comes out of the house.

IRENE: No, no, it's OK; they're here, we'd left them outside.
(Picks up the wineglasses and sees something on the roof of the shed.)
Víctor, I think there's something on the shed roof. 'Osvaldo Tamera agricultural pest control: send the plane, save the crops. Osvaldo Tamera, Route 23, Kilometre 821, by the General Galindez roundabout, 2234-551-273.' If I don't say the whole thing I don't remember the number; did you write it down? Víctor! I think it moved. What was that programme called where they locked those kids up in a castle and they had to put their hands in fish tanks? Do you remember? It was an abandoned castle; it was full of scorpions or wild animals inside. It was really shocking, Víctor. Do you remember? I don't know what it is on the roof but it's moving. *(Goes inside.)* That man used to host it, the really funny one… Talented… 'Osvaldo Tamera agricultural pest…'

IRENE goes inside and POXI comes out of the window waving the bottle of wine in one hand. He walks to the shed and climbs up onto the roof.

POXI: This is the one my dad drinks every day.

ESPINOSA: One day less; cheers. *(Pushes the cork down into the bottle.)*

POXI: Dad says when I turn eighteen he's gonna teach me his wine recipe. What he doesn't know is I'm leaving home when I turn eighteen.

ESPINOSA: Won't be any use to you then.

POXI: Maybe you can have the wine recipe.

ESPINOSA: I'm leaving too.

POXI: But you only just moved here.

ESPINOSA: Not planning on staying.

POXI: I think when someone's just moved somewhere they shouldn't think about leaving. I don't know; maybe I'm talking rubbish.

ESPINOSA: You want me to stay? I'll stay if you want me to stay.

POXI: Er… Yeah! I want you to stay. I think I'm gonna go back in the house; they'll come out to see what I'm doing.

ESPINOSA: Go on; see you tomorrow.

POXI: See you tomorrow.

ESPINOSA: See you tomorrow.

POXI climbs down from the roof and walks to the house. In a dark corner, close to the veranda, OMAR is seated on his bag. POXI sees him.

POXI: That you, Uncle Omar?

OMAR: Who's that?

POXI: Lucas.

OMAR: Oh, hello, kidda.

POXI: Erm… What you doing here?

OMAR: Sitting on my bag.

POXI: Yeah, but I didn't know you were coming. Why aren't you inside?

OMAR: Oh. True… I get a thought stuck in my head sometimes; don't notice the time passing. I'll clap my hands.

POXI: What for?

OMAR: To… To announce my arrival. I didn't bring the taxi; I'd honk the horn otherwise.

POXI: Oh, no. But I don't think you need to. Come inside.

OMAR: I'm tired.

POXI and OMAR enter the house.

POXI: *(Going in.)* Mum! Uncle Omar was at the door.

VILLA REAL
OR, THAT POOR BOY

Day. The valley bathed in sunshine. IRENE and OMAR on the veranda drinking their morning maté.

OMAR: And according to what they said I was stationary with a customer in the taxi on a slip road off the motorway and I wasn't moving. And apparently she got out the taxi and ran away. And after a while they found me with my hands on the steering wheel staring into space. There was nothing there.

IRENE: Nothing?

OMAR: Well, the road.

IRENE: Oh, Omar.

OMAR: I try to remember and nothing. White. Black. Nothing. The last thing is me in the hospital waiting room. There's another four drivers; it was similar apparently; someone from the union. They kept us there a few hours; we talked to a few doctors. Then they put us in a room with two doctors and a bloke from the highways agency and they tell Róbera and me we have to hand our cab licences in.

IRENE: But it cost you so much money!

OMAR: Curiosities.

IRENE: What?

OMAR: There was one of those magazines about scientific curiosities there and me and Róbera were talking about how they'd found the longest sea snake in the world off the coast of Japan. Twelve metres long it was.

IRENE: What's that got to do with it?

OMAR: No, no… I tell a lie: fifteen metres. From the radiation.

Silence. Maté.

OMAR: Róbera went to live with his father-in-law in the mountains. He sent me a letter, said it'd done him good to get out of the city.

IRENE: And that's when you thought, 'I'll go to Irene's.'

Silence. Maté.

OMAR: It's me and Róbera. It's not a coincidence.

IRENE: The magazine?

OMAR: No, not the magazine… This is just between me and you… Me and Róbera had been saying… We talked a lot with Rolando… And talking about how… No, no, I tell a lie, I tell a lie…

IRENE: What?

OMAR: No, I just get confused.

IRENE: Come on, Omar: you're frightening me.

OMAR: Some kids. We were saying that. Kids standing there on their own stopping the taxis.

IRENE: Robbing them? There was something on the television about that.

OMAR: They stop you, at sunset, when you're finishing up for the day, on the road, and they ask to go to Villa Real.

IRENE: Villa Real's just a pile of rubble now.

OMAR: 'Villa Real's just a pile of rubble now,' that's what we said. And those kids act like the earthquake never happened.

IRENE: 'Modus operandi: approach and mislead.' They said that today.

OMAR: When you try and explain there's just twisted steel and mountains of concrete left there they say, 'So that's where I am: underneath the rubble?' and then – wham! – you turn 'round and they're gone.

IRENE: What do you mean, 'they're gone'?

OMAR: Just that… The place where they were is there, but they're not in it.

IRENE: They get out of the car?

OMAR: They disappear.

IRENE: Goosebumps.

VÍCTOR walks in from the valley.

VÍCTOR: Irene! Irene!

IRENE: What is it?

VÍCTOR: The new lad, the one from the city.

IRENE: *(To OMAR.)* The new assistant, that poor boy.

VÍCTOR: He threw himself in the fermentation tank.

IRENE: Huh?! It can't be!

IRENE stands and goes into the house. OMAR stands, looks towards the house, looks at VÍCTOR.

VÍCTOR: I couldn't find him anywhere this morning; he was nowhere to be seen; I went to his cabin to look for him but nothing. The blades in the fermentation tank had got jammed and Don Zorega went to fix it and he found him there. The body. The body wedged between the steel blades.

OMAR: That's horrible.

IRENE returns from the house.

IRENE: So… So… So… What are we going to do?

VÍCTOR: How do I know what we're going to do?

OMAR: Did you get him out?

VÍCTOR: Yes. Zorega took him out and covered him with a tarpaulin.

IRENE: That poor boy.

OMAR: But he…

IRENE: They said it on television one afternoon: 'Thirty per cent of young people who lose their families in disasters suffer from suicidal tendencies.' They had an expert on.

OMAR: Is an earthquake a disaster or a phenomenon?

VÍCTOR: We tried to help him out after what happened. That's why he came to work here. I can't believe it.

IRENE: He was Lucas's friend, poor thing.

VÍCTOR: They've got a band.

IRENE: They did have.

OMAR: I've come at a bad time. Don't you need to tell someone?

IRENE: Yes. What do we do now?

VÍCTOR: It's just he doesn't have any family any more... He's got no one.

OMAR: I wish I could help.

VÍCTOR: I think we all have to think. I'll go and help Zorega.

OMAR: I'll go with you.

IRENE: Yes... What do we do with the body? Oh, the poor boy.

OMAR: I think I'm in shock.

VÍCTOR and OMAR walk towards the valley. POXI comes out from the house.

POXI: Morning...

IRENE: The weather said very, very cold today; you're not going out like that.

POXI: Mum, imagine if something happened one day and you didn't have telly any more.

IRENE: Why would that happen?

POXI: It's a hypothesis: something happens and the whole world... Well, not the whole world, the whole country is left without television. Something like the earthquake but different, that only affects signals.

IRENE: Oh, I don't know if I understand what you're saying.

POXI: Never mind; I'm off to the shed.

IRENE: Luqui, come here.

POXI: What?

IRENE: No, no, nothing... Off you go.

POXI walks to the shed and picks up ESPINOSA's bass. He plays a note and sustains it. In the valley, OMAR and VÍCTOR can be seen in silhouette dragging ESPINOSA's body covered in a tarpaulin.

VÍCTOR: That's it; here'll do.

OMAR: His face.

VÍCTOR: What?

OMAR: Look at it.

VÍCTOR: I'll never fathom why these things happen, I really won't.

OMAR: What shocks me is he's not making any particular face. If I tried to make the same face he's making now, I'd not be able to, 'cause he's not making one.

VÍCTOR: We should fetch the shovel from the shed.

OMAR: You know Róbera lost a nephew like this, too, more or less the same age.

VÍCTOR: Are we burying him or not?

OMAR: Shouldn't we tell someone?

VÍCTOR: Who? He's got no one.

OMAR: Oh.

VÍCTOR: I just thought it's the best thing: bury him before he starts to smell.

OMAR: I think whatever you think is fine; I don't know… *(Looks back and forth from ESPINOSA's body to VÍCTOR.)* Don't look at me; I only just got here. Oh… Sorry, I got a bit confused.

VÍCTOR: Don't worry, Omar. Have a seat and wait for me; I'll be right back.

VÍCTOR walks to the shed. OMAR sits on the ground; he looks at the covered body. In the shed, POXI stops playing.

VÍCTOR: Carry on playing; I don't mind; I've just come to fetch something.

POXI: No, it's OK; do you need a hand?

VÍCTOR: No, no, thanks… Did you talk to your mum?

POXI: Just now?

VÍCTOR: Yes.

POXI: Yeah, we talked a bit.

VÍCTOR: And?

POXI: What?

VÍCTOR: What about?

POXI: Nothing major; I don't remember now.

VÍCTOR: Ha ha, well… Carry on, carry on…

POXI: Why d'you ask me that?

VÍCTOR: No, no, nothing…

POXI: All right, I'll carry on.

POXI starts playing a slow bass line. VÍCTOR walks over towards a pile of tools, picks up a shovel and stops at the door to look at POXI.

VÍCTOR: Lucas.

POXI stops playing.

VÍCTOR: Your friend won't be working with us any more. He told me this morning and left.

POXI: No, that can't be right; he told me he'd see me today.

VÍCTOR: I don't know what to say. I know you'd become friends.

A note from the bass resounds in the air. In the valley, ESPINOSA†emerges from the tarpaulin, but his body remains lying on the grass. OMAR crawls backwards, stands up.

OMAR: No, no, Omar, it's not what you think; don't make eye contact; the boy's dead; don't look at him, don't look at him.

POXI: Where can he have gone?

OMAR: Don't look at him…

VÍCTOR: I don't know where he went, Lucas; I'm not his father; he's a grown lad; he'll sort himself out somewhere else.

OMAR: Oh… Is he looking at me? Is he looking at me?

VÍCTOR: And you have to accept he's decided what he's decided. You knew him. Lad from the city. Must have felt lonely here, sad, and well, he's moving on. He didn't tell me where.

POXI: What about his guitar?

OMAR: Er… Hell… Hello.

VÍCTOR: I don't know… Clearly a lad who doesn't know what he wants.

POXI takes off the bass, lays it on the floor and stares at VÍCTOR.

POXI: Was that everything? Off you go, then.

VÍCTOR: Don't shoot the messenger.

OMAR: Nice... Nice to meet you; I'm Omar, Irene's... Irene's brother... Er... Er... Everything's OK... All OK.

POXI sits at the drum-kit and starts drumming angrily. He strikes the drums loudly and badly. VÍCTOR exits the shed and drags the shovel towards the valley. ESPINOSA⁺ walks slowly towards the shed. He passes VÍCTOR, but VÍCTOR does not see him. The beat of the drums matches ESPINOSA⁺'s footsteps. He arrives at the shed and picks up the bass. He starts to play a bass line and sings. In the valley, VÍCTOR and OMAR dig.

ESPINOSA⁺: Buddy
Gonna tell you
Something big
Do me a favour
Don't quit the music
And if there's something you don't get
You should play
Play
Play
Play
Buddy
Gonna tell you
Something big
Don't quit the wine
They don't love you
And if there's something you don't get
You should drink
Drink
Drink
Buddy
Gonna tell you
Something big
I love you
I loved you
And I came back
And if there's something you don't get
You should dig

Dig
Dig
Dig
Dig
Dig
Dig
Dig
Dig

POXI: I knew you hadn't left.

ESPINOSA†: I'm not gonna let you play the bass so much.

POXI: What happened to you?

ESPINOSA†: This? Oh, you won't believe it. I finished the bottle you brought last night and I remembered the fermentation tank was full of wine so I went down to find it. Got a few stains on me.

POXI: Ha ha! It's not even wine yet!

ESPINOSA†: In the city they call it being cracked.

POXI: Cracked?

ESPINOSA†: Yeah.

POXI: But that's nothing to do with the earthquake, or is it?

ESPINOSA†: Everything's to do with the earthquake now.

POXI: That's true.

ESPINOSA†: Mate.

POXI: What?

ESPINOSA†: Don't tell anyone I'm here. They think I left and it's best that way.

POXI: OK, fine.

WHEN I DIE
OR, CAB-DRIVER LIMBO

VÍCTOR is seated on the veranda with a notebook. He thinks and writes. Writes and thinks. IRENE rushes out from the house.

IRENE: Lucas! Come inside; it's starting!

VÍCTOR: Irene, could you not shout?

IRENE: He won't hear me from the shed otherwise. What are you doing?

VÍCTOR: Trying to write the recipe down.

IRENE: That boy spends all day in that shed, the whole day in the shed. The wine recipe?

VÍCTOR: Of course the wine.

IRENE: First you have to put all the ingredients and then the method, and then you put the ingredients again, but you can write them sort of on a different background.

VÍCTOR: No, this is different. A wine recipe has to be narrated. It has to describe the whole process clearly. Can't miss a single detail out.

IRENE: *(Intro music sounds.)* Lucas! It's starting!

VÍCTOR: Can you tell me what he does in the shed all day?

IRENE: Lucas!

VÍCTOR: Clearly doesn't want to watch soaps today, Irene; do me a favour and go inside.

IRENE: All right, but he needn't come asking me when he doesn't know what's going on because he's missed an episode.

VÍCTOR: Fine, I'll tell him.

IRENE: Not to come asking me.

VÍCTOR: I'll tell him.

IRENE: *(Going into the house.)* Because he asks...

VÍCTOR: *(Writing.)* The border between... bitterness... and... mmm...

POXI comes out of the shed with ESPINOSA†. POXI walks towards the house and ESPINOSA†climbs onto the shed roof and lies down.

VÍCTOR: *(Writes.)* Mmmmm... com... pos... i... tion....

POXI: Has it started?

VÍCTOR: She said not to go asking her later about the soap; don't ask her.

POXI: I never ask her.

VÍCTOR: Do you want to read this later?

POXI: Read what?

VÍCTOR: What I'm writing.

POXI: Er… OK, fine, one day. *(Goes into the house.)*

VÍCTOR writes. In the valley, ESPINOSA†sits up on the roof of the shed.

VÍCTOR: …Mmmm… The process should last approximately… mmm

ESPINOSA†: 'If you're lucky, someone's body will fall straight into the fermentation tank and spend the whole night filling its lungs with wine. That will give the recipe that topical touch.'

VÍCTOR: …Depending on the type of grape… mmm… opaqueness does not always mean… mmm…

ESPINOSA†: Not a lot of people know this but the people who died in the earthquake are getting together and travelling from one place to another in a gang. It looks like an exodus but they're just wandering around; they're not going anywhere in particular; they're not scaring anyone. They huddle together like they're cold. Now I'm dead, I know they don't feel anything. Not cold or hot. Not bitter, not frustrated. They don't feel anything in particular. From here, you don't feel the need for anything in particular to happen. But all the same they huddle together. The dead. From the earthquake, like school friends. My family must be among that crowd. They always liked getting together in groups just because. I never did. I see them from a distance, like looking at a mountain or a giraffe. My dad, for example, used to like telling jokes with no punchlines or telling everyone his son liked guys, because that was something that got other people's attention. 'My son likes men; he fancies his classmates.' He must be doing that right now. Getting attention from people with too much time on their hands 'cause they don't feel anything and they've nowhere to go. And in the city, the waiting room in the provincial hospital fills up with taxi drivers. The same thing happens to all of them: passengers get in on the road and ask to be taken back to their homes which now are nothing more than a pile of concrete, steel and pieces of furniture with drawers where people like my dad stored a few old Havana cigars and ladies like my mum collected tickets from long-distance travel. And those taxi drivers get disoriented; they lose their minds and wonder if they're the ones who are dead, in a cab-driver limbo, because the waiting room of a hospital is a bit like that. No, no, but here we feel nothing. Or almost nothing. I mean, because sometimes something… When I get distracted and I'm talking to Poxi, I could believe for a second I'm still alive.

OMAR walks in from the valley, looking dishevelled, with a bottle of wine in one hand and a bunch of wild flowers that he has picked in the other. He stops and looks at the patch of earth where ESPINOSA is buried. ESPINOSA⁺ comes down from the roof and walks towards OMAR.

ESPINOSA⁺: What you doing?

OMAR: Argh!

ESPINOSA⁺: Calm down.

OMAR: What are you doing here?

ESPINOSA⁺: I'm here.

OMAR: But you're there. *(Points to the patch of soil.)*

ESPINOSA⁺: Yeah, I am there, actually.

OMAR: But where are you really?

ESPINOSA⁺: 'Really' I'm under there. Did you know that when the earthquake happened, after two days of piling up bodies, the rescuers looked for people to ID them and there were so many of them that most of the people who could've ID'd them were dead too?

OMAR: I didn't know.

ESPINOSA⁺: But you must know what happened next; you're from there too.

OMAR: What do you want? What are you looking for?

ESPINOSA⁺: What happened was they started to smell; the air started smelling of death, so the government set a deadline and buried them all.

OMAR: Buried them? I don't understand what you mean.

ESPINOSA[†]: Person doesn't always have to mean something. Is there any of that left?

OMAR: I'll be off.

ESPINOSA[†]: Did you see Poxi?

OMAR: No offence but I'm leaving now.

OMAR throws the flowers onto the patch of earth where ESPINOSA is buried and walks towards the valley with the bottle in his hand.

ESPINOSA[†]: Come on: gimme a swig.

POXI and IRENE come out of the house talking. ESPINOSA[†] walks towards the shed and picks up the bass. Isolated notes that resonate as much as possible.

IRENE: …situation they can't cope with.

POXI: All right, but she's been in love with him for ages, but she goes and tells his mate instead of going straight to him and telling him; do you understand it? If you understand it, tell me why, 'cause I don't.

IRENE: It's not that simple.

POXI: That was one thing I thought was bad about this soap, 'cause telling his mate is practically the same as telling him.

IRENE: I think it's fine: people are like that; people do do that sort of thing.

VÍCTOR: *(Writing.)* Mmm… the tanning…

POXI: 'Tanning'? Isn't it just 'tannin'?

VÍCTOR: 'In', not 'ing'?

IRENE: Tannin, tan-IN; no, I don't think so.

VÍCTOR: It's taking shape; want to read?

POXI: I'm off to the shed to practice for a bit. Maybe later.

POXI walks quickly towards the shed.

IRENE: Leave him… Leave him…

VÍCTOR: No interest in the recipe whatsoever.

IRENE: 'Be rebellious,' they said on the television. And then they said, 'In times of crisis, there are lots of things to think about.'

POXI sits at the drum-kit. Unstable beat, slow rhythm, repeated cymbal. ESPINOSA†plays a sad but energetic melody, a symptom of the fever of a whole generation.

ESPINOSA†: The ground moved
Let's bury them all
The ground moved
The world no longer has
The same shape
The ground moved
Let's bury them all
Beneath the rubble
There's me
Beneath the rubble
There's all of us
Let's bury ourselves
Like so many other times
Let's bury ourselves
Like one more of them
The ground moved
And you
Move the ground for me
I'm no longer here
But all the same
The ground moved
And you
You move the ground
For me.

POXI: I don't know if I'd want to be buried when I die.

ESPINOSA†: No, I don't think I would either; we could change it.

POXI: When I die I want my body to be burned and what's left of me to be put in the bass drum.

ESPINOSA†: When I die I want to be butchered and fed to the animals. It's called cremation.

POXI: When I die I want people to pogo dance on top of me.

ESPINOSA†: When I die I want to be used for anatomy lectures.

POXI: Can they do that? That'd be awesome; they should do that.

ESPINOSA†: When I die I want to be hung upside down from my feet and for people to write messages on my face and my body with a marker pen.

POXI: I want to be thrown off a really high cliff.

ESPINOSA†: I want to be wrapped in plastic and left on my bed forever.

POXI: I want to be cut into six pieces and one piece to be thrown onto each continent.

ESPINOSA†: That's a pain: leaving a lot of work for the people who are still alive.

POXI: Yeah, that's what I'd want. Leave a lot of work for the living. But not being buried; I don't know if I'd like that.

ESPINOSA†: No, that's true; it's not good being underground.

THE BEST WINE OF ALL
OR, THE SILENT CABBIES

IRENE and OMAR are on the veranda. VÍCTOR appears from the valley with a bottle of wine with no label. ESPINOSA† climbs up into the shed roof.

IRENE: Here he comes! Go and tell Lucas.

OMAR: What?

VÍCTOR: Here it is… The first bottle of the harvest.

IRENE: The cheese, I forgot the cheese.

IRENE and VÍCTOR go into the house. OMAR stares at ESPINOSA† who is standing on the shed roof.

ESPINOSA†: First wine of the harvest. The first bottle from the harvest is here. You can nearly see the road from here. When you see the road, the city looks just like an afterthought. I can't even remember what the tarmac smells like, what the exhaust fumes smell like. It's weird being dead and wanting to drink wine, wanting to pour wine into this mouth only for it to fall through the empty space and land on the floor, because you have to be something to contain something else. If I'm anything, I'm that very wine that's come to the table today, and that tomorrow, at the wine festival, they'll celebrate as the best wine in the region, and Víctor will celebrate being better than his neighbour, he'll go and celebrate his recipe, and he'll baptise his son with his recipe, but the wine road will never reach here, because there'll never be anything like the wine road ever again. There's the taxi driver looking at me. He does remember the exhaust fumes and the tarmac. Omar, tell me something: have you been frozen, staring into space, like when you were holding the steering wheel on the road? Your friend Róbera's back in town now, and, you know what? The dead of the earthquake visit him every day and take turns to tell him things. And he doesn't speak any more; doesn't say a single word. Omar? Are you there? Hello. Omar? Are you there?

VÍCTOR, POXI and IRENE come out onto the veranda. IRENE has a cheeseboard.

VÍCTOR: OK, OK, let's all stay calm; I'm a little bit emotional. Omar? Please, do me the honour of being the first.

OMAR: *(Looks at the shed roof.)* No, thanks, no… Er… It has to be you, Víctor.

VÍCTOR pours three glasses of wine. The reddish liquid falls into the glasses and settles. A ray of light shines through them and the red glows more intensely. OMAR, VÍCTOR and IRENE look at the glasses of wine, as if hypnotised. Time passes.

POXI: What is it?

VÍCTOR: Nothing. *(Lifts the glass, swirls it around, smells it, looks at it and drinks.)*

IRENE: So?

POXI: Is it good?

VÍCTOR: Full-bodied. Notes of blackberry and tobacco. Smooth aftertaste. The best. Simply the best wine. A distinct wine. Let's all stay calm. Let's have a toast. Let's pour one for Lucas; this is a good time for him to try it.

OMAR: No.

IRENE: What's the matter? Are you all right?

OMAR: No, don't give him any, because I... Er... I'm not feeling too well; I'm a bit confused... He can have my glass... I tell a lie... Your glass. I'm going for a lie down. Excuse me.

OMAR goes into the house.

VÍCTOR: Let's sit down. Enjoy the moment.

IRENE: I'll go and see if he's OK...

VÍCTOR: No, no, stay here, Irene... You can go in a minute. *(To POXI.)* So?

POXI: What?

VÍCTOR: Try it.

POXI: Oh...

IRENE: Just a mouthful. There was a doctor today saying, 'Young people aren't assimilating alcohol properly.'

POXI takes a swig of wine. ESPINOSA†plays an arpeggio on the bass from the shed.

VÍCTOR: So?

POXI: It's all right.

VÍCTOR: Your palate just hasn't developed yet.

IRENE: His palate's not used to it.

VÍCTOR: *(Raises his glass.)* To his first glass of wine, to the grape and to your palate, son. To the recipe. My recipe today will be your recipe tomorrow. Cheers.

ESPINOSA†: Cheers.

OMAR comes out from the house, walking very quickly. He walks past all of them and goes to the shed. He stands looking at ESPINOSA†on the roof.

OMAR: What is it you want? Please tell me what you want and how long you're going to stay here.

IRENE: What's wrong with Omar?

ESPINOSA†: I'll stay here as long as I like.

POXI: Uncle Omar?

OMAR: I can't stand it any more; I can't stand it any more; go away.

ESPINOSA[†]: Could you do me a favour and get me some of that wine?

OMAR: Stop! Stop!

VÍCTOR: Who's he talking to, Irenita?

IRENE: To nothing.

VÍCTOR: There's no one there.

ESPINOSA[†]: You're getting all these idiots worked up. Come on: get me that wine and don't make a scene; I don't want any fuss here.

POXI: What do you mean, 'no one'? That's Espinosa on the roof, isn't it?

IRENE: The assistant? Oh… God save us.

ESPINOSA[†]: I want to see if I can still drink wine even though I'm dead.

VÍCTOR: No, it can't be; is it Zorega? I can't see properly from here.

ESPINOSA[†]: It's not that I need it, you understand.

POXI: No, I think it's him; it's him; he didn't leave.

VÍCTOR: 'You think', you say, son, but it's Zorega, or some animal or I don't know, but it can't be him.

ESPINOSA[†]: I know it's unbelievable, but I haven't tried it yet.

IRENE: Oh, God protect and save us; I don't feel well.

VÍCTOR: Zorega! You see? He turned around. Come on: let's go inside, Irene.

IRENE: …Please, make him go away… Víctor, I think I saw him; is there something on the roof?

VÍCTOR: Let's all go inside. Everyone inside, damn it! Omar! Lucas! Come inside! Damn it! Let's go, let's go in.

VÍCTOR takes IRENE into the house; she is very distressed. POXI walks to the shed.

ESPINOSA[†]: Are you gonna bring me that wine now or what? Here comes Poxi.

OMAR: You want wine?

POXI: What's going on?

OMAR: I'll bring you some wine.

ESPINOSA[†]: No, nothing's going on, Poxi; everything's fine.

POXI: Don't you want to come down?

OMAR: Tell your uncle to bring me the wine and then leave. Bring us the wine and leave us alone. Tell him that, and then we have to talk. We have to talk about our business.

POXI: I swear I don't understand any of this.

ESPINOSA[†]: It's not easy to understand and I don't really know how to tell you, but I swear it's quite simple. It's simple if I explain it to you bit by bit.

POXI: What bit? What are you talking about? Can you just come down?

ESPINOSA[†]: OK, I'll come down; I'm coming down.

ESPINOSA[†]comes down from the shed roof. OMAR walks with the bottle of wine to the place where ESPINOSA is buried and empties the wine onto the ground. ESPINOSA[†]and POXI stare at him. The wine falls as if in slow motion and soaks the black soil forming a puddle. POXI walks over to OMAR, sees the flowers on the ground soaked in wine. He returns to the shed, takes the shovel, walks to where ESPINOSA's body is and starts digging. OMAR walks quickly away to the valley. ESPINOSA[†]puts on the bass and plays one last melancholic, distorted melody.

ESPINOSA[†]: All I wanted to tell you is
Kept somewhere
Buried
All I wanted to give you
Is buried there
And it's me
It's my body
When the shovel hits something hard

Covered in plastic
You'll understand me
And your uncle won't be able to talk any more
He'll want to tell you something and he won't be able to
And my wrapped-up body will be
The last you know of me
And then you'll leave
You'll leave this place
And go somewhere else
To the city
To wherever you want
Without the recipe
And my wrapped-up body will be
The last you hear of me
And my wrapped-up body will be
The last you hear of me.

POXI stops digging. He seems to have found something. ESPINOSA†puts down the bass. He walks to the hole in the ground and climbs back into his body. ESPINOSA is now just ESPINOSA's body wrapped in the tarpaulin. POXI takes the body and lifts it in his arms. OMAR appears, walking along the valley with a bunch of flowers he has picked, and throws them onto them.

END

(POEMA ORDINARIO) / POOR MEN'S POETRY

JUAN IGNACIO FERNÁNDEZ
TRANSLATED BY WILLIAM GREGORY

Juan Ignacio Fernández

Juan Ignacio Fernández is a playwright. He studied Communication Sciences at the University of Buenos Aires. His plays have been performed in Buenos Aires at the Teatro Nacional Cervantes and the Teatro Municipal General San Martín, in Chile, in Uruguay and at various venues on the alternative theatre scene. *Poema ordinario* was written at the 2016 Andrés Binetti playwriting workshop.

Characters

FEDERICA
CRISTIAN
LORENZO
OLIVIA

San Pedro. 1982. February.

SCENE 1

Beneath a white wooden porch, on a creaking wooden floor, a swing seat lit by a bare, hanging light bulb. Behind the seat, a large, double window leading into the living room of the house. The window is covered by an almost transparent curtain that floods the room with yellow tones. Opposite the porch, a garden that extends into the darkness, barely lit from above by the light from the house, and ending at a balcony overlooking the Paraná River. A waning moon and the white reflection on the water. FEDERICA (55) is dressed in a robe with a white tee-shirt underneath. Her hair is sun- and smoke-stained. She smokes and drinks beer. An open bottle stands on the floor waiting to refill her glass. Behind the curtain the silhouette of a young woman can be seen, seated at the piano with her back turned. She is playing Schubert's 'Divertissement' with great skill.

FEDERICA: *(Shouting into the house.)* Play... Play louder. I feel like dancing. I have a wild urge to dance. To dance and dance, Olivia. Like this, like this. *(Performs a few amused steps around the porch.)* When a man dances with you, you have to look at his hands, Olivia; always look at his hands... *(Continues dancing.)* Look at his hands, because anyone can move their feet, but look at his hands. *(She looks at her own hands as she dances and continues drinking.)* Look to see if they're relaxed, or if they're like crowbars; if he moves them gracefully or roughly, because he'll do the same with your body, Olivia. If a man doesn't move his hands gracefully when he dances, he won't be able to make you happy. Oh, the gentle hands I've fallen in love with. Louder, Olivia; play louder. Like bellowing laughter, like you're the happiest girl in the world. Like this, like this, like this, let him hold you by the waist and lead you off to be condemned to love. *(Picks up the bottle and drinks straight from it as she continues dancing.)* Look at his hands, Olivia; look at his hands... Let's dance, Olivia; dance so we don't waste time... Everything goes so quickly...

The screen door opens and CRISTIAN (28) comes out in jeans and a white vest, with a glass of beer.

FEDERICA: Oh, darling, don't listen to me. Don't listen to me. Dance; come on: dance.

179

CRISTIAN: No thanks.

FEDERICA: See how good it feels in the moonlight! Loudly, Olivia, with desperation. Loudly! Come on, darling: dance.

CRISTIAN: I don't know how to dance.

FEDERICA: I'll teach you. See how light it feels. See how light everything feels when you dance. Like this: move like this...

CRISTIAN: You're a good dancer.

FEDERICA: I can't believe a nice young man like you doesn't know how to dance... I don't believe it.

CRISTIAN: I don't know... I don't even know how I'm supposed to move...

FEDERICA: Oh, you're so sweet. Like this: move like this. It's lovely when a man dances with a woman. It's very lovely... Oh... I feel light-headed. *(Sits on the swing seat.)*

CRISTIAN: Are you all right?

FEDERICA: Very. Very all right, darling.

CRISTIAN: Do you want some water?

FEDERICA: No. I'm fine. You don't realise how much you drink in this heat, do you.

The sound of the piano stops. The sound of crickets fills the space.

OLIVIA: *(From the living room.)* I'm going for a bath. *(She stands and exits to the bathroom.)*

FEDERICA: I never asked you about your mother, darling. Is she pretty?

CRISTIAN: Yes.

FEDERICA: That's good; that's good... And does your father love her very much?

CRISTIAN: Yes. They love each other.

FEDERICA: How lucky... And you love them very much.

CRISTIAN: Yes.

FEDERICA: How lovely... Do you have brothers and sisters?

CRISTIAN: A sister.

FEDERICA: *(Interrupts.)* And you love her too?

CRISTIAN: Yes.

FEDERICA: Tell me more...

CRISTIAN: She's older than me, she has long hair...

FEDERICA: *(Interrupts.)* No, I mean... Tell me what it's like to be happy. All of you loving each other...

CRISTIAN: It's nice.

FEDERICA: Nice. Just nice. When it must be such hard work... It must be like sadness: you end up getting used to it. Don't you have lovely hands... Very lovely hands... I knew a young man once... What was his name? I sometimes wonder what became of that young man... Claudio. Yes. His name was Claudio. Hands just like yours... Tell me. What do you think of Olivia?

CRISTIAN: She's nice... She's a nice girl.

FEDERICA: She has a great gift. A great gift; not everyone sees it. Everything she lacks on the outside, she makes up for on the inside. I can assure you of that. Such a generous girl...

CRISTIAN: Seems so, yes.

FEDERICA: Generous and strong despite those thin, pitiful arms she has. Such a delicate thing. We gave her up for dead more than once, but she always bounced back... She clung onto life like she'd been overwhelmed with blessings. I'm so grateful I had her: she's my support now. I'd tell you I get up every morning thinking how I can leave a happy, beautiful future for her, because there's not much I can do about her present, or her past, but I still harbour some hope that the future will be happier and she'll get used to it, if it's that easy. That she'll get used to being happy. I'm boring you, prattling on...

CRISTIAN: No, ma'am. *(Drinks the rest of the beer.)*

FEDERICA: Federica.

CRISTIAN: Yes, sorry.

FEDERICA: I love that you know how to drink. It's a quality I value in a man. Darling, I don't want to put you out; you know we're very happy to have you here with us. Do you think you could give me an advance on the next few weeks tomorrow?

CRISTIAN: Sure. Yes. I can ask for an advance tomorrow and pay the next few weeks up front.

FEDERICA: If it's not a bother... This town isn't made for the weak.

CRISTIAN: I'll ask for an advance tomorrow; don't worry... I think I'll be off to bed.

FEDERICA: So early... On a beautiful night light this.

CRISTIAN: Early start tomorrow.

FEDERICA: Of course. Poor soul... I love the night. If I had my way, I'd sleep all day and only live at night time... Look at the moon, Cristian. It's waning... That must be what's making me happy... It stops the damp and heals all wounds. The moon is so wise.

FEDERICA hears a sound and stands up. CRISTIAN hears it too.

LORENZO: *(Off, approaching the house from the darkness of the grass.)* Federica...

FEDERICA takes a few slow steps towards the house.

LORENZO: *(Off, nearing the house.)* Federica... Olivia...

FEDERICA enters the house and closes the screen door. CRISTIAN stays on the porch, looking into the darkness. FEDERICA looks out from the window, but at a distance, like a ghost behind the curtains. LORENZO (28) comes out of the dark and steps up onto the porch. He has a beard and wears jeans, a somewhat dirty tee-shirt and a green rucksack like a stomach about to burst.

LORENZO: Hello.

CRISTIAN: Hello.

LORENZO: Who are you?

CRISTIAN: Cristian. I rent... I've been renting the room downstairs... for a few weeks.

LORENZO: How much you paying?

CRISTIAN: Fifteen hundred...

LORENZO: *(To FEDERICA, who is watching from the window.)* Where do I sleep?

FEDERICA: *(From the living room.)* You can sleep in your sister's room; there's a mattress.

FEDERICA disappears.

LORENZO: I'm taking my pillow.

CRISTIAN: I didn't know the room… that you'd be coming…

LORENZO goes into the house, leaving CRISTIAN with the last words. A few seconds pass. FEDERICA comes out onto the porch with a cigarette and a plate of food.

CRISTIAN: I didn't know… your son was coming back.

FEDERICA: Neither did I.

CRISTIAN: I can find a hotel tomorrow if you want…

FEDERICA: No, darling. That room's yours. Please don't forget the advance.

CRISTIAN: I don't think your son should have to sleep on a mattress…

FEDERICA: *(As if she hadn't heard.)* He's changing… I haven't seen him for three or four years. The waning moon, what surprises it brings. That room's yours… At what age does a man become a man…? He wasn't a man when he left…

CRISTIAN: I'll be off to my room… *(Goes inside.)*

FEDERICA: Of course, darling. Off you go. Sleep well.

She stares at the dark lawn, her gaze lost. OLIVIA's shouts of joy can be heard inside the house, gradually diminishing. The sound of the crickets is deafening. FEDERICA approaches the edge of the porch and throws a scrap of food from her plate onto the grass. She calls out, as if to a pet.

FEDERICA: Tuuuutu… Tuutu… Here, little piggy… Tuuuutu. *(The sound of the crickets starts to fade until they grow completely silent.)* Tutuuu, old piggy, greedy-guts… Tuuutu, you angry beast.

Tuuutu, you soppy girl. I've thrown some chicken out for you, darling. Eat that and don't make a fuss: we have guests.

Something is heard moving in the grass, but the darkness is total. Then, the sounds of something eating. Silence. Slowly, the sound of the crickets takes over the night.

SCENE 2

LORENZO and OLIVIA (20) are on the porch. LORENZO is on all fours and OLIVIA is on his back as if riding a horse. It is night. There are three empty glasses on the floor.

OLIVIA: She's not moving… She's blonde. And she's in the ocean, but you only realise later it's an ocean, because it looks like a river; it looks like this river, but not so brown. It's like night time, but it looks like the sun's coming out. It's not dusk; it must be the morning, the first light of the morning, and she's alone, there in the water, and it's a terrifying image. Why is someone alone in the water terrifying? You know there's something down there, and by then my hands had already started sweating, and my breath was quickening, and then the music started. Da-dum. Da-dum. Da-dum da-dum… And on and on like that, just those two notes and the darkness and I had to stand up… and I had to leave.

CRISTIAN comes out with a bottle of beer and looks at them for a moment. He starts pouring the beer.

OLIVIA: After a while Cristian came to look for me in the bathroom because I didn't come out… *(Laughs.)* I'll never be able to go in the river again, Lorenzo. I can't stop thinking about it every time I see it, about what might be under there.

LORENZO: Mud.

OLIVIA: There's so many animals in there, Lorenzo. Cristian's working: he builds roads.

CRISTIAN: Engineer. *(Hands out the beers.)*

OLIVIA: They're building a whole new neighbourhood down in Las Canaletas and they found a whole load of animals there: snakes, caimans. Children have disappeared, Lorenzo. That's what they say.

LORENZO: People shouldn't throw themselves in the river there.

OLIVIA: No, Lorenzo. They say they find their bones and hair, like they've been swallowed and spat back out. Bones and hair, Lorenzo…

CRISTIAN: Don't listen to them, Olivia.

OLIVIA: Hair and little bones… It terrifies me. Really. We could go to the cinema and see it if it's still on. Maybe I'll be able to watch if there's three of us… And when I don't want to see I'll cover my eyes… But you can't cover your ears. That's useless, and da-dum, da-dum, da-dum….

CRISTIAN: Dum, dum, dum, dum, dum, dum. *(Approaches OLIVIA as if to scare her.)*

OLIVIA: Don't scare me!

LORENZO makes a movement with his back. OLIVIA understands she needs to get off.

LORENZO: Good job you weren't on your own.

CRISTIAN: I like the cinema.

LORENZO: Good.

OLIVIA: He likes sitting right near the front. And everything vibrates. The sound makes the walls shake, and I think, 'how many more films can it take before it falls down?'

CRISTIAN: *(Laughs.)* It's not going to fall down.

LORENZO: Why not?

CRISTIAN: Because… It won't. Those buildings are specially designed. The foundations…

LORENZO: But vibration and time can make anything fall down.

CRISTIAN: Yes. But, well, it'd take a long time…

LORENZO: But it could happen.

CRISTIAN: Yes.

OLIVIA: Whenever you want, we can go for tea at La Perla and watch the people go by. So many new people are coming because of the new neighbourhood they're building.

LORENZO: Federica must be pleased about that. New people…

FEDERICA appears in the living room and stops behind the window.

OLIVIA: Mum loves new people and chatting.

CRISTIAN: Yes. Well, at least someone in the house spoke to me. This one didn't speak to me at all for the first few weeks. Not a word.

LORENZO: It's not shyness. She's weighing you up.

OLIVIA: I like to get to know people before I speak to them.

LORENZO: Every time Olivia starts speaking, Federica gets a new boyfriend.

OLIVIA: *(Laughs.)* That's why I didn't speak to Joaquín for months. Because he was a good man.

LORENZO: He was unbearable.

OLIVIA: He was a good man. But he left.

LORENZO: Like all of them.

OLIVIA: Did you see Dad?

LORENZO: No.

FEDERICA comes out onto the porch smoking and looking for beer with an empty glass. CRISTIAN hurries over to pour her what little is left in the bottle.

OLIVIA: Did you at least look for him?

LORENZO: No.

OLIVIA: So why did you leave?

FEDERICA: I slept a lot, didn't I. *(Drinks.)* My siesta overran… Have you eaten?

CRISTIAN: Yes. We ate, but there's quite a lot left in the fridge… Chicken and rice.

FEDERICA: No. That's all right, darling. I'm fine… It makes me happy, you three eating together. What a lovely night… One doesn't even feel like lying on a night like this. Look, Olivia. It's waning. It's a dark moon tomorrow. Is there any cold beer left, darling?

CRISTIAN: Yes, Federica. I'll get you some. *(Goes into the house.)*

FEDERICA: Such a nice man…

LORENZO: Isn't he a bit young, Mum?

FEDERICA: Sarcasm twice in one question. You've been practicing.

LORENZO: We're enjoying ourselves, Federica.

FEDERICA: Do you remember, Olivia, how good your brother was at talking back?

LORENZO: Don't drag her into it.

FEDERICA: Just like your father's talent for playing the piano: quick, skilful, and accurate.

LORENZO: Is it in the blood?

FEDERICA: It helped him get away and not come back.

LORENZO: You need me here to keep you from going off the rails, Federica. You can't be left on your own for too long.

FEDERICA: Do you remember, Olivia, when he left the last time? He swore he'd never come back and he destroyed the bedroom you'd painted and I'd fixed up?

LORENZO: Don't drag her into it.

CRISTIAN: *(Coming out to the porch with a glass and a bottle of beer.)* I'll go to the shop tomorrow. Maybe I'll take the empties in the morning...

FEDERICA: Oh, would you be so kind...? Those bags get heavier every time. Pour me a beer, darling; this heat's frightful...

CRISTIAN: *(Pouring.)* Anyone else want some?

LORENZO: Isn't it hard work being like this all the time?

CRISTIAN: Like what?

FEDERICA: There's only three of us, Lorenzo.

CRISTIAN: What am I like all the time?

FEDERICA: If you attack all three of us today, you'll be bored tomorrow.

CRISTIAN: What am I like?

LORENZO: Someone who acts like he's found paradise while his feet are being burned.

FEDERICA: Listen to that, Olivia. What poetry!

LORENZO: Why are you dragging her into it?

FEDERICA: Tell me: could he not have been a poet, a writer, or something, if only… Well, if only he'd tried.

LORENZO: I should have wasted less hours kicking drunks out of your bedroom.

OLIVIA: Did you know, Cristian, that my mum and dad tried to abort me, but the doctor messed it up and I grew anyway? I died three times those first two weeks in the clinic. But I don't remember any of that now. *(Laughs.)* I was a baby, and a baby only starts to remember from two or three years old.

LORENZO goes into the house.

FEDERICA: Maybe I will heat myself up some of that rice. You're such a good cook; it's a shame not to take advantage. *(Goes inside.)*

OLIVIA: I frighten them off like flies. *(Laughs.)* Don't pay too much attention to what we say.

CRISTIAN: No… It's all right… I'm not used… We don't talk so much in our family. Not like this. We don't say these things to each other…

OLIVIA: So what do you say? It's only words.

CRISTIAN: Still, they hurt.

OLIVIA: It's words. We can go to the cinema tomorrow, can't we?

CRISTIAN: I'm working late tomorrow.

OLIVIA: Oh. Sunday, then. Or Saturday evening. And Lorenzo can come, and we'll watch whatever's on. It doesn't matter.

CRISTIAN: I don't think your brother wants me here.

OLIVIA: Is that what you think?

CRISTIAN: He's not particularly nice to me.

OLIVIA: Do you know how crickets find a mate?

CRISTIAN: No.

OLIVIA: By making as much noise as they can. Listen to them… So, cinema Saturday?

CRISTIAN: Yes.

OLIVIA approaches him and tugs on his tee-shirt. CRISTIAN clumsily lowers his head and she gives him a short kiss on the lips. She goes into the house. CRISTIAN is left alone on the porch; the sound of the crickets is deafening. LORENZO comes out. He is wearing a new shirt, and his hair is wet and combed. FEDERICA's silhouette can be seen in the living room.

CRISTIAN: Going out?

LORENZO: What?

CRISTIAN: No... I mean, are you going out... You look like you're going out...

LORENZO: Yes. Why?

CRISTIAN: No. It just looked like you were going out.

LORENZO: Do I need your permission?

CRISTIAN: No... No... I was just asking...

LORENZO: Are you scared of me?

CRISTIAN: No... Why should I be...? No.

LORENZO: When I come close, you move away.

CRISTIAN: No... I don't.

LORENZO takes a step towards him and CRISTIAN backs away.

CRISTIAN: I'm not scared of you.

LORENZO takes a step towards him but CRISTIAN stays where he is. He takes another step towards him. They end up face to face. They hold this position for a few seconds. The sound of glass smashing on the floor comes from inside the house.

FEDERICA: *(Off.)* I'm such an idiot!

LORENZO keeps looking at CRISTIAN as he slowly steps down off the porch and heads out into the night. CRISTIAN stands and watches as LORENZO leaves, almost shaken. FEDERICA comes out with a glass of beer.

FEDERICA: Be careful when you go inside: there's glass on the floor. I didn't eat the rice in the end: I prefer something cooler in this heat... But it does smell delicious... Delicious...

CRISTIAN: Must be the rosemary. It can be quite pungent.

FEDERICA: Must be. Of course, it must be. Because rice and chicken always taste the same; what's different is the spices; it's the subtleties that change everything, isn't it. Not that I know what I'm talking about: I can barely cook. No one ever demanded I cook. And Esteban, the children's father, didn't much care. He used to spend the whole day at the piano and he'd forget to eat. Did you know Schubert died at thirty-one years old? Thirty-one years old… My husband was obsessed with Schubert. And when he saw thirty on the horizon, he started with his attacks, his fears. It was a terribly anxious time for us; I was pregnant with Olivia. He thought he was going to die and that everything he was doing was going to suffer, poor man… The worst illnesses are in the head. He looked at my belly, big with Olivia, with such fear and hatred that he couldn't even swallow. I used to sleep with my arms around my belly to protect it. He told me all the time that no one should ever have to go through what he was going through. That no one should suffer the way he was suffering. Suffering brings out the worst in people. The worst. Until he left and saved us, saved himself. And I always forgave him because leaving this place is almost impossible, and the pain that that man must have suffered in his bones when he left, I can't imagine it. I could never have left. Never… There are some people who are special. The rest of us are more ordinary, more earthly… I adore living here… Don't you like it?

CRISTIAN: Very much.

FEDERICA: He felt fenced in here… Suffocated. He was born different, but he realised late. And here, you either kill yourself or you leave. There aren't many options here. I don't blame him for trying to be happy somehow. I tried too. I try… Some people think that words… that words don't have substance… Do you understand? That something so light, something that floats in the wind, can't do any harm. But it can; it can. A whisper can change a whole life and it's just words and silences; just a few words joined together can make you cry. Words have weight… Oh, I'm talking a lot… Oh, God… It's the beer loosening my tongue. Don't listen to me… Listen to me, but don't pay me any mind… My words are worth very little, they weigh very little... They're like poor men's poetry. *(The crickets begin to murmur more quietly. FEDERICA watches the grass.)* Did I tell you about Tutu, darling?

CRISTIAN: The animal?

FEDERICA: She's coming... Can you hear? She was washed in when the river burst its banks... Years ago now. Many years ago... The water washed everything along with it and poor Tutu, she came down from who knows where and clung to this piece of earth and never left... She was tiny, so tiny when I found her. I fed her and, the next day, when night fell, she came back and I fed her again... She looks at you and she understands everything. Everything. And it's been like that ever since; every day, she grew and grew, and her movements slowed down, and at some point every night she comes to visit. And she's cleared out all the rats we had down in the stream. She's cleaned everything out, the hungry thing... Tutu...

Silence begins to flood the night.

FEDERICA: There's nothing, Tutu.

CRISTIAN takes a few steps back.

FEDERICA: Nothing at all, Tutu... Not today. Go on...

The silence remains.

FEDERICA: Nothing, Tutu. Go on, I said. Don't be a nuisance. Go on.

The silence remains. FEDERICA takes a step back and waits in silence. CRISTIAN leans back on the wall of the house. A few seconds of complete silence pass, then the sound of the crickets returns.

FEDERICA: She's hungry. Very hungry.

CRISTIAN: What's... Federica? What... is it?

FEDERICA: Don't look at her like that. She's not doing any harm. Don't worry.

CRISTIAN: What does she eat?

FEDERICA: She's like a dustbin.

CRISTIAN: She eats chicken?

FEDERICA: She loves it.

CRISTIAN: She eats whole chickens?

FEDERICA: Yes... But we can't allow ourselves those luxuries now. Don't be frightened, darling; she's not doing any harm.

The piano is heard from the living room. CRISTIAN watches the grass in the darkness.

FEDERICA: Oh, how beautiful, Olivia. I needed that. Listen to her play. Just like her father. Play, Olivia! Loudly. Play loudly. What a lovely night... I do love the summer... It's Schubert's 'Divertissement'. Always the same piece. Sometimes I think she's calling her father. 'Divertissements' they call them. These little songs. Light entertainment between acts.

CRISTIAN: Federica.

FEDERICA: Yes, darling.

CRISTIAN: I think... it would be better if I went... somewhere else.

FEDERICA: Is this because of Lorenzo? You needn't listen to him. He's like the crickets. Only a bother if you pay attention.

CRISTIAN: I think it's the best thing.

FEDERICA: It'll break Olivia's heart.

CRISTIAN: I don't...

FEDERICA: *(Interrupting.)* I know. I know. But she's got her hopes up. She'd almost stopped playing the piano, and now listen to her. Every night. Listen to her. I don't mind begging. I'm not proud that way. Make us happy; we need that so much...

CRISTIAN: I can't make anyone happy, Federica.

FEDERICA: Don't leave us alone with him. The first time he left, he tried to burn the piano; the second time, he destroyed his bedroom... Who knows what'll happen the third time? Maybe having you here will calm him down a bit. He always needed boundaries that I couldn't give him. I don't know how to set boundaries for men. I've seen the way he looks at you and I know that look, darling. He doesn't look at everyone that way. He won't dare do anything like that if you're here with us. He wouldn't dare.

The piano stops.

OLIVIA: *(Off.)* I'm going for a bath. Don't use the water, Federica.

FEDERICA: I met a young man once with just the same eyes as yours. The self-same eyes. He looked like he was always scared. Where could that boy be now…? Ramiro… I never saw him again. I'm going to wash the dishes; it's late. I love the summer. It's easier to talk in summer, isn't it. *(Going inside.)* It's a dark moon tomorrow.

CRISTIAN sits on the motionless swing seat and looks thoughtfully out into the darkness. He comes back to reality and, when he notices he is alone, goes back into the house.

SCENE 3

LORENZO swings slowly on the porch and smokes a cigarette. The reddish sun is already giving way to the darkness of the night with a dark moon. Footsteps are heard on the wooden floorboards inside the house and the silhouettes of FEDERICA and OLIVIA can be seen walking to and fro behind the curtain in the yellowish light of the living room.

FEDERICA: Olivia.

OLIVIA: No.

FEDERICA: Olivia, darling.

OLIVIA: No! Stop following me. Stop following me. Stop following me. Stop following me.

FEDERICA: I'm not following you, darling; I just want you to stay still and stop throwing the music around.

OLIVIA crosses to one side, throwing sheets of music into the air. FEDERICA follows behind her, picking them up.

OLIVIA: Leave them on the floor; I want to walk on them!

FEDERICA: Darling, I'm begging you, please.

OLIVIA: I hate you. I hate you with all my soul; I hate you. You're a monster, Mum. You're a monster. You're all monsters. I hope you all die.

FEDERICA: Olivia, this isn't like you.

OLIVIA: All of you. I hate all of you! I hate you and him and him and Dad! I hate you all, and even if I wanted to I couldn't stop hating you!

FEDERICA: You'll make yourself ill!

OLIVIA: You make me ill. He makes me ill. No one makes me ill! I'm a bad person too. I'm a bad person too. I'm not different and I hate you all so much, Mum. I hate you all so much.

She runs away; seconds later her bedroom door is heard slamming. CRISTIAN comes out onto the porch with his back packed, fresh from the bathroom, his hair wet and combed; he is disturbed by the shouting. When the house falls silent, the crickets fill the space once more.

LORENZO: Did you find something?

CRISTIAN: There's a room come free at the Hotel Turismo.

LORENZO: It's a dump there.

CRISTIAN: Is it?

LORENZO: Full of old people.

CRISTIAN: It's close to the council offices. It's where the truck leaves from for Las Canaletas.

LORENZO: You won't have this view there.

CRISTIAN: No.

LORENZO: Or good company for the beer.

CRISTIAN: I think it's best for everyone… *(Picks up his bag.)*

LORENZO: Best for you.

CRISTIAN: For everyone.

LORENZO: For you.

CRISTIAN: No. For everyone.

LORENZO: For you. You shouldn't be scared.

CRISTIAN: I'm not scared.

LORENZO: I think you are.

CRISTIAN: Can I tell you something? I don't want to frighten you. But what your sister said... yesterday... about the children who disappear. The bones and the hair. It's true. I don't want to frighten her but we are finding them there. We found three when we started the work and two the following week and we keep on finding them. People thought they'd been swallowed up by the river but there's something else, Lorenzo. That animal that comes... the one your mother feeds at night... Your mother said it eats a whole chicken. That meat's similar to human flesh. I don't think it's very safe for your sister. Do you know what I'm talking about? Have you seen it?

LORENZO: It doesn't let anyone see it any more.

CRISTIAN: I think you need to be careful.

LORENZO: Thanks for looking after her.

CRISTIAN: I wouldn't want her getting hurt.

LORENZO: Do you love her?

CRISTIAN: Yes... But... But like a sister. She's very sweet. I wouldn't want anything to happen to you. To any of you. You either...

LORENZO: I can take care of it.

CRISTIAN: I can help you if you want.

LORENZO: You're leaving.

LORENZO stands and approaches CRISTIAN.

CRISTIAN: I can still help you.

LORENZO brings his mouth close to CRISTIAN's face.

LORENZO: But you're leaving.

CRISTIAN: It's dangerous, and I don't want anyone getting hurt.

LORENZO: We're not going to hurt anyone. *(Kisses him on the mouth.)*

CRISTIAN drops the bag on the floor and moves him away slowly.

LORENZO: What are you doing?

CRISTIAN: I didn't do anything.

LORENZO kisses him again.

LORENZO: What are you doing?

CRISTIAN: I... I didn't... You... You... What are you doing?

LORENZO kisses him again, more violently.

LORENZO: I'm doing what I want.

The look at each other. Now it is CRISTIAN who approaches clumsily and passionately and kisses him on the mouth. LORENZO responds and gradually brings the kiss to a stop. Finally LORENZO pulls away, crouches down as if his movement might startle a fearful prey, takes the bag, lifts it up and takes it slowly into the house. CRISTIAN does not move. FEDERICA comes out onto the porch with a cigarette and a beer and looks at the sky.

FEDERICA: Didn't I tell you, darling? The moon can't be seen when it's a dark moon. With no warning, it leaves the Paraná River in darkness... Dark night. Just the February heat. The river's frightening without the silvery reflection; it's frightening because no one knows what's there beneath the treacherous waters. The beer's ice cold; fetch yourself a glass if you like.

CRISTIAN looks at her, unable to speak. He goes into the house.

FEDERICA: Olivia, darling... Olivia... Look at the sky; there's a dark moon... Olivia, your father and I met under a dark moon. Olivia, darling...

OLIVIA comes out slowly.

FEDERICA: Look for it. It can't be seen. Only imagined.

OLIVIA: Is he staying?

FEDERICA: Isn't that what you wanted?

OLIVIA: I don't want him to be angry.

FEDERICA: No, darling. Why would he be angry?

A loud noise is heard inside the house. OLIVIA looks towards the living room.

FEDERICA: When I was your age, or maybe a couple of years older, when I was living alone with your grandfather, the house used to fill up with young men wanting to court me. One, two, three, four, five, some nights it was like a birthday party. They were fascinated by the pretty girl who lived far from the village, somewhat wild, somewhat submissive…

A loud bang inside the house.

OLIVIA: Are they fighting?

FEDERICA: Your grandfather used to let them in; he didn't ask many questions, as long as they brought something to drink. He was permissive: he never set boundaries. Not even for himself. I don't blame him. When you love someone very much it's hard to set boundaries. One night, two young men arrived with a younger one in tow; skinny; they'd got him rather drunk and he could barely stand up.

A loud and now repetitive, rhythmic banging.

OLIVIA: Mum…

FEDERICA: He wasn't the prettiest; he wasn't the most attractive. But he looked at me with pity behind his glasses while the others shouted and played cards.

OLIVIA: Are they fighting?

FEDERICA: He looked at me and he understood me. It's so hard to be understood in this life. So difficult to find that look. A few years later we were married. He saved me, Olivia. Just like I saved him too, when the time came. This boy has that look. That's why I'd like him to stay.

OLIVIA: Mum…

FEDERICA: No, darling. They're not fighting. He's staying.

The bangs grow faster and faster, with no space in between them. OLIVIA approaches FEDERICA, who hugs her as she continues looking at the sky searching for the moon. The banging begins to slow down, gradually, until it stops.

FEDERICA: There's cold beer; do you want some?

OLIVIA: He said he didn't look for Dad.

FEDERICA: Who knows what your brother does?

OLIVIA: I know he lies. You do, too.

FEDERICA: I've lied my whole life. Lying is a weapon no one can take from you. The option of lying. When someone tells the truth all the time it's not because they're a Christian: it's because they can. And the rest of us lie.

OLIVIA: I'm going to tell Father Gabriel you said that.

FEDERICA: I like Father Gabriel. Don't tell him; be nice to your mother; if I can't go to mass I can't meet new people... Besides, I do listen to him. He says such interesting things. He's so wise. Have you seen the way he looks when he talks about God? Watch him this Sunday. Watch him, because he's riddled with doubt and that's what wisdom is. Oh, your mother. She falls in love so easily with looks and hands. Tell me what you fall in love with.

OLIVIA: I'm embarrassed.

FEDERICA: Dirty girl.

OLIVIA: He won't stay for me.

FEDERICA: He'll stay.

OLIVIA: But he'll stay for him.

LORENZO comes slowly out onto the porch. FEDERICA passes him a cigarette; he lights it.

OLIVIA: Sometimes I think everything that's given to me gets taken away.

FEDERICA: So hold tighter.

LORENZO: With those little arms...

FEDERICA: Those fingers are strong. You could play an allegretto to go with the dark moon.

OLIVIA: I'm never playing again.

LORENZO: Why are you being so contrary?

OLIVIA: Why didn't you look for Dad?

LORENZO: I did.

OLIVIA: Are you lying now or were you lying before?

FEDERICA: Olivia, darling, do you think that town's like this one? It's not like here, darling. There's buildings, so many buildings, one after another. And no one knows anyone.

LORENZO: He lives in Calle Austria. In Barrio Norte.

The sound of the crickets fades gradually.

OLIVIA: Did you see him? Did you speak to him? Did you tell him I play the piano? What did he say to you?

FEDERICA: Go away, Tutu.

OLIVIA: Lorenzo, what did he say?

FEDERICA: Go away, Tutu; there's nothing for you here. Don't be a nuisance.

OLIVIA: Lorenzo.

LORENZO: He's got a sideboard with lots of drawers and each drawer has a lock. And he opened one of the drawers with a little key and showed me a photo. Federica's pregnant with you and she's looking at the camera, smiling. He's sitting at the piano staring at the keys. And I'm standing to one side. You can only see half of me but the one eye you can see is staring at the ground.

FEDERICA: My father took that picture... Let's go inside; she's not listening to me.

OLIVIA: What did he say to you, Lorenzo?

LORENZO: He said he's not my father.

FEDERICA: Tutu. Go away, I said.

LORENZO: And I should ask Federica to tell me the truth.

FEDERICA: Go away, Tutu.

OLIVIA: Mum... Is that true?

FEDERICA: Let's go inside.

LORENZO: I'm going to set the grass on fire.

FEDERICA: No. Of course not. Let's go inside.

OLIVIA: Federica, is it true what he said?

LORENZO: I'm going to burn it all.

FEDERICA: You're not going to do anything. Tutu! Go away!

LORENZO: Just like Granddad used to burn.

FEDERICA: Tutu! Go away, I said!

LORENZO: Those weeds have grown a lot.

FEDERICA: Inside, Olivia.

LORENZO: We'll have to close the windows so the smoke doesn't get in the house.

FEDERICA: Stop punishing us, Lorenzo.

LORENZO: I'll burn it tomorrow.

FEDERICA: You can't treat me like this; I'm not a child.

LORENZO: I'm doing what I have to do.

FEDERICA: Stop punishing us. You're not…

LORENZO: Your father?

OLIVIA takes a step forwards. Then another, then another, until she steps down off the porch and into the grass. Her body seems to disappear from the waist down into the thickness of the dark garden. LORENZO hurries to the edge of the porch and, grabbing OLIVIA by her clothing and torso, takes her back to the porch. He puts her down on the wooden floor and holds her arms firmly.

OLIVIA: Get off me, you queer.

LORENZO releases her and goes into the house.

OLIVIA: *(To FEDERICA.)* Slut.

OLIVIA goes into the house.

FEDERICA: Are you feeling sad? You do know how to survive, don't you, beautiful. Don't come here. Disappear for a few days; you get too hungry… When you get like this you don't have boundaries. And I don't know how to set boundaries.

SCENE 4

The sunset floods the front of the house in red. Empty bottles of beer lie on the wooden porch floor. Some on their sides, some standing up. Gradually the voices of LORENZO, OLIVIA and CRISTIAN become audible in the distance, coming up the path that leads to the porch. LORENZO is carrying OLIVIA on his back.

OLIVIA: You were scared.

LORENZO: No.

OLIVIA: You were scared! Your hands were sweating.

LORENZO: No.

OLIVIA: Oh, you're such a liar, Lorenzo. There's nothing wrong with being scared. It's a horror film. If it scares you it's because it's good. Cristian was scared too the first time.

CRISTIAN: No, not scared. Nervous.

OLIVIA: You say 'nervous', I say 'scared', but it's the same thing. Put me down.

LORENZO: I'm not putting you down.

OLIVIA: Put me down.

LORENZO: No.

OLIVIA: Tell him to put me down.

CRISTIAN: She says to put her down.

LORENZO: Oh, does she? And who are you to boss me about?

OLIVIA: He's a surveyor. Put me down.

CRISTIAN: Engineer.

LORENZO: The engineer can't help you.

OLIVIA: Help me.

CRISTIAN: Put her down.

OLIVIA stretches her arms out to CRISTIAN; he lets himself be hugged by her thin arms. LORENZO begins to pull her to one side, holding onto her legs; OLIVIA tries to stay clinging to CRISTIAN with her arms.

CRISTIAN: Put her down; she'll get hurt.

201

OLIVIA: No! Save me.

CRISTIAN: You'll hurt yourself.

OLIVIA: Save me; it wants to eat me!

LORENZO: Dum dum dum dum dum dum dum dum.

OLIVIA screams, scared but enjoying herself; CRISTIAN pulls her body towards him with more force; she ends up hugging him. LORENZO approaches them slowly.

LORENZO: Dum, dum, dum, dum, dum, dum…

OLIVIA: No! Not me! Eat him!

LORENZO: Him?

OLIVIA: Yes! Not me!

LORENZO: Dum, dum, dum, dum, dum…

OLIVIA hugs CRISTIAN and hides her face in his chest. LORENZO approaches, still making the same sound, until he is close to both of them; he stretches out an arm and gropes CRISTIAN between the legs; uncomfortable, CRISTIAN releases OLIVIA, who remains hanging from his body with her own strength for a few seconds until her feet touch the floor.

OLIVIA: Did you kill him?

LORENZO: Obviously.

CRISTIAN: I'll go and get something to drink.

LORENZO: If Federica hasn't drunk it all.

CRISTIAN goes into the house.

OLIVIA: Did he get scared?

LORENZO: I make a good monster.

OLIVIA: Stop it now.

FEDERICA slams the screen door open, staggering, with a large glass of beer and a crumpled cigarette between her fingers.

FEDERICA: Who… Who paid for the tickets?

OLIVIA: What's going on, Mum?

FEDERICA: Did you pay for the tickets or did the other... the other boy?

LORENZO: Why don't you go and lie down for a bit?

FEDERICA: Just because, Lorenzo. Who told you...? Did he tell you?

LORENZO: Calm down, Federica.

OLIVIA: Mum, what's going on?

FEDERICA: What's going on... is that your brother is a greedy swine. Why did you come back, hmm? Why?

OLIVIA: What's happened?

FEDERICA: Did he pay?

LORENZO: I did.

FEDERICA: How did you afford that? Give me that key back. So now you're a thief as well.

LORENZO puts his hand in his pocket, takes out a small key on a keyring that is just two strands of wool tied to the metal and holds it out to FEDERICA. CRISTIAN watches all of this from the living room, silent and motionless.

OLIVIA: What's that?

LORENZO: Tell her.

OLIVIA: What is it, Mum?

FEDERICA holds out her hand clumsily to take the key but LORENZO plays at not giving it to her and FEDERICA does not have the reflexes to take it on her first attempts.

FEDERICA: It's mine. It's ours.

She tries again and this time succeeds in snatching it from LORENZO, who finds the game fun.

LORENZO: It's the key to a post office box. Your dad leaves money there every month to make sure you're doing OK.

FEDERICA: And how is she doing, hmm? Tell me: how are you doing? She's the happiest girl in the world and you're a bastard. She doesn't want for anything... For anything! And you've got nothing, Lorenzo. Nothing. Why do you come back? Why do you come back every time you leave?

OLIVIA: Dad gives you money?

LORENZO: He writes to her too, to see how you are.

FEDERICA: You have nothing. Nothing.

LORENZO: He knows you play the piano and you like Schubert.

FEDERICA: I'm wounded all over.

LORENZO: She sends photos of you every Christmas.

FEDERICA: Wounded all over, inside.

OLIVIA: He knows everything? Why can't I write to him, Federica?

FEDERICA: Destruction makes you happy, Lorenzo. It makes you so happy. I know that look and it doesn't end well. Look at your face. The piano, the... the... bedroom... your sister. You've no limits.

OLIVIA: I want to see him.

FEDERICA: No!

OLIVIA: At least let me write to him.

FEDERICA: Inside, Olivia.

OLIVIA: I want to write to him.

FEDERICA: No, Olivia. Go to your room.

OLIVIA: Lorenzo, did he listen to the tape? Lorenzo... Did he listen to the tape? Tell me. Tell me he heard me, please. Stop lying to me... please. Tell me if he heard me... Lorenzo... Please, look at me and tell me if he heard me playing the piano, playing the allegretto... I swear I'll never ask you anything again... Tell me if he heard me... Did he have something to play it on? Did you remember, Lorenzo? Tell me if he heard me... Tell me, please. Please...

LORENZO: Yes, he heard you.

OLIVIA: Why didn't you tell me, Lorenzo? Why didn't you tell me? Did he say anything? Did he look at you? Did he say anything?

LORENZO: He cried.

OLIVIA: Because he liked it?

LORENZO cannot answer and simply nods.

LORENZO: And... he put the tape on and played.

OLIVIA: He liked it, Federica. He liked it. Why can't I see him? Let me see him, please. Why can't I see him? Why don't you let me see him? Federica, please!

FEDERICA: Because he already killed you once... And we're not letting that happen again. Him or me.

OLIVIA: You kill me too and we see each other every day.

OLIVIA goes inside. When she sees CRISTIAN in the living room she stops. She hugs him tightly and goes to her room. LORENZO sits on the swing seat. FEDERICA looks out to the horizon.

FEDERICA: When you were born I found it hard to look you in the face. I was so frightened, so frightened. They laid you on my chest and I felt your skin... all warm... but I couldn't look at you... It took me a long time to look at you. I don't know how long it was until I dared... I remember we were alone... We were often alone, you and I... And we got on well together... It's words that hurt us... Words... We cast them into the air, they're so light, and you don't imagine they could hurt... Father Gabriel said that the other day... It stayed with me... And you know I've never paid much attention to priests... But that man has something special. He said we should take care of the people we love. Take care of the people we love and don't want to hurt... Because when you hurt someone without meaning to, that's the worst kind of hurt, because it's infinite. We have no choice but to hurt each other because we're filth, the same tawdry blood, but she's like her father, and they're special... They break easily, and when you see them break it tears you apart. Almost unbearable.

LORENZO: And what was Granddad like? Did he mean to hurt people or did he do it without meaning to?

FEDERICA: When I looked at you for the first time, we were alone. I looked down, so scared. So scared. I didn't want to see your face... I didn't want to see the look in your eyes. And when we did look each other in the eye it was like you'd been waiting days for me to look at you. You started feeding and from that moment on I couldn't take my eyes off you... And we were alone for a long time. A long time.

They both fall silent. FEDERICA lights a cigarette and offers another to LORENZO. FEDERICA looks towards the living room and sees CRISTIAN.

FEDERICA: Come out here, darling. Come on.

CRISTIAN comes slowly out onto the porch with his beer in his hand.

FEDERICA: It's so nice having you here with us... I like having lots of people in the house... Lots of people... I got used to that when I was a girl... We rented a room once to a young man from... where was it he lived?

LORENZO: Esquel.

FEDERICA: Somewhere far away. It snows there. He had lips just like yours. Just the same... What was his name, Lorenzo?

LORENZO: Ezequiel.

FEDERICA: Oh, yes. Of course. You used to tease him about his name. Ezequiel from Esquel. He used to laugh a lot. A deep laugh and then a high-pitched one. We used to laugh so much. What can have become of him? The last quarter's starting... You can already feel it, can't you.

FEDERICA goes inside. CRISTIAN and LORENZO fall silent. CRISTIAN dares to speak.

CRISTIAN: We could leave here... I'll ask for a transfer this week... We could live in Buenos Aires. My parents have a flat there. It's small but we could stay there for a while, for as long as we need. As long as you want... I... I'd like that... I'd really like it... Really.

Schubert's 'Divertissement à l'hongroise', the allegretto, can be heard from the living room.

CRISTIAN: Your sister plays well.

LORENZO: It's my dad... *(Gestures to CRISTIAN to wait until a second pair of hands is heard playing, then ends the gesture and speaks again.)* That's where she starts. That's both of them playing now. Playing with four hands. Dad left one part on one of the tapes and my sister always plays it and plays along with him. Can you take her back to the cinema tomorrow?

CRISTIAN: Yes. But they're still showing the same film.

LORENZO: I don't want her here when I set fire to everything.

CRISTIAN: Let me help you.

LORENZO: No. I'd rather you take her and she doesn't see.

CRISTIAN: I don't want to leave you alone with this.

LORENZO: It'll be all right.

CRISTIAN: I'm scared you'll hurt yourself.

LORENZO: I'll be fine.

CRISTIAN: I've never felt like this before.

LORENZO: It'll be all right.

CRISTIAN: I feel... a bit stupid... I don't want you getting hurt.

LORENZO: Take her to the cinema. And I'll meet you outside La Perla.

CRISTIAN: OK.

LORENZO: And then we'll leave... You and me.

CRISTIAN: Really?

LORENZO: Yes.

CRISTIAN: What about your sister?

LORENZO: She'll be fine. She always survives.

CRISTIAN: I can ask for a transfer on Monday.

LORENZO: Yes.

CRISTIAN: I'd really like to... leave with you. Live there with you.

LORENZO: So would I. Being with you makes me happy.

CRISTIAN: I thought I couldn't make anyone happy. I never... I've never felt like this before. I don't feel right... But I feel good. But I'm sort of dizzy all the time. I go to work and think about coming back and being here with you... And at night...

LORENZO: Steady...

CRISTIAN: I'd really like for us to be together. I don't like being like this... I'm not like this... I feel like I'm going to... die if anything happens to you.

LORENZO: Nothing's going to happen to me. Or to you. Take her to the cinema tomorrow. And then we'll leave this shit together.

SCENE 5

FEDERICA, distressed and drunk, paces to and fro on the porch with a cigarette in her hand. Her body and clothes glow in the heat and the red light coming from the fire that has started to rise up in the grass. Every footstep she takes on the white wooden floor of the porch leaves a black mark.

FEDERICA: I understand you're angry; how could I not understand? I feel it all the time here, darling, all the time here. But this isn't the way, darling. This isn't the way. Lorenzo, if I could change what happened, don't you think I would? Please... Stop now... You're hurting us; you're all we have. We only have each other; we have no one else, darling... Lorenzo, son... Don't be like him... You don't have to be like him if you don't want... Hug me... All I want is for you to hug me... It's been so long since I've felt you hug me... Since I've felt you... Let's not talk to each other any more; we hurt each other; let's just hug each other... Come here... Come here... A hug and we'll smell the smell... That's it... It'd calm us down a bit... Smelling the smell again... Like when you were a baby... And looking at each other's faces 'til we fall asleep... You're not like him. You're not like him, so hurtful... I can't leave here, Lorenzo... You'll make her angry... And leaving us without the grass... You're leaving us unprotected... Lorenzo... I only lie to protect you... The truth leaves us... You understand? Alone. The harm; why does the harm get passed down? Is harm in the blood? Lorenzo...

SCENE 6

OLIVIA is standing on the porch, looking at the open door into the house, which seems to have detached from one of its hinges and is almost falling off. The destroyed interior can be seen through the open window and the curtains flapping in the wind. On the porch, black handprints are imprinted onto the wood and the smell of burnt grass sticks to the skin in the damp of the burgeoning night. There is only silence.

OLIVIA: Mum… *(Takes a step towards the door.)* Mum…

CRISTIAN can be heard calling in the distance as he approaches the porch.

CRISTIAN: Lorenzo! Lorenzo! Federica! *(He arrives at the porch and approaches OLIVIA.)*

OLIVIA: I'm going in.

CRISTIAN: No. Wait. Federica!

OLIVIA: I want to go inside.

CRISTIAN: No, let me.

CRISTIAN goes slowly into the house. OLIVIA waits on the porch. FEDERICA walks from the burnt grass to the porch in her dress, which is darkened with soot just like her face and hair.

OLIVIA: Federica.

FEDERICA: Olivia, darling.

OLIVIA: What happened, Mum?

FEDERICA: Come here, darling; don't go in there.

OLIVIA: What happened, Mum?

FEDERICA: Nothing, darling. Nothing.

OLIVIA: Where's Lorenzo?

FEDERICA: I don't know, darling. I don't know.

CRISTIAN comes out of the house and stops.

CRISTIAN: Federica.

OLIVIA: Where's my brother?

CRISTIAN: He's not there.

OLIVIA: What happened to him, Mum?

FEDERICA: Nothing, darling, nothing. Tell me, darling: is my son's rucksack there? I'd go in myself but you must understand I've had such a scare I can barely move.

CRISTIAN runs into the bedroom. With the last of her strength, FEDERICA sits. CRISTIAN rushes back out.

CRISTIAN: No. The rucksack's not there.

FEDERICA: Oh, that's good, darling. That's good.

OLIVIA approaches the swing seat slowly and sits next to FEDERICA. CRISTIAN looks at the burnt grass and the red sun starts to set.

CRISTIAN: I can't hear the crickets.

FEDERICA: I can't hear anything... But everything grows again; it all grows again. That's the thing with weeds, darling; they grow back stronger and protect us.

CRISTIAN: Where is he, Federica?

FEDERICA: There's nothing left. Nothing left alive. Left us naked.

CRISTIAN: Federica... Please, where is he?

FEDERICA: Back soon, darling. Won't be gone forever. A whole lifetime by my side. Finds somewhere to hide, then comes back... Isn't that right, darling? That's why we stayed inside today.

OLIVIA: Won't be gone forever.

FEDERICA: Always comes back. Never left me alone. Always comes back. But every time, I'm more and more frightened.

CRISTIAN: Where's Lorenzo, Federica? Lorenzo.

FEDERICA: Did he tell you to wait for him, darling?

CRISTIAN: Where is he? Please, Federica...

FEDERICA: He always does these things... Hurts without limits... Do you remember, Olivia, how that boy cried? What was his name?

OLIVIA: Patricio.

FEDERICA: Patricio. Poor boy, we never saw him again... But looking in his eyes that afternoon, it felt like having your soul torn out. And I understand the pain. There are few things I understand like pain.

CRISTIAN: Where is he?

OLIVIA: He always leaves. Always. It's not your fault; it's no one's fault. He's like this. He always leaves.

FEDERICA: But he comes back, doesn't he, darling. He always comes back.

OLIVIA: He always comes back.

FEDERICA: We're going to wait for him. But inside. Tonight's not a night for being outside. We'll mend the door and put the sofa against it... And we'll have to board up the back door; he broke that too... We'll have to board everything up... Everything...

CRISTIAN freezes. OLIVIA starts to sway gently in the swing seat.

FEDERICA: It's a new moon today. The grass will grow quick and strong. We have to close the windows and doors... We have to close everything properly today, darling, because he's left us naked in the middle of nothing, and she's very hungry... I can feel her here. *(Touches her stomach.)* She's very hungry... Very hungry... We're going to go inside and close everything up because she's ravenous and we don't have the crickets to warn us...

CRISTIAN: He was going to kill her.

FEDERICA: They grew up together, darling; he could never kill her. Let's go inside, Olivia; let's go inside, nights like this have no boundaries. When she's angry she hurts people without meaning to.

FEDERICA and OLIVIA go into the house. OLIVIA returns and looks at him for a moment.

OLIVIA: Shall we go to the cinema next Saturday? I think they're changing the film, and if they don't, we can see the same one. I don't mind as long as I don't see it on my own.

OLIVIA goes inside.

FEDERICA: *(From inside the house.)* Darling... I'm sorry, but could you ask for an advance at work? There's so many things to mend, it would be a real help… It's not an easy world for the weak.

CRISTIAN looks at the burnt grass. OLIVIA can be heard playing Schubert's allegretto with her father. CRISTIAN takes a step forwards, then another, and stands on the edge of the porch. He takes one more step forwards and stands on the grass watching the horizon.

END

FUEGO DE DRAGÓN SOBRE DRAGÓN DE MADERA. / DRAGON FIRE OVER WOOD DRAGON

MARIA CANDELARIA SABAGH
TRANSLATED BY KATE EATON

Maria Candelaria Sabagh

Candelaria Sabagh is a teacher, dramatist, director and theatrical researcher. She was born in Río Ceballos in Córdoba, Argentina, in 1976. She began her training as a young girl by getting involved in theatre workshops and became a dedicated reader of philosophical texts as an adolescent. Nowadays she defines herself as an artist-political-activist. She graduated with a degree in stage direction from U.N.A (National University of the Arts), and a degree in teaching philosophy from U.N.C (National University of Córdoba). She is currently working on her dissertation for a master's degree in playwrighting (U.N.A). Her teaching activity includes working as an assistant on The Semiotics of Theatre and Analysis of Text II (Department of Dramatic Art, U.N.A) and Project Design I to IV (Department of Visual Arts, U.N.A,). Since 2002, she has headed-up the theatre company Amarillo en Escena Trajo Mala Suerte (Yellow on Stage Brings Bad Luck) with whom she has staged numerous shows. Some notable productions include *Ofiuco*, her graduation projects from U.N.A., *Zoom in 90's* and *The Canterville Residence, No More Zzzzs* and *Ego*; With these last two shows she toured nationally and internationally to Córdoba, Chile, The Netherlands and England.

Characters

HER
Woman-child

She projects a specific kind of femininity
through her gestures which indicate a
vulnerability, a fragility.

Acts out the strength she doesn't have

A danger to herself.

HIM
Twelve years older than her

Dangerous to everyone else.

ACTOR STAGE-HAND 1

ACTOR STAGE-HAND 2

Act One

PROLOGUE TO HAPPINESS

(She is sitting on a bed or sofa; broken-down, worn-out She wears a light nightdress. Barefoot. She gnaws at a part of herself, a knee or perhaps an arm. She has her laptop, which is open, with her. The image on the screen saver is the title of the play 'Dragon Fire over Wood Dragon'. This image is projected, greatly magnified, onto the back of the stage. Everything that happens on the screen will be replicated in the projection.

She weeps. It is the weeping of an inconsolable child. She tires of wiping away tears that fall steadily with a sustained rhythm. Sometimes she sighs before an empty firmament. She gets up, she goes towards some sort of boundary, a frame, or a door if you like, which she looks through. She looks towards an adjoining space. She speaks, camouflaging the weeping, which grows.)

HER: – Sweetheart, you've got an hour of *play* left and then we'll go and get Vicky. I told her nanny I'd take you both to the playground today. OK? Tommy? *(…)* Did you finish your hot chocolate and your rice cakes? I love you, honeybun, answer me once in a while… *(She blows him a kiss. She looks at him a few seconds longer. As she goes back to her laptop she says automatically.)* Not so close to the screen, Tomás… *(She returns to her laptop and moves the mouse. Instantly, the greatly magnified image of the desktop with its icons and files, appears projected. The wallpaper photo is of Tommy, a five-year-old boy who stares at the camera with glowing eyes. She chooses a Word file from the desktop 'Dragon Fire over Wood Dragon' and opens it. She puts:* Edit – Select all – Copy. *She clicks on the icon for the new file and pastes the contents of the old one. The file copies rapidly. The page that can be seen, as usually happens, is the last one. In this case it's from a play that concludes with the words:*

The End

She scrolls up to the beginning. She selects and deletes the first scene. In its place she writes:

• HAPPINESS

HER: *(Writing.)* – Summer. Siesta at my family home in Córdoba. I am in what we call 'the woodland grove', an area of the park that offers the possibility of a unique perspective. If you're lying on the ground and looking up at it from below, depending on how the breeze stirs the branches of the trees, pieces of sky appear, intermittently. These turquoise landscapes shape shift with the swirling of dense branches, canopies of leaves and the impressively three-dimensional yellow flowers that twist and twine around each other. *(She opens a file showing a photo of this woodland. As she starts to speak, she contemplates the image on her screen and then on the projection that expands the wood to its natural size above the stage. She gets up and walks around, going over it.)* An unexpected phenomenon: various acacias, whose growth rate some landscape gardener had failed to calculate and had ordered to be planted too close together, unwittingly creating a micro-universe. Birds, insects and small furry animals rest there, side-by-side, more or less hidden from any predators. The unexpected happenstance of a verdant oasis in the midst of an arid, ragged, mountainous terrain. It was there that I was sleeping, abundantly empty, when in the blink of an eye my whole world changed. *(She takes her mobile phone and listens attentively, frozen like a mouse that knows it has been seen.)*

HIM: – I've been dreaming about you for months. I long to walk down the street holding your hand. Last night I couldn't bear it, it was too much. I was imagining you with me all the time, I had bought a *Glenlivet* – the one they drink in *The Sopranos* – for the midnight hour and I was smoking a *Cohiba*. I yearned to have you by my side, for you to be the woman who moved with me to this house, to share my world, to be close enough to me for me to see you. You inhabited my thoughts. All the time, your face, your intelligence, your smile... you were present the whole time. Perhaps it's really selfish of me but I can't go on like this with Laura. Everyday I've been imagining my life with you, with you and with our children. Carrie, Tommy and us, the four of us. It will hurt my daughter and hurt me to break the news to her, but I can't go on like this, I'm done. I'm going to get a separation. It'll take a while, so I'll need your patience, but I realise that I love you, I want you and I dream about you. You are my love, *you* are my woman and I want us to be together, Maria Sol… my little Sunshine.

HER: *(She turns off the phone. She runs towards HIM, jumps into his arms. He spins her around as she hangs onto his neck, like in an advert. They look at each other, they caress, their eyes filled with tears. They kiss, they look at each other; they separate still looking at each other until each last finger has said its goodbye. She returns to her place. Euphoric.)* This is it, I thought. This is one of those immense, superlative, foundational moments in life, like when Tomás was born, and I knew straightaway that nothing would ever be the same. This grove is the landscape that will be immortalised in my memory. It is where I am when I discover that indescribable happiness is mine for the first time ever in my story. This is how it must be (I wager) how a princess feels when at last she sees, arriving from afar, the armoured knight who is coming to save her forever from the icy solitude of the tower. I see the turquoise sky between the branches, the yellow of the flowers, the greens, the browns. The birds sing, two commonplace butterflies, white ones, fly by and then fly off again, butterflying happily. A hare passes close to me. There are dragonflies, ladybirds, bees. A breeze gets up and some flowers rain down, softly, delicately.

HIM: – 'The landscape is a state of mind'.

HER: Yes, he had told me that once. Now I understand. Now everything makes sense. What I wanted, what I cried for, the love that I gave to him so completely. Now is the moment when my true heart receives benediction for the unblemished zeal of its devotion. I am completely happy, and the world and nature kiss me. Today is 25th December 2012. Christmas in the Year of the Dragon. I am the Fire Dragon, a dragoness who senses for the first time that she won't be burnt to death by the fire of her own flames. I unfold my wings. I am not afraid, and I am ready to fly. *(She heads rapidly towards her laptop. She starts to search for something on the Internet, but the image of the woodland is still projected onto the stage. Her speech is giddy and euphoric.)* I would like to shout it to the furthest corners of the universe, but I can't. I've managed to keep the secret for a whole year now, an epic endeavour, desperate to share it with the whole world as I was. Oh, Gero, Gero, my love, my big fat sweetie, love of my life, my love…! I don't know if you could tell how happy I was to hear from you. *(Taking her phone.)* Urgent: text message. *(The message which she types rapidly is projected over the image of the woodland.)*

'We will love each other limitlessly. You will be inside of me a thousand times over. My

eyes are filled with tears. It's a dream.'

(She leaves the phone and concentrates energetically on the laptop. She has copied a link from You Tube.)

HER: He and I have a secret code. We say things to each other via our Facebook walls. He uploads songs onto his with the mood and the lyrics to suit each situation and I respond from mine. All these months we have communicated this way, especially when it seemed we had split forever. That's where the importance of the songs came in. To go into his wall after days of agony and absence to find songs secretly dedicated to me was one of the best gifts that Gero could give me. He chose them so well... We've been reconciled hundreds of times that way. Other people, unaware of the situation, generously distributed their 'likes', and some friends opined upon the technical merits or otherwise of the songs Gero had uploaded. (Gero has Facebook friends he doesn't even know, he is that rare beast, the well-known 'thinking-person's actor'; He does TV and cinema and – lately – a lot of commercial theatre, something that I continually taunt him about, ha.) Geronimo is fat, it's important to know that to understand some elements of his psyche (I don't care, he's so handsome!) The truth is, nobody suspects us or that those songs are part of the intimate language of our love. I find that so magical... HIM Facebook! *(She opens her Facebook wall.)* 'How are you feeling, SUNSHINE?' 'SUNSHINE' that's me. *(She pastes in the link that she copied. It's the video of Amy Winehouse 'Our Day Will Come', a version with Spanish subtitles.)* For you. This is how I feel today, love of my life.

(The song starts. She dances, sings, replicates, responds to Amy's movements which are projected onto the stage. It becomes a sort of 'musical number' between the two of them whilst at the same time SHE is dressing for the next scene. The space transforms into the area of a bar, with the help of the two STAGE-HANDS, actors who

*also engage in tiny choreographic movements or carry some piece of
furniture upon which she perches in the style of a musical from the
golden-age of Hollywood.)*

HIM: – *(Watching her dance, applauding a little.)* Isn't she gorgeous?
I met her a few years ago on the interview panel for
candidates hoping to be accepted onto the Scenic Arts Course
at EMAD, the Municipal School of Dramatic Art. I was a
mandatory member of the panel along with two colleagues
and they told us at the last minute that one of us wouldn't be
able to make it. (Luckily it wasn't me.) The authorities had
managed to get hold of a girl who had recently graduated and
was already teaching classes in theory at the college. As soon
as she walked into the room, I felt something special. An
immense desire to have her. To really possess her. She was
wearing a sky-blue blouse, which was buttoned up to here
but that still couldn't disguise her perky tits. She introduced
herself, rather nervously. 'Maria Sol, pleased to meet you',
she said, and she sat down with us to complete the panel.
And there she was, as luminous as her name. Timid and
curious, she couldn't disguise her enthusiasm at getting stuck
in with the applicants for the directing course. Provincial,
hysterical and lovely. If it had been up to her, she'd have
given them all the green light. Each applicant seemed
acceptable to her. She couldn't distinguish between the young
boy from Palermo who lived for theatre from the psychopath
who at the first dropped grade would have been mowing-
down the lecturers with a machine-gun. She was naïve, but
– hey – very intelligent the little madam. We laughed during
the interviews; it was great. We exchanged a few words on
the way out, I walked with her towards the block where she
lived, it was on my way. She told me that she had a little kid
of about a year, her partner had left her *twice* the so-and-so,
once during the pregnancy and again afterwards, for good,
the day the child turned six months old. I also told her about
my kid, Carrie, who was nearly two then and the absolute
apple of my eye. We agreed that children are the purest and
most complete kind of love and the full stop to what is known
as freedom. She gave me a flyer for her play and insisted
that I go to see it. There were only a few performances left
before they went on tour. She didn't stop talking about it

her eyes aglow 'You've got to come and see it before we go, Gero! We're going to England, Holland, Finland and Spain! We're going to Europe, Gerónimo, Europe!' I was moved. I remembered my early touring days. A while ago now. She was so proud. She had written the play and directed it. She was 'really, really' interested in my opinion, she said. As I am a generous person, I went.

(She continues working on the Word document. The text is projected onto the onstage screen as she simultaneously writes and reads aloud the following:)

BRIDGING SCENE

- Five years later

- Premiere of new play

- No money for press, so I open a Facebook account to promote it. I add all the 'loaded' people that I know. Gerónimo is one of them.

- I invite him to see my new work (he'd liked the last one I remember).

- He comes

- The play ends. Gerónimo waves at me without saying anything and leaves.

*(She minimizes Word and goes to Facebook. She is bored for a microsecond when suddenly a chat window appears with Gerónimo X. He is chatting from a small device (Blackberry, Smartphone, iPhone). She chats from her laptop. The conversation is projected. What appears **in bold** is what HIM and HER comment to themselves whilst they chat – it is material from which the actors can improvise as they go along –)*

GERONIMO X: – Hi Sol, are you there?

SUNSHINE: – (**Oh it's the deaf-mute from the pavement**) Yes, hi Gero! What happened, didn't you like my play or something? You just stood there by the exit, said nothing and left… ☹

GERONIMO X: – (**I wasn't going to stay to see you getting hysterical with each idiot that congratulated you.**) I saw you were excited and had a big crowd of people around you.

I'm shy.

SUNSHINE: – I got all upset, I thought you didn't like the play which is why you didn't say anything to me…! *(She says this sentence aloud to herself as she types it.)*

GERONIMO X: – I've got a lot to say to you. (**And a lot to give you, you've no idea…**) But I'd rather do it in person, if you're interested, it'll be easier to talk. (**easier to devour you**)

SUNSHINE: Obvioooooooooo….!!!!!! I am super-interested!!!!!!

☺ ☺ ☺

(**Smiley face, smiley face, smiley… He'd better not be hitting on me…**)

GERONIMO X: – Look. If you're not doing anything tonight come with me to a premiere at the Bafici. It's my latest film. The press will be there. You could invite them to your play, it might work… (**Let's see if you turn me down now you ambitious little minx…**)

SUNSHINE: – That would be great!!!! (**Does he think I'm going to return one favour with another the fat pervert…?**)

GERONIMO X: – 20:45 I'll be there, making notes, the show starts 23:15

SUNSHINE: – Oh, he's making notes, very good….

GERONIMO X: 😆

SUNSHINE: – You've left it a bit late to invite me, though!!!! *(She says the phrase aloud and completes it adding* **motherfucker…***)* I need to find someone to leave the boy with…

GERONOMO X: -My wife's not coming (**Thank the Lord!**) because we couldn't get a babysitter.

SUNSHINE: Ah, do you want me to help you find one then? (**Is this guy trying to get off with me or does he just want**

me to look after his kid so that he can go to the Bafici with his wife?)

GERONIMO X: Just find yourself a babysitter and come.

BOTH TOGETHER: (**You/I want to get off with you/me**).

SUNSHINE: No, but really: do you want me to see if I can find you a babysitter, Gero? How old's the little one? (I've got a VERY large babysitter I can lend you!) (**Just so you're clear I don't want anything with you, fatso**)

GERONIMO X: – Nooooo… We've got two but neither of them are available today. Come with me. (**Come on. Baby. Come, come, come, come!**)

SUNSHINE: – OK, I'll come.

GERONIMO X: – Done. We'll meet at the top of the steps at the entrance to Aguero, around 22.30, if that suits you?

SUNSHINE: Great. I'll bring some flyers for my play and you can hand them out?

GERONIMO X: – Can't wait! And afterwards I'll give you my critique.

SUNSHINE: – My promised critique at last! But how many days had to pass before the huge and venerated actor managed to think of what to say to the poor little director of Off…!!!

GERONIMO X;– *(Laughs.)* (**What a bitch…**) Huge because of the size of my belly, you mean?

SUNSHINE: – Nooo… What belly?

GERONIMO X: – What an absolute torrent of self-indulgent narcissism you are my dear.

SUNSHINE: – A torrent is too small for me. My narcissism is a perfect storm and it carries me high.

GERONIMO X: – Fine by me. I'm a storm pilot. I specialise in emergency landings. I'll bring you down whenever you want. (**She laughs and says, 'Dickhead!'**) See you in a while. And stop drinking aviation fuel it's a little bit scary.

(She replies carelessly with a random emoji.)

(They both laugh as she gets up immediately from her laptop and he puts his phone away. They sit facing each other at a table in a bar. Night. They have been there a while. She drinks beer and he coffee. She is fascinated by what she hears.)

HIM: There's a kind of flowering. In the botanical sense I mean. As though suddenly there are territories that converge and spring up creating new terrain, does that make sense…?

HER: *(With an enormous smile.)* – Absolutely.

HIM: – There's something about the acting *(–)* which is fine by the way, not a problem eh. Something unimputable, punkish, as though it's capable of absorbing everything with its energy. It's a good experience, I like it. It's happened to me with other plays, some years ago… seeing a particular world, a place that didn't exist. Good job.

HER: *(Happy.)* – …

HIM: And then there's you, you, spreading your obsessions around onstage with impunity, standing there, guileless, showing-off your intelligence. I was watching the play and I thought: 'How she loves to play the *enfant terrible* that one, what a whimsical, insecure little girl, how I'd like to grab hold of her, the narcissistic idiot.'

(His mobile rings)

HIM: – Sorry, I have to get this. *(Smiles.)* Right now, look… Hi Euge, darling. How are you? How's it going? *(…)* Good, good, I'm glad *(…)* Yes, good. The TV thing same as ever. The theatre all a bit boring *(…)* Slow, really slow. Trying to concentrate on what's in hand, yeah? Getting on with the things I need to finish, the cop show, the classes. So, how are you? *(…)* so not too bad generally. *(…)* Aha! Ah, OK, OK *(…)* yep, that's not a bad gig… No, it's all good, it's just that… you know what I said, right… I'm a bit tired of being typecast *(…)* Yes, no I know it's not a case of drawing the short straw either, but look, I'm always either the fat best friend of the protagonist or the fat thug friend of the villain… and I can't get beyond it. I'm a bit fed-up, if you know what I mean? *(He winks an eye at HER.)* *(…)* *(Greatly amused.)* Yes, I know

I'm not Leo Sbaraglia, Eugenia! And I don't want to play
the leading man either, it's just that in the real world we fat
people aren't just friends with thin people who get to see all
the action, dammit! *(He makes another knowing gesture to HER.)*
Of course, of course *(...)* and yes, eternally ungrateful *(...)*
OK, yes, kiss, kiss. *(Turns off his phone.)* Sorry, my agent.

HER: – You don't know what it means to me to hear that.

HIM: – That I'm tired of playing the fatty?

HER: *(Laughs. Rapid-fire, verbal diarrhoea.)* – What you said to me
about the play, because I believe in myself, a lot but I never
could – I mean I don't know – *lobby* and it's all such an uphill
struggle, you know? The press either insult me or completely
ignore me… And I do it all with so much passion and apart
from the kids who follow me, it's crazy that they've followed
me for years and years and there are a lot of us you know?
We rehearse so much, I change the text a thousand times,
we all put money in, no-one gives us any fucking subsidies,
the actors go overboard filling out applications and nothing!
We rehearsed this play for three years, nineteen actors, my
assistant… all without a penny, exhausting. And well, things
happen to me. I'm on my own with the kid, his father's no
help, it's like having another child, a disaster. And I've got a
whole load of problems, my emotional intelligence is zero,
it's been decreed, psychologists, psychiatrist, the whole lot.
They made me do a very long test once, they said I've got a
triangle instead of a rhombus and *(–)*

HIM: – Sorry? What was all that about Euclidean geometry…?

HER: *(Laughs)* – I use one part of my brain a lot, but another part
is completely under-developed which turns me into a kind
of emotional idiot… They gave me medication once, but it
didn't work; adjusted I'm even worse. And well, basically, my
emotional intelligence will be that of a thirteen to fifteen-year-
old girl my entire life, so there you have it… I try to make it
work in my favour, with fire in my ascendant, I turn it into
creativity.

HIM: – You teach, direct, you're a mother, you write, you make
interesting theatre. Your unresolved infantile triangle seems
fascinating to me. I've started to feel burnt out these last

few years by doing too many commercial gigs. It's great to have so much work, I'm not complaining, but the truth is I'd love to return to working more creatively. I really like this philosophical-theatrical-torrent that you produce. I don't know, I thought maybe we could write something together if you're interested…

HER: – Um… Yes… Can you hang on a minute while I go to the loo? *(She gets up from the table and moves away a couple of metres. Stamps her foot. Stops. Thinks. Returns).* Write together no. I don't think I can write with another person. But if you want, I can write something for you, even if someone else directs it, I'd love it if an actor like you played one of my characters! I really like your work; there's an in-depth organic quality to it which I enjoy each time I see you. I could write a play for two or three characters, you know. Two. Maybe you could be the psychoanalyst to some crazy woman like me?

HIM: – I studied psychoanalysis. I worked in institutions… For a while now I've thought that the transference that analysts seek is part of the process of acting, I'm interested in the idea… What drives you or *(–)*?

HER: – The port city thing. I am Cancer with Aries in the ascendant and I move with the pure dynamic of water and fire: melancholy and desire.

HIM: – And all the theoretical references in your play?

HER: – A nod to a philosophical past that I dredged up.

HIM: – 'Philosophical past', how do you mean?

HER: – I studied philosophy when I lived in Córdoba, but during a journey I had an epiphany as the result of an extraordinary incident – it was in Barcelona – and I decided there and then to change my life for theatre and move to Buenos Aires.

HIM: – 'Career-changing epiphany caused by extraordinary incident in City of Barcelona'. Let's hear it then.

HER: – Now?

HIM: – Please!

HER: – It was twelve years ago, in 2000. It was the year of the Dragon, like this one, 2012, which is also the year of the Dragon – did you know that?

HIM: – It's my year. I'm a Dragon. Born '64. Wood.

HER: – Aha, fancy that. Me too! Born '76. Fire.

HIM: – Fire eats wood. Out with it.

HER: – In 2002, I ran into a guy, another Dragon. I met him on a Granada-Barcelona train. Compartments full of stoned Spaniards. In one, I was the star attraction, making them think that I had an Aztec great-great-grandmother who had taught me an ancient technique for reading people's palms and revealing their true selves. *Not the past nor the future, but who you really are,* I would say. Everyone wanted a go, hands outstretched and me gloriously inventive and believable; the girlfriends I was travelling with, killing themselves with laughter. At one point it was the turn of a fat lad whose friends obviously made fun of him. I was very serious as I read his hand. I said that nobody knew what he was really like inside. That his hand revealed someone who perceived the world in a very special way. The consequences of this were insane.

HIM: – I can imagine, you made someone undervalued feel special, how could it fail. *(Laughs.)*

HER: – The fat boy erupted. Tears, snot, he was yelling that none of his friends really knew him, he leapt up and accused them of terrible things from the past, he even chucked a couple of pineapples at the sealed windows of the train…

HIM: – Poor kid…

HER: – Then one of the other lads, he hadn't asked me to read his palm but had been staring at me in silence *(–)*

HIM: – He became your lover later, I bet.

HER: *(Nods.)* – Amadís his name was. His eyes were a very dark blue, slanting and looking right at you, like a cat.

HIM: – You fell in love.

HER: – I nearly went to live in Barcelona! I'll tell you the rest in a minute, I need to pee, it's the beer.

HIM: – Keep calm.

(She gets up and he watches her go. She returns immediately. She has loosened her hair which before was tied back with a clasp.)

228

HER: – I'm back. So, Amadís. He grabbed my arm and we went flying through various carriages until we reached a goods car. We opened the side door and sat down together, our legs half hanging out of the train. From time to time you could see the orange and lilac horizon of the Mediterranean. It was freezing. Amadís stared at me intently. He murmured into my ear: 'Do you want to know who you really are?'

HIM: – So much mystery. It's not true. Made-up story.

HER: – I swear to you on my son's life, that apart from my occasional verbal embellishments, it is true!

HIM: – Carry on, dramatist.

HER: – We agreed to meet each other in the Plaza de Cataluña the following night at ten. On getting down from the train he indicated that I should make myself 'elegant and sexy'.

HIM: – It's a brothel that square at night, I know it.

HER: – (I was on time and he wasn't, I can't tell you what a fright it gave me.) Anyway, he took me to dine at a lovely little place in the Gothic Quarter. Violin. Candles. Amadís and me. Connection. He cracked up laughing at my philosophical academic training, he thought all that stuff was a complete joke. Suddenly a diner two tables away starts to cough. He's choking on his food. The man's wife doesn't know what to do, she's desperate. A man gets up from another table, by luck he's a doctor, he performs the Heimlich manoeuvre on the diner and saves him. Relief and commotion all around, as you might imagine. When everything calms down, the wife of the choking man stands up and 'chink, chinks' a knife against her wine glass. She makes a speech – it seems lovely – in Catalan. Everyone gets emotional, they toast, applaud, we all cry, even me who didn't understand a thing. The *Maître D* says something, and Amadís – who was half translating for me –, says that dinner is on the house adding that it's just as well as he didn't have enough to pay the bill anyway and that now we're going to another place.

HIM: – My God... what a jerk.

HER: He takes me to a small bar down one hundred steps, in a neighbourhood of labyrinthine corners and passageways. We enter. Darkness. Velvet, worn out screens. Suspended in time. He tells me that this is the only place left in Europe where they still sell the authentic absinthe, which isn't what the tourists buy in Prague. He explained to me that it was like opening the door to madness little by little. This is where Piaf came, he said, to drink it. (Amadís and I both liked the same Piaf song as we had discovered earlier while dining.) I had never heard of something as extraordinary as absinthe, I wanted to try it. Soon two cut glasses arrived alongside two small bottles filled with a green amber liquid suffused with its own light. We raised our glasses. I drank it straight down. It was warm. 'I need to go to the bathroom urgently.'

HIM: – Go on then.

HER: No. 'I need to go to the bathroom urgently.' I said to him.

HIM: – It's that door you can see, over there.

(She gets up and goes out, then enters again straightaway.)

HIM: – You are elegant and very sexy, just as I asked you to be, You're obedient. That's good.

HER: – Thanks.

HIM: – I like those stockings, I didn't know Argentinian women still wore them. They don't exist here.

HER: – How can silk stockings not exist, what are you saying?

HIM: – Women here wear panty-hose – all in one piece. Not like yours, in two pieces and held up by those sexy fastenings.

HER: – The garter belt?

HIM: Garter belt.

HER: – But how can you tell I'm wearing a garter belt if this is a knee-length skirt?

HIM: – Come on, you did it on purpose.

HER: – Did what?

HIM: – Went to the bathroom and left the door open to show us everything. We all saw you.

HER: – What?!

HIM: – Didn't you realise you went to the toilet without closing the door?

HER: – I didn't do that. It's a lie!

HIM: – You did do it sweetheart. Hey, you're already as clever as they come! Let's go outside, OK.

(He takes her arm and helps her put on her coat. They're about to leave. She stops suddenly.)

HER: – Look! There's that couple from the restaurant. That's the man who choked and look! The doctor who helped them is also here. They're all friends it seems. They know each other! But why are they all here?

HIM: – I asked them to come.

HER: I don't understand. When, if we left together and *(–)*

HIM: – We planned it yesterday. It was all for you. Of course, we didn't know it was going to turn out so delightfully. Getting a free dinner was a fantastic denouement, a beautiful surprise. We've been working together for a while. We do these kind of things, surprise performances and set-ups. People often hire us to do them.

HER: Like that film about the game, the Michael Douglas one!

HIM: – Fuck that. We were doing this long before any of that American crap came out. You are already one of us, even though you don't know it. On the train that night, you gave a unique gift to that idiot Darío. Telling him that he was special, that he had a secret. It takes a good eye to be able to do that. You achieved an effect. The effect is sacred. You should forget about studying philosophy which is a load of wank. It's not for you. Your ship sails in different waters, princess. It's no accident that we met. Do you believe in destiny?

HER: – ...

HIM: – Come on. You need some air. The absinthe has got to you. Now everything starts to seem like a film.

HER: – *(Shouting as she points to a projection that says:* 'I see subtitles! Yellow subtitles, I see, there they are! You said "film" and now I see everything with subtitles. They seem real!'*)* – I see subtitles! Yellow subtitles, I see, there they are! You said "film" and now I see everything with subtitles. They seem real!

HIM: – All this is real. *(A huge subtitle is projected which says:* 'All this is real'.*)*

(He runs towards the laptop and plays a video that combines perspectives and images of the City of Barcelona by night which at times fuse with mobile trencadís mosaics in a kaleidoscopic style. This video is projected to the soundtrack of 'Comic Strip' by Serge Gainsbourg. HIM and HER go all over the city excitedly and at great speed. Sometimes they hold each other by the waist, sometimes by the hand. They run around, they're clumsy, they trip, laugh and continue. They take photos, they dance. There is the feeling of one of those popular film sequences from the 1950s or 1960s, which narrates the whole story of a date, using signs and some shots of a couple dancing, eating, going to the theatre etc. A pair of ACTOR-STAGEHANDS in code as the 'ensemble' of the musical can carry or move a streetlamp or a flower stall etc. From time to time HIM and HER stop to point out something or to comment on what they see. During these fleeting moments the following subtitles will be projected to translate what they are saying whilst the music plays.

– La Oveja Negra is a place where all the stupid tourists go. We frequent it a lot to make them freak out.

– Just follow me and do exactly what I say.

– See that guy sitting over there drinking with his friends? He is our target. We're going to produce an effect for him.

(They have arrived during this sequence at 'La Oveja Negra' tavern, this means that the scene can be played out in the same area with tables and chairs as the beginning of the scene.)

HIM: *(He clasps her round the waist from behind and talks to her whilst supposedly looking at a man sitting at the same table that they were sitting at previously and sitting in the same place where He had been sitting.)* I'll go and talk to that guy, the Mexican with that bunch of people. Looks like he's the leader of the group. Don't be scared, he's only a tourist, OK? You're all over the place. You're dizzy so you just have to trust me. The fact that you're a knockout is your trump card.

HER: – A what-out...?

HIM: – A knockout. You're really beautiful, you've got a great chance of success. And you know it of course. Things aren't going well for you. You arrived here three days ago from your country because this guy promised to place you with an exclusive escort agency. Escorts – beautiful girls who offer services.

HER: – Prostitutes

HIM: – Right. You came to Barcelona without a cent and the sonofabitch has done you over.

HER: – Done me what?

HIM: – Done you over – tricked you. You urgently need to make some dough. Quick and easy money so that you can get to Paris where your best friend lives. You met me in the airport, and I've been letting you stay with me in exchange for sex. I'm going to speak to the guy, I'll sell him the story and ask him if he wants a fuck.

HER: – Oh my God! What an idea… alright, go on. But tell him I've never worked as a prostitute before so if I seem uncomfortable, there's a reason, OK?

HIM: – Perfect. Can't you see you were born for this?

HER: – Prostitution?

HIM: – No way, babe. Inventing stories for other people. Stay there until I call you, love. I'll speak to him and then I'll give you a sign.

HER: OK. Wait, wait, Amadís!

HIM: – …

HER: – What's the name of the airport in Barcelona, just in case it comes up, they might have flown here, me too supposedly…

HIM: – *(Laughs.)* El Prat. OK?

HER: – El Prat!

(He walks over to the table and sits down occupying the Mexican's place. She takes off her coat and lights a cigarette, rather nervous. She remains standing. HIM and HER hold their gaze. Brief silence.)

HIM: – So… This fella tells us that you're a party girl… We can all see you're a real good looker. *(Drinks.)* So, he's kind of made us this proposition which I personally find very interesting, not because I'm thinking of my own pleasure, as my *mamita* in Mexico City would say, but because we're celebrating the birthday of our *hermano* Sergio here…

HER: – Happy birthday Sergio…

HIM: – So charming. *(Someone sitting next to him says something into his ear. He laughs.)* Don't fuck around, jerk… *(He drinks. Continues talking to HER.)* I haven't personally given my friend here a present yet. We're squashed into this bar like all the damn tourists. I'm looking at your hair, your face and your clothes. Great tits. *(Drinks.)* I don't think it's enough though for my *hermano* to receive a one-off gift as some sort of mark of his social status.

HER: – …

HIM: – OK: Let me explain it to you more slowly. Frankly I think you're a little bit uptight and I'm wondering what you can do to help yourself relax.

HER: – I don't understand.

HIM: – Hey, don't stress baby doll. Your boyfriend told us everything and it's all fine and dandy but he's asking for a lot of money. *(As he takes out some notes from his inside jacket pocket, he counts them and lays them on the table.)* Now I don't have a problem with that, much less for *un hermano* like Sergio. Thing is, these Spanish guys and these Argentinian women have a tendency to exaggerate *(Drinks.)* Why don't you come a bit closer and convince us that the goods are worth what your boyfriend's asking for?

HER: – Amadís was sitting to one side. There were four friends. The table was a longish plank of wood. It was your typical dirty bar, acne-ridden tourists proliferated. Smoke, bursts of laughter, mugs of beer clanking against each other. I must have been about two metres away from the Mexican who was fat and sweaty. His half-open shirt revealed the little medallion of the Virgin glinting on his chest. I held his gaze. For a fleeting moment I glanced at Amadís, seeking his support. He winked at me, furtively. And then… *(She lifts her skirt up level with her hips)* ... I get creative and inventive. *(She takes off her panties and plays with them between her hands. She stares at HIM.)* I could feel the silence of a thousand eyes looking at me. *(She advances towards the table. She gets up. Crawls. She is face to face with HIM. She takes his left hand, plays for a moment with his fingers, chooses one and licks it like it's the only popsicle left at the party. Brief pause. Now she speaks, as she does so the action will play out exactly in the way she tells it.)* The guy grabs the money and offers it to me. Amadís gripping onto my arm like a vice, yanks me down from the table, kicks a chair, snatches the money, throws it in the air and shouts:

HIM: – *(Throwing the notes in the air.)* Shove it up your arsehole, motherfucker!

HER: – *(Helpless with laughter, she runs out alongside HIM.)* The notes float down like they're dancing. The greasy tourists go crazy. The commotion intensifies as we get to the street and Amadís yells something in Catalan at a police officer who immediately orders the evacuation of the tavern. And we run and run and run and I feel like I did when I was a kid playing knock down ginger. *(There could be a small reprise of Comic Strip here, the song itself has a brief separate ending. Helpless with laughter, ending the encounter.)* Life...

HIM: – Such is life!

HER: – Do any taxis go this way? Wouldn't it be better to walk towards Corrientes and Anchorena?

HIM: – Let's take a look...So the upshot of it all was that you decided to give up philosophy *(–)*

HER: – And to dedicate myself to producing effect after effect.

HIM: – And here we are. *(/)* They go this way...

HER: – Here we are!

HIM: – Playing at knock down ginger, Freud would have a field day.

HER: – You liked my telling of it.

HIM: – What a child you are.

HER: – Exactly as it happened, eh! *(Looking towards the street.)* Here come two.

HIM: – *(Raising his arm to stop the taxis.)* You take the first one.

HER: – *(She goes to say a quick goodbye, but he hugs her, it's a rather awkward embrace.)* Well, thanks for everything. I'll think about some scenes for the psychoanalysis play, if you like the idea and I'll try to have something to send you in a few days?

HIM: – Yes, perfect. Put your mind to it.

HER: – I'm super excited by the idea, I would just die to write something for you to act, I still can't believe it, are you really serious?

HIM: – Of course. We'll meet again in fifteen days; how does that sound?

(They separate. They have scarcely parted when He takes his mobile and writes the following text message which is projected immediately as She receives it and reads it).

HIM: – 'I am going to help you assemble the rhombus. You will help me return to poetry.'

She responds straightaway, also by text message:

'I promise to use all my mental instability to achieve it'

He replies:

'Ah… I have to tell you: I think I'm going to fall in love with you. Sorry, I know I'm a horrible guy.'

She laughs to herself as she replies

'As long as it's not me who falls in love… because then we'll all be lost. Get some rest now. Ciao.'

DIEGESIS AND MIMESIS OF LOVE

HIM: – The meeting to see what she had written for me happens earlier than agreed. The text messages multiply markedly over the next seventy-two hours. On the fourth day, during a sunlit siesta, I am between her sheets. I give her a good time. A seriously good time.

HER: – Afterwards I remember, he said to me smiling 'What happened to you, baby girl: Did someone put an old man in your bed?'

HIM: – And that's how it was, inevitably. Stealthily I etched my signature into her folds and creases. Masterfully I conquered each nook and cranny of her being, how vulnerable she was, I knew how close I was to her secrets... the materiality of her gestures and her gaze turned from fire to water without any seeming restriction. The more deeply I knew that I touched her, the rapidity with which she changed, the more excited I became and very soon we were falling more and more deeply in love.

HER: – Incredible his kisses, so sweet and hot. Gentle and obscene caresses. Heavenly fucks. His steady gaze, completely unfathomable. Friendly words, honest advice, conversation. Electric laughter. Affection, a whole heap. Longed-for liaisons, ardent and fleeting and agonising absences that only served to accentuate a thousand-fold the ecstasy of each moment spent with him. And I didn't even see him as fat!

HIM: – We needed each other. We sent fifteen, twenty messages a day.

HER: – The heaviness of time without him was so painful. Longing for him drove me mad. Necessity, appetite, the lack of them marked of every moment of his absence.

HIM: – And because of that, from time to time, all hell broke loose. The pretext, always the same. What I gave her wasn't enough *(–)*

HER: – Because you gave me so little...

HIM: – So little? Look at all that stuff you just said about being together...

HER: – You give me so little.

HIM: – Yes, I give you so little.

HER: – And it hurts me so much *(–)*

HIM: – I know baby, and then you get angry and leave and end the relationship.

HER: – I really believe it's over.

HIM: – You say dreadful things to me, you shoot to kill.

HER: – More like I'm defending myself.

HIM: – Defending yourself from what?

HER: – …

HIM: – You become murderous.

HER: – Yes. I told him once that I wished he'd die of a heart attack. That to him I was no more than a whore who opened her legs for him a couple of hours a week. That the house he'd built for his family four years ago was just a pile of bricks. What's more…

HIM: – That I use you to spice up my life. That my selfishness has no limits or borders. That I turn you into a psychopath. That you're just a thing to me. That I don't understand you, that I don't love you, that I don't take care of you.

HER: – That you don't take care of me.

HIM: – You would attack me, and we would stop seeing each other. And always, each and every time we would think that the split was final.

HER: – That's because every time we left each other it was 'forever'!

HIM: – And then would come the separation.

HER: – And the desperation of the days and nights without him.

HIM: – A fucking nightmare.

HER: – Unbearable pain.

HIM: – The unbearable, never-fucking-ending pain. How many times did we live through that hell, how many times did we try to leave each other forever *(–)*?

HER: – Eleven times in eight months. *(She takes off her shoes and walks, she staggers a little.)* I remember that once I came back home sad and alone after a party. Pissed off because some jerk had been trying it on with me all evening. One of the shittiest things about doing independent theatre is that every so often you have to have a party to get some money together. It's the only way; new costumes, Party! Want to print a pair of fucking flyers in colour? Party! And if you're the director you can't be stand-offish. So, some little indie actor shit who wants to be in one of my plays decides to dedicate himself, like a madman, to cheering me up. He

238

brings me drinks, he pays me compliments, he tries to get me to dance... Now, when I'm in love, I don't want anyone else to look at me, I don't like it if someone puts their hand on my back or speaks right into my ear because the music is loud... I don't want to have anything to do with anyone, me. I love Gero, it's been twelve days since we split-up, no messages or anything and naturally I'm imagining that he's sleeping with his wife. But I am Cancer with the moon in Sagittarius – the most faithful combination in the zodiac – so of course he goes to touch me the little actor shit – and when I'm in love, another body trying to get close to mine is like a desecration of my unsullied devotion. So, I arrive home sad, alone and drunk. I unblock him on Facebook without much hope to see if he has posted anything on his wall and I find a stream of songs... They chart the course of everything my love was feeling during those days, what he wished he could have said to me.

HIM: – She was listening to them in the same order that I'd uploaded them. *(He – playing the DJ – puts on some big earphones and plays music through Her laptop. The videos do not appear on the screen instead there are some of those moving abstract images that are used in some programmes that play music.)* 'I am a DJ of Love, baby!' *(The linked songs are the following)* That's the way it goes – My heart's a dirty traitor – my hands have slipped the handcuffs once again.../ I met you, I know, in a moment of heavenly rapture – you are the luminous place where the waves kiss the shore/ How can I find my way through the deep blue night if your eyes don't see me anymore...? – I want to be inside you one more time/ I can't be happy – I can't forget you – I know I've lost you and the pain is so sharp – I gave you up – burning with passion – it's impossible to have – a conscience and a heart / I don't know if this zamba will reach you – beneath the stars it drifts through the night – searching for the village where I left you – to hear again – the sound of your voice – girl with the olive-green eyes – I travel with the zamba, pilgrim of love. *(She listens to the fragments of the songs as she gets undressed, she puts on some pyjama bottoms with a vest top, she sits on her bed and cries. When the Zamba de Usted starts HIM and HER look at each other then he gets her up to dance. They dance the zamba. They end up barely a metre apart, facing each other.)*

HIM: Hallo gorgeous, lovely, beautiful, my love... *(He hugs her, he rubs her back, her buttocks, her arms. He sniffs at her desperately.)*

HER: Hallo...

HIM: – How I've missed you, bitch. These jim-jams, how I've missed them.

HER: I put them on just now, when I got back from teaching.

HIM: – Very good... daddy has really missed getting you out of them... *(She cries.)* No, no, no... *(He licks her tears.)*

HER: Dirty pig.

HIM: – I had a searing pain in my shoulder, a massive spasm.

HER: *(Laughs a little)* – Because you didn't see me, the spasm.

HIM: – Of course! I was circling you the whole time; it was driving me crazy to see your little green dot in the *chat* and not be able to speak to you. The little green dot was you. I climbed up to the water tank to howl with misery, that's how much I missed you, sweetheart.

HER: – I listened to the songs you uploaded...

HIM: – Did you like them my love?

HER: – They were beautiful. I didn't know that Zamba... It seemed as though you had written it for me.

HIM: – Well there you are then; it can be our song.

HER: – I really wanted to be able to leave you this time, I tried very hard, for Tommy more than anything, but I couldn't *(–)*

HIM: – How beautiful you are.

HER: – No...

HIM: – I don't know if I want to look at you from near or afar... Stay there *(He moves away.)* Beautiful, beautiful, beautiful you are. You are a beautiful woman!

HER: No... I'm horrible, my eyes are all puffy... The house is a disaster zone, I've been so detached from Tommy, crying all the time... Such a bad mother I've been these last days...

HIM: – That's not true. Did he go out to play in the garden? Did you feed him? Give him a bath?

HER: – Yes, obviously. And I read him stories, but with a sadness, with an emptiness he doesn't deserve. What a miserable mother my little boy has…

HIM: – Well, baby, you have to learn to control your emotions *(–)*

HER: – I told you that I can't! *(Bursts into tears.)*

HIM: – *(He hugs her.)* – There, there… Tell me, have you been writing for me. How's it going? You promised to return me to poetry, I want to see it *(–)*

HER: I already told you, the psychoanalysis thing is toast. I'm just capturing what's happening between us. I don't know if it'll be poetic but it's truthful, I don't want to talk about it now, it stresses me out…!

HIM: – *(Laughs.)* – What a pretty little thing you are.

HER: – Everything's a problem. By chance a critic from one of the daily papers came – newspaper, critic! – to see my play and then said he wasn't going to write a review. Nothing! The guy watches a show that took three years to make and doesn't want *(–)*

HIM: – But didn't you write a satirical song about the critics, honey bunch?

HER: – Yes, it's a lovely *Bossa Nova…*!

HIM: – But the lyrics are quite defamatory aren't they my love? What did you expect baby? If life gives you lemons…

HER: – *(She moves away, bursts into uncontrollable tears and points at him as she speaks.)* – That's the exact same thing you say about our relationship, I hate it when you use that expression, I hate it!

HIM: – What?

HER:- When I suffer because I miss you, because I need you or because I have to hide on a dark street corner waiting for you to pick me up in a taxi after one of your shows in one of your mega theatres which of course are reviewed in the papers, you always say that thing about the bloody lemons *(–)*

HIM: – You knew from the start that getting involved with me meant having to deal with all that. I never lied to you sweetheart. I always told you that I had a family. *(Laughing)* And so yes, 'If life gives you lemons, make lemonade, baby.'

HER: – You're laughing at me! *(Cries even more.)*

HIM: *(Laughs a bit more.)* Oh, baby, baby… You can't give the same weight to everything. The critic who saw your show, being a good mother, the fact that I'm married… You have to learn to be able to separate things, sweetheart. Life is a mass of different things, multiple outlooks. Decompress, my love. Listen to me, lovely. How I would love to nurture you *(–)*

HER: – Nurture me then…

HIM: – I can't…

HER: – *(She grabs his cock.)* Nurture me… You are the only one who can nurture me…

HIM: – I can't do it sweetheart… I can't nurture you, but at least I can support you a little. Don't be such an extremist, doll.

HER: It's the rhombus…

HIM: What rhombus?

HER: – The thing I told you about my emotional problems when we were chatting that night at the Bafici… chemical imbalance, fire and water, triangle and not rhombus…

HIM: – When you were telling me those things, I was looking at your skin… *(He caresses her. He takes her by both arms, slightly distancing himself from her.)* Listen to what I'm telling you, trust me.

HER: – …

HIM: – Know what's going to happen now?

HER: –

HIM: – I'm going to lick your pussy…

HER: – No.

HIM: – Why not?

HER: – Because not.

HIM: – Why?

HER: – No.

HIM: – But there's nothing in the world that makes me happier, you know it…!

HER: I said no! I haven't washed; I spent the morning rushing around, and I had to pee in the faculty and there's never any paper in those toilets.

HIM: – Well there's a simple solution to that…

HER: – No. No. I don't want to wash myself in the *bidet,* it's too premeditated and it ruins the spontaneity of the moment, no.

HIM: *(Laughing as he takes her by the hand and leads her.)* – Come on, baby doll… come on, daddy's going to wash his little girl and leave her all nice and clean…

HER: No! What are you saying?! You're mad!

HIM: – Mad with love, sweetie pie… *(He laughs and leads her away.)*

HER: God how embarrassing, you're a pervert, Gerónimo, I don't want…!

HIM: – It's all good, sweetheart. Daddy's not going to lose the chance of spending hours eating that soft, pink little pussy, that's not going to happen, my love… *(They leave. From off.)* I don't want to scald you, precious… better add a bit of cold…

HER: *(From off.)* Careful when you turn on the cold, it spurts out suddenly!

(One ACTOR-STAGEHAND enters carrying an umbrella with which he protects the laptop and another ACTOR-STAGEHAND enters with a hose.)

HER: – Careful with the cold tap, I said!

THE CREASE

(The ACTOR-STAGEHAND makes an abundant rain shower with the hose for a few brief seconds. The stage area becomes wet, apart from the laptop which is protected by the umbrella held by the other ACTOR-STAGEHAND. The rain stops and both ACTOR-STAGEHANDS exit. She enters wrapped in a towel with another towel wrapped around her head. She carries a

243

mop; she dries the floor. This scene could take place in the area with the table and chairs.)

HER: – I can't stand it anymore. I want a separation; I'm not going on like this. This is no kind of life.

HIM: *(He's half-dressed, he has a cup of coffee in one hand and some pages written in Times New Roman 12 in the other. He sits down in one of the chairs at the table. Reads.)* – What's wrong now, I don't understand…

HER: – Ah, you don't understand.

HIM: *(Reads.)* – No. I get here, you're locked in the bathroom, you don't say hallo. *(Without reading.)* What's this?

HER: *(Pointing to the pages.)* I'm not stupid you know!

HIM: *(Continues reading.)* – Keep it down can you, Carrie will hear. What's wrong, Laura?

HER: – Tell me something, are you fucking eighteen-year-old girls, is that it?

HIM: – What?

HER: – Are you fucking teenagers?

HIM: – What are you talking about, Laura?

HER: – Is that why you won't touch me?

HIM: – …

HER: – It's so long since we've screwed.

HIM: *(Reads.)* Laura darling, we've already talked about this. Again *(–)*

HER: – It'll be two months next week! Two! And it's always me who has to initiate it. Never you! I'm tired of your shit. I want a separation.

HIM: *(Reads.)* What's going on, we had a lovely breakfast this morning the three of us and now you start saying *(–)*

HER: – Do you think I'm some kind of idiot?

HIM: – But what is this, what's happening, what are you playing at, Laura?

HER: – Last night, when I stuck my head round the door to show you the little note in Carrie's exercise book, you were at the computer, you were very jumpy, and I saw you, quite clearly, close a window in a rush. I registered it but I didn't say anything. This morning I sat down, calmly, to check my emails and suddenly all these porn ads start popping up: 'Would you like a date with Lucy?' and a photo of some twenty-year old floozy sucking a dick.

HIM: – You're crazy, Laura... You accuse me of screwing teenagers, just because an ad for a prostitute popped up – the internet's full of these things, they just appear of their own accord, all the time.

HER: – Go on, take me for a fool, be my guest.

HIM: – Laura! *(–)*

HER: – I had a look at your search history, Gerónimo; you'd been looking at your emails, you'd been on *Facebook* and you'd been Googling porn. You'd visited seven porn sites, seven! Are you fucking teenage prostitutes, is that it? And what about me, Gerónimo? The last time we had sex, you looked right through me. Your eyes were completely empty! It was as though you'd been extinguished. I looked at you, sprawled beneath me, with all your weight on the bed. You had the glassy stare of a dead wart hog.

HIM: *(He stops reading.)* – OK, OK. Let's stop for a bit.

HER: *(As she takes the towel off her head and leaves the mop.)* – You didn't like it. What is it? Her speech patterns are too like mine; she hasn't got her own rhythm? She wouldn't use a word like 'extinguished'? She wouldn't express herself like that *(–)*

HIM: – You are crazy.

HER: – ...

HIM: – You really want the shit to hit the fan for me, babe...

HER: – *(Unable to contain her glee.)* Yesss! Yes, yes, yes! I've nailed it! It was almost exactly as I've imagined it, I know it! You told me about that episode in passing, the night we went to dine in China Town (China Town where you told me you took 'all your lovers' But you never had a lover like this one, eh, baby?!)

HIM: – I've certainly never had the mayhem that I've known with you.

HER: *(Laughs.)* – I love you!

HIM: – I love you, but not this.

HER: – Oh come on, don't get all arsey now, big boy… You've known since the first time we fucked that I ditched the psychoanalyst and the crazy woman story in favour of making the play more autobiographical, and you absolutely loved the idea.

HIM: – I told you it was OK, not that I 'absolutely loved' it…

HER: – I always work with what I have! And I've never written a love story before! It just so happens that I'm in love and I have a pressing need to work with that material. It's so overwhelming, it'll eat me up if I don't get it out of my system, baby, if I don't air it. I am suffering so much because of the insignificant part I play in your life.

HIM: – It's not insignificant, for fuck's sake! You're really important to me.

HER: – I hear you say that every so often, but I don't feel it. The only thing that saves me is channelling my emotions, doing what I do. I write and direct, Gero. I write and direct things that very few people see and for which I have to virtually starve myself. I am not well. I am not whole. I would fall to pieces if you took it away from me. I won't survive this relationship if I don't have theatre. Do you understand that, my love?

HIM: … *(He tenderly kisses her neck and face.)*

HER: *(Smiles and cries.)* 'If life gives you lemons', I can say that to you now… And 'you knew from the start that getting involved with me meant having to deal with all that', right?

HIM: *(Laughs.)* – Bitch…

HER: – We can change a few things, lover boy… Instead of a wart hog for example we can have a camel. Instead of saying there were seven links in your search history we'll say four. Stuff like that. I also thought I should choose another physical peculiarity as a substitute for your actual one.

HIM: – I hope that you do.

HER: – So what occurred to me that night, if you remember, when your agent rang, and I heard you complaining *(–)*

HIM: – Oh, yes. I was protesting because I don't like being typecast as a *(–)*

HER: – Fat guy!

HIM: – What?

HER: – I came up with that idea to disguise your true identity.

HIM: – You made me fat?

HER: – Yes. In the play you are fat instead of… well… what your actual issue and predominant physical type is, *physique du role,* as Stanislavski would say. But as I love you and I see you as beautiful, so it's exactly the same for the character. Indeed, the actor could be an overweight fifty-something or all skin and bones as long as in Maria Sol's eyes, he's as sexy as hell.

HIM: – Aha! And Maria Sol could be a young woman playing a little girl of twelve because that's who you are in my eyes and that's how you behave.

HER: Fine by me. Anyway, it's for you to create the role. You'll be brilliant, zero typecasting. All the little pussies in the city will be aching for you when they see you. (There won't be a dry seat in the house, handsome!)

HIM: – …

HER: What. What's up?

HIM: – You are beautiful.

HER: – And super-talented, don't you forget it!

HIM: – God help me if I do!

HER: – Right. Do you want to read on? *(Pulling out a couple of pages from the ones he's holding.)*

HIM: – Of course, …

HER: *(She kisses him briefly and noisily on the forehead as if to comply but clearly concentrating on the pages she's looking at. Pointing at a particular part of one of the pages.)* – Here I need to resolve the transition between the argument with Laura over the porn and what happens next. It's the bit where she wants to fuck but you don't. Let's have a look. *(She puts the towel around her head again and picks up the mop.)* 'If you say that you love me, then why don't you show me, bunnykins? Show me because otherwise I'll think you don't want me anymore. Kiss me my angel, come on…'

(He strokes her legs, slips his hands under the towel and massages her buttocks)

HER: – No, no, stop! That's not what it says here. Do you really do that to your wife? All the stuff you say to me about being your one true love, True or false?

HIM: *(As he continues touching her.)* – True, sweetheart…

HER: – Get off me, Gerónimo. *(She lets go of the mop, handing it over to him.)* I presume it doesn't excite you. Don't make me jealous, don't be a shit, babe! Come on. I'm her. 'What's the matter, bunnykins? Don't I turn you on anymore…?'

HIM: – What's the point of this infantile and ridiculous scene, Little Miss Sunshine? It has nothing to do with you. I can't even mention my wife without you getting all teary-eyed and hysterical? Who are you trying to impress with your perversity?

HER: – No one…

HIM: – It is pure adolescent provocation, sweetie. There's no need.

HER: – I'm doing it for dramatic effect…

HIM: – What a masochistic idiot you are.

HER: You're going to love this though. Your lumpen aestheticism will delight in all this… *(She opens the towel. She has her back to the audience and is facing HIM, so that the audience can't see HER. Just HIM looking at HER.)* How can I not be a masochist, a neo-baroque dame like me, going to bed with a fat, bald guy like you?

HIM: – Oh, so I'm bald now too, am I?

HER: – Yep, I've just made you bald!

HIM: – Come here, you delicious little bitch. *(He pulls her towards him like a shot).*

(The following text messages are projected onto the screen:

'I've just turned the corner from your house and I already feel like I miss you. This has been happening a lot recently.'

'Sorry! It's just that I'm addicted to your fucks, your tongue, your eyes and your love.'

'I already told you: I can't nurture you, but I'll support you a little.'

GERONIMO DIXIT.

HIM: – In therapy I work a lot with the theme of absence. My analyst explores with me the reasons why I can't relax, right? On accepting that it is possible to have an amorous relationship with one woman in spite of living with another woman with whom I share a daughter as well as other mutual projects. Why can't love exist within a different framework? Love can negotiate its own territory wherever it wants, or rather wherever it is allowed to.

(She is facing her laptop. She watches a video on YouTube, with headphones. This video is not projected onto the screen yet. It is 'Don't let him waste your time', by Nancy Sinatra.)

HIM: – But She doesn't understand that. Maria Sol doesn't understand that. And what happens is that she suffers from the tremendous absence of everything that she considers should occupy the territory of love. What she doesn't realise is that it isn't free love that she yearns for, but rather one that adheres to a script, a script that she finds desirable, but that within the framework of our relationship cannot be followed through. She believed the fairy-tale that the princess always ends up in the castle with the prince. And she has such contradictory outbursts, my little one. She senses that I love her, she knows it and she also loves me and knows that I know it. But in spite of all her reading, the lucid and critical thinking that she displays to the world, she suffers because we cannot be together 'truly' as she puts it, 'truly be together'. And there are things that I cannot – and will never be able to – give her. The fact that I'm already a big name, that I have a daughter and a new house that my wife and I have spent years in the planning and construction of, mean that, effectively, there are many things that I can't give her, despite the fact that I love her, That I genuinely love her.

NIGHTS OF LOVE AND BIRTHDAY

(She writes on Word 5, Nights of Love and Birthday. Then she puts 'expand screen' on her laptop whilst she takes off her headphones and at the same time the sound is heard, and the video is projected onto the stage (finally) from 2:12 into the video until the end of the song – with subtitles – on the screen. Towards the end of the song she opens a photo that she has on her desktop, it is of an infinity of lighted candles that occupy the whole screen, these will remain projected during the following scene. He is dressed smartly and carries a medium-sized book which is gift-wrapped. She has on an evening dress and wears an apron.)

HIM: – These little candles that you've put everywhere are so pretty, my love.

HER: – I remember when I was little my mother did the same whenever we ate *bourguignon*. The flickering flames and the bubbling casserole create a lovely ambience *(–)*

HIM: – You want to be like your mother.

HER: – Shut up!

HIM: – I think you do… *(Giving her the book.)* A small gift, nothing really…

HER: – *(Tearing the paper.)* – For my birthday? It's not for two days yet! On Monday, it's a holiday maybe we could *(–)*

HIM: – No, my love… public holidays are impossible for me.

HER: – *(She has succeeded in taking the book out of the wrapping.)* let's see… aha. A Deleuzian re-reading of Nietzsche: how lovely, Gero. Thank you.

HIM: – You don't like it.

HER: – Of course I like it! It's just that what with the literature of abandonment and the feeling I sometimes get that you want me to go back to my previous career, you…

HIM: – It doesn't mean anything. It's just that you're the only woman I can talk philosophy with,

HER: – I love it when you say that!

HIM: – Did you know about it, my love, had you read it?

HER: – No, no. *(Searching through the first few pages.)* Let's have look at the dedication: it has one I suppose. Can you read it to me, pretty please?

HIM: – I'm embarrassed. *(Reads.)* 'How many selves am I? I have never counted, but I hope that I am many, and that some of these many selves can immerse themselves in the semi-clear, semi-cloudy vistas of your eyes. And that as we immerse ourselves what all of us will feel is love.' Gerónimo, July 2012.

HER: – *(She re-reads the dedication in silence, on the point of tears.)* How beautiful, my sweet… *(She jumps into his arms and kisses him desperately.)*

HIM: – How pretty you look. Gorgeous! *(He sniffs at her like a bear.)*

HER: – It's because today at last I had a chance to dress up! You've never been here at night before!

HIM: – I love your house at night. And your eyes… they're beautiful at night.

HER: – I've made six kinds of dips: black olive, palm hearts, carrot, a sweet and sour that'll go really well with the meat… umm… avocado, beetroot and my favourite one, which is garlic and parsley.

HIM: – Sounds delicious, sweetie…

HER: – All for my fat little piggy-wiggy. *(She takes off her apron.)* I told a friend of mine exactly what you did to me the other day, Mr piggy-wigg….

HIM: – What?

HER: – You know… that thing with the fingers and the tongue…

HIM: – Ah. You said that if I first licked your *(–)*

HER: *(Putting her hands over her ears.)* – No! No! Don't say it, it's embarrassing!

HIM: – You make me laugh when you do that *(He imitates her)*. You look like the idiot from *There's Something about Mary*, who does it every time he gets nervous.

HER: – Fuck off!

HIM: – No, but I love it. I've always wanted to play a character with some kind of developmental disability. You know like Sean Penn in *I am Sam*, Di Caprio in *What's Eating Gilbert Grape?* Those parts are like Hollywood Oscar gold! Mental disorders really interest me – as long as I'm given free rein of course – and fuck political correctness.

HER: Uff! The creative and phenomenological prison that is political correctness!

HIM: I'm great as the idiot. I can do a really good imitation!

HER: – Go on – show me!

HIM: – No!

HER: – Go on, just a bit!

HIM: – No!

HER: – *(Laughs)* – I remember once that Juan and I, a couple of months before I got pregnant, went up to the doors of the Alvear, Laurie Anderson was playing. She'd come for a theatre festival. A few years back.

HIM: – I saw her, I saw her.

HER: – Well, anyway, the thing was, the tickets had already sold out months ago and an ex-friend of mine had nicked poor Juan's ticket. People didn't know what to do except turn up at the theatre. The queue was massive, it snaked all the way back on itself, they'd put up those stretchy barriers they use for crowd control. Juan, in despair, was watching all the people with tickets happily walking past the ropes, the house was already open, and he was obviously not going to get in. Then we saw a very sorrowful looking woman go by; she was dragging a tiny girl by the hand and carried a sign that read. 'I need a ticket.'

HIM: – No! What a calculating bitch, trying to increase her chances by using the child!

HER: – Yeah, complete bitch. Then I saw Juan's face light up and in the middle of all those people he starts, *(Behaving like someone with a pronounced cognitive-behavioural disorder)* 'Laurie… Laurie Anderson…'

HIM: *(He laughs and starts running through his repertoire of behavioural disorders as he says* 'Laurie... Laurie...Anderson'*)*

HER: – *(Helpless with laughter.)* Yes, just like that. Brilliant!

HIM: – *(Completely taken over by the character.)* 'I want a ticket for Laurie Anderson... Lauri...Anderson...' *(Begging, he tugs at her clothes.)* 'I need to see Laurie...'

HER: *(Helpless with laughter.)* He played it to the hilt, totally despondent and desperate and every time the queue zig-zagged past him, I would see him again, imploring people; he kept it up the whole time, son of a bitch...!

HIM: – 'Laurie! Laurie Anderson! I want a ticket!' *(He runs around the space; perhaps even into the auditorium.)*

HER: – He made me laugh Juan, he was shameless. One of a kind.

HIM: – So why did you separate?

HER: – He has a galloping Peter Pan complex.

HIM: – And didn't you tell me he was half Irish, poor thing? Bloody-minded: resists all forms of psychoanalysis.

HER: – That's one hundred percent imperialist bullshit. The Irish are a spiritual people. Juan's a loser because he's a loser. Well, he loves Tommy in his own way, I don't know... he treats him like an equal, it's as though he were an uncle who comes to visit when he feels like it. He eats everything in the fridge, they go on the Playst...

HIM: – It's good that you allow him to be here in your house, it's good for Tomás... *(He goes over to the laptop.)* Shall we put a song on, sweetheart?

HER: – Whatever you want, my love. I adore the way you express your opinion on how I bring up Tommy... Everything you say, the advice you give me *(–)*

HIM: – I want to see you directing something in the commercial theatre soon, that's my best advice. *(He puts on the Serge Gainsbourg song, 'Je t'aime moi non plus'.)* Enough of all these hippie happenings. I told you I've got a possible actress who would be perfect for your play. She's going out with a producer, he might... well I'm sure he will, put up the readies. Do you like the idea, baby doll?

HER: – Why wouldn't I?

HIM: – Do you want that actress to play you?

HER: – Of course, she's divine! I'm so happy when I feel that you care...

HIM: – My love...

(They kiss. The two ACTOR-STAGEHANDS enter, they turn up the music and 'set' the scene. They help undress the actors, who remain half-dressed and wrapped in a sheet, creating the idea that they have dined and then gone to bed together. The ACTOR-STAGEHANDS exit. The candles remain projected on the backdrop. HIM and HER relax on the bed or in the armchair. He holds her by the waist from behind with his arms and legs wrapped around her. Silent caresses.)

HER: – ...Where are you?

HIM: – Here, my love...

HER: – No. Where are you supposed to be at the moment?

HIM: – Ah. I said I was going to eat with Tadeo after the show, he's depressed because his boyfriend left him.

HER: – Has he really left him?

HIM: – A few months ago now, but he did leave him, yes.

HER: – Aren't you worried it might look suspicious? Eating out so late, I mean?

HIM: – No, no. Tadeo is such a gossip. We can spend hours chatting. I took a huge risk the other day however when we walked hand in hand down Abasto for twenty blocks. And the *sushi* (–)

HER: – Oh yes, the *sushi* bar, that was a bit of a disaster. Those people staring at us had obviously recognised you off the telly,

HIM: – When you are near my need to touch you overwhelms me... I find it difficult to keep my hands off you. I probably shouldn't tell you this (but as I'm an old geezer I don't care, I wouldn't have said it when I was young) but when I'm with you I feel like a dog. *(She laughs.)* Seriously. I follow you like a dog follows its master with its eyes. You are the centre. I don't mind saying it as our relationship's not like that.

HER: – *Au contraire...*!

HIM: When you go to the kitchen or the bathroom, I just stand there completely empty. You are so incredible, so intense, such a treasure trove you are *(–)*

HER: – My darling... I dream that you will truly be my boyfriend and that we can walk everywhere together, and go out... That you can stay the night...

HIM: – I would love to be able to stay over one day...

HER: – And I dream that in the morning we'll wake up together and that the kids, Carrie and Tommy will come to our bed to say hallo...

HIM: – Beautiful... *(He kisses her on her brow.)*

HER: – It's so cool they're almost the same age, isn't it?

HIM: – ...

HER: – When do you move to the new house?

HIM: – I don't know... It's already been delayed by months, a nightmare... now it just needs cleaning. Laura wants to do it herself.

HER: – That's crazy. Why don't you call one of those companies that do an end of project clean-up?

HIM: – End of project clean-up, what's...

HER: – Those firms that send a pair of guys in overalls to your house, they scour everything, vacuum up the dust, scrape off any paint still lurking around on sockets, or glass or in corners. A final clean-up. Since you're well able to afford it they'll sort you out in an instant!

HIM: – I adore the ease with which you say certain things...

HER: – What?

HIM: – Nothing. I love our cultural differences. Let's see that Chinese Astrological thing you wanted me to read.

HER: Oh yes! *(She jumps up. She goes to look for a book and returns to his side.)* It's a bit of a mishmash this book. It borrows so much from other works, that occasionally whole paragraphs appear that quite by chance are true. *(She gives him the book, open at a particular page.)* Here it is.

HIM: *(Reads.)* – 'Dragons tend to become obsessed with other dragons; they put them on a pedestal and refuse to accept the reality of the situation.' I told you I was an obsession of yours.

HER: – No you're not. Go on.

HIM: 'A relationship between a Fire Dragon and a Wood Dragon can prove fatal for the wood element…'

HER: – You're going to burn with my love, baby. *(She kisses his neck and his face, tenderly and very noisily.)* I'm going gobble you all up…

HIM: – All these kilos, seriously?

HER: – Were you a fat as a kid?

HIM: Yes.

HER: – What a bummer…

HIM: – Yeah. I paid a high price in primary school. Always on my own. Huh! I got together with the other unpopular kids like me. The weak and the lame. I was always a herd animal. Grubbing around in the mud.

HER: – Sweetheart…

HIM: – That's why I like being interviewed. Doing television is a way of saying to the world 'Hey, look, the little fat boy made it' …

HER: – I love you. You won't let yourself love me, but I love you.

HIM: – What do you mean I won't let myself? I let myself every day. I carry it with me everywhere. I love you all the time!

HER: – I dread the thought of summer.

HIM: – Baby…

HER: – It's like a barrier that's there, a line that's getting closer every day. I'm going to take a plane and fly to my house in Córdoba and I'm not going to see you for two whole months.

And that will give us a major opportunity to leave each other. It has to be. I can't go on suffering like this next year, Gero *(–)*

HIM: – But it's still ages until summer, sweetie… who knows what might happen to you in the next four months?

HER: – What could happen? You're never going to get a separation. You've told me that so many times. If I at least had that assurance, even if it wasn't for a few years, at least then *(–)*

HIM: – I would never give you that assurance. Those guys who keep a woman hanging on, counting the hours for a day that will never come… they're miserable creatures… I don't want to give you false hope, my love. Let's enjoy what we have. That's what life is, moments, nothing more. Yes, baby doll?

HER: – Give me your hand. I want to read your palm.

HIM: *(Holding out his hand.)* – Are you going to treat me like that dimwit on the train?

HER: – I read his present, for you… *(Reading his palm.)* Aha! Near future. It says here that in a little over two months it will be your birthday…

HIM: – That's right.

HER: – And it says we're going to spend it together.

HIM: – Look…

HER: – Yes. You are going to spend the first few minutes of your birthday with me… It says here it's going to be wonderful. Mmm, it seems that on that very day I will have been to see you in the play that you will have have recently premiered in one of the big theatres on Corrientes!

HIM: – A scary prospect, I know you'll be critical. 'Very commercial, Very commercial…'

HER: – We will have just eaten a delicious little appetiser that I made for you… *(She gets up and exits. From off.)* The play was very commercial, but you were amazing, love!

HIM: – I enjoyed that *brie,* it was perfect, very *(–)*

HER: *(From off.)* – I took it out of the fridge before leaving to see your play so we could eat it runny and at room temperature!

(She sticks her head in.) You are a fermentation zone! *(Exits.)* Is it starting?

HIM: *(Looking at what would be a television set.)* Nearly, hey! Come on, come and see him make his entrance! *(Laughs.)* He's the greatest, Martinez!

HER: *(From off.)* – I love him! Dad and I have followed him for ages, we adore him. It's lucky that you wanted to watch it too, sweetheart...

HIM: – Of course I did, are you kidding me?!

HER: *(She enters with a cup cake decorated with a candle and a tiny porcelain figurine. The figurine is a 'pin-up girl' that looks like HER.)* 'Happy birthday to you/ happy birthday to you/ happy birthday-hurry-up-and-discover-that-your-marriage-can't-be-mended-so-you-need-to-get-a-separation-and-move-in-at-last-with-meeeeeee/ Happy birthday to you...' You have three wishes!

HIM: *(He makes the wishes and blows the candle out in silence)* – This figurine looks like you...

HER: – That was the idea. The cup-cake is passionfruit. It's small because of your diet. Look: he's making his entrance!

HIM: – The full performance!

HER: – And the singer from Calle 13, amazing!

HIM: – He's smiling the sonofabitch, even though the crowd is against him!

HER: – Is it nerves making him laugh?

HIM: – No! He's full of confidence, hyped up! His last fight was against an Irish guy on Saint Patrick's Day and he was happy!

HER: – He's a master!

HIM: – And this is against a Mexican on Mexican Independence Day.

HER: – Oh my God, what an occasion! I'm scared of the other guy!

HIM: – Twenty-four fights in a row, Chavez.

HER: – How come they're in the same category? He looks so much smaller.

HIM: – He's actually taller, and I read, after the weigh-in, that he's got some brutal recovery techniques. But Maravilla's arms are six centimetres longer, look.

HER: – What do you reckon, babe? Who's going to win?

HIM: – It all depends on the first round, I'll tell you after it finishes, sweetie. *(Patting the chair.)* Come here baby and sit next to me so that I can kiss you from time to time.

HER: *(She takes away a glass that he is holding, which he has recently drained of beer or champagne, and places it on the table, she pops a piece of cupcake into his mouth. He chews it distractedly. She takes his hand, kisses it and continues reading his palm.)* And that is how you will spend the first few minutes of your birthday, my love: watching a fight with an extraordinary ending.

HIM: – Which I, obviously, will have predicted. I like how you read the future. Where did you learn it?

HER: – It comes to me intuitively. Like the end of a project.

HIM: – That cleaning company you were telling me about?

HER: – No you numbskull, the ending of one of my plays. They arrive without warning, and when they do, they're irreversible.

HIM: – Spooky! *(Holding out his hand.)* What else does it say about my birthday?

HER: *(Reads.)* – That the last round will be extraordinary, that *(–)*

HIM: – *(Jumping up from the chair.)* Oh, no, he's down, he's down! He's down, oh no! Get up you motherfucker, get the fuck up! Look, he fell… he slipped. The ref isn't counting it. He's up… Come on, come on! Get those punches in, nooo…!

HER: *(To herself.)* – I will be thinking that this is the first thing we've done together that isn't talking, fucking or eating *(–)*

HIM: – Look: he's destroying him, he's a hero, a legend! He's destroying him! *(–)*

HER: – … I feel so complete when I'm with you *(–)*

HIM: – Hit him, hit him, hit him Sergio, hit him! *(–)*

HER: – As if my whole life had been a rehearsal to prepare me for this love *(–)*

HIM: Hey! He can't lose the fight, for a fall, he can't lose the fight! For one fucking fall, arseholes!

HER: – I will think that natural forces bring us together, that our destiny is *(–)*

HIM: – Those motherfuckers have to give it to him!

HER: – *(She leaps up.)* – Of course, my love! *(To the imaginary television.)* Give the fight to Martinez you fucking Yanks!

HIM: – Yankee motherfuckers!

HER: Viva Perón, damn it!

> *(They laugh. They high five. The following text messages are projected onto the backdrop:*
>
> – 'Tonight, we lived something close to happiness. You are my sunshine, baby.'
>
> – 'I'm still using the messages we sent each other to write the play, my love. Sometimes that makes it more difficult for me than you can imagine.')*

THE WOODLAND GROVE AGAIN

HER: *(Sitting at her laptop writing; she says the words she types which are projected.)* – I am having what writers call a 'block'. This never usually happens to me; it must be because I'm really ashamed to relate the even *(She crosses out 'the even')* the contents of the events that follow. *(She opens the photo of the woodland grove from Scene 1. It is projected. She doesn't write now. She speaks.)* I am in the Woodland Grove and his phone call has unleashed a vast slew of emotions. White butterflies, unfurl my wings, etc. There is an overwhelming sensation that total happiness is real, and it is ours. 'Ours'. 'Us'. It's really happening; there exists an 'us'.

HIM: – I told her that I was dying to have her by my side, that she should be the woman who moved with me to this house *(–)*

HER: – My dreams were fed by the echo of his words for days *(–)*

HIM: – You are my love, *you* are my woman and I want us to be together, my Sunshine *(–)*

HER: *(Verbal diarrhoea, rapidly.)* Text messages come and go like crazy. They arrive at all hours of the day and night. Our future together is populated by ever more blissful scenes.

(The following messages are projected onto the screen at great speed, one after the other, over the woodland: 'Imagine us walking down the street, hand in hand, darling.' 'I can't wait for us to be in a night club, smooching to our heart's content, baby.' 'Holding each other all night long', 'One day we'll go to Disney World with Carrie and Tommy, the four of us, my love!'*)*

HER: (That last one was mine: 'go to Disney World' *(Laughs.)* What a ridiculously bourgeois thing to say…*)* I think giving Tommy and Carrie a sibling was something that we'd both secretly wanted. *(Pause.)* I confess that I'd even dreamt we'd have a child together, Gero and I. A baby of our own. *(Pause. She imagines or remembers something.)* That summer passed in a fever of happiness. *(She breathes, gathers her strength to continue, rapidly,)* I finish writing the first version of the play, basically scenes from our life during the past year. I am in Córdoba, Gero in Buenos Aires. Two whole months without seeing each other it would have been, but halfway through, he invents a glorious lie to keep his wife happy *(–)*

HIM: – Filming in Córdoba for an overseas commercial, I told her.

HER: – He's going to come and spend a whole afternoon with me. We agree to meet in a small country hotel *(–)*

HIM: – I want to see her so much. I'm scared too. Since I promised her at Christmas that I would leave Laura, the pure blood of anxiety has been racing through my head. Nightmarish phantoms hover over my skull. The thought of telling my daughter that I'm going to live in another house petrifies me. I feel sorry for my wife, I love her like a sister. She's tenacious, it distresses me to think of her *(–)*

HER: – I condition my hair and cut off the split-ends, I paint my toes, I sunbathe and get a tan. I make myself lovely for him. My heart beats wildly as I wait for him where we agreed to meet. I get there first.

HIM: – We have just moved into a beautiful house that has taken us years to complete and now I will have to go out and find what will probably be a dark, damp flat to rent, so that I can be near my daughter? ... Something doesn't add up.

HER: – Gero and I will make love for the first time knowing that we want to spend the rest of our lives together. I never got married, so I lived that encounter as though it were our wedding night. Well, a 'wedding siesta" it would be, really...

HIM: – When I saw her again, I couldn't believe how lovely she was. Bronzed and radiant. We went into the bedroom, we talked, and we kissed. Something feels right when we're together. As well as the pure animal eroticism that we have between us, there is also a deep love that flows around us. And we have such fun. She is like a mirror in which I see myself aroused, and I am like the sun before her eyes.

HER: – We both cried with love, I remember...

HIM: – Any doubts I brought with me disappeared completely during that siesta.

HER: – My happiness depends on you my darling, I told him. We said goodbye.

HIM: – See you in a month, my love. Don't cry baby, soon we will be together...

HER: – The illusion lasted almost until my return to Buenos Aires.

HIM: – Almost.

HER: – Three weeks of messages, dreams, calls and love flew by. Just four days left until we would see each other again. I am flicking through a gossip magazine while I'm waiting to be seen at the waxing salon (I want to be smooth for him) and then it happens: I see an interview with my love, from just a few days previously. It was immediate. The article, his words, what he said about the plans he and his wife had for the coming year. I felt stabbed in the back. I knew. I knew then and there that Gerónimo wasn't thinking of leaving his wife. My whole world collapses.

(The trees in the woodland photo start to rain little red drops which increase to until they become a down pour. The whole screen goes red.)

HER: – This heartbreak has so much of me in it. He will not be able to contain me. I will not be able to contain myself either.

(The scarlet screen explodes and breaks like glass, making a tremendous noise. The pieces fall, the screen goes completely black for the first time.)

A KIND OF THERAPY.

(The ACTOR-STAGEHANDS enter and place the armchair where HIM and HER are sitting centre stage and facing the audience who will represent the therapist to whom they are speaking. She cries like a child, there is a large box of tissues which she uses to dry her tears.

HIM: – I am so, so sorry. Forgive me, I beg of you. Please, please don't cry any more.

HER: – Why can't you be truthful? Why don't you value our love?

HIM: – Because it's not just our love, sweetheart. I have to think about other things as well, things that are just as important as our love. I'm not an eighteen-year-old boy, you know, I've got a daughter who *(–)*

HER: – You could still be an excellent father. Ninety-five percent of people *(–)*

HIM: – I am not ninety-five percent of people.

HER: But what are you teaching your daughter about *love*, Gero? What will it mean to her when she grows up and finds a partner: someone by her side who doesn't desire her?

HIM: – ...

HER: – Do you want her to grow up thinking that all women are bitter and cheated on, like her mother?

HIM: – Laura is not cheated-on.

HER: Sorry?! You've been cheating on her for years? Or do you think that because all those girls meant nothing to you, she doesn't *(–)*

HIM: – Stop it, Maria Sol, that's enough. I've got other things going on as well, dammit!

HER: – What things, Gerónimo?

HIM: – Some situations of mine, that I have to sort out...

HER: – ...

HIM: – I'm worried about not living with my daughter every day and that the same thing will happen with you that seems to happen with all my partners – our love will grow stale; everything will become routine and our sex life will suffer.

HER: – Oh don't talk crap! If we were truly together, we would have a huge amount of resilience and you know it.

HIM: – I've just moved house, my daughter seems so happy, I want to spend time with her there, making her toasties, rearing little terrapins together *(–)*

HER: – Well you should have thought about the little terrapins *before* you told me you were going to leave your wife, Gerónimo!

HIM: Yes, you're right there. I'm a horrible person, forgive me.

HER: – You did it because you saw that I'd stopped communicating with you, you did it to keep hold of me! The summer was my only chance to leave you and you knew it. Instead of which I spent it planning to be with you. Someone like me *doesn't have what it takes* to get over a trauma like this. Are you aware of that?

HIM: – And it was true, she didn't. She had clung on so strongly to the idea of being together that she felt that her life was over now all hope was gone. She cries for hours in front of her son. She can't help it. I try to explain to her that despite not being able *(–)*

HER: – Not wanting.

HIM: – ... Neither wanting nor being able to ask for a separation, I am still in love with her. That I truly want us to find a way to be together, because I miss her, and I need her.

HER: – The way that he wants to find is to fuck me once a week, avoid phone calls and have a minimal exchange of texts to avoid a repetition of last year *(–)*

HIM: – I don't want to lose her *(–)*

HER: – Or rather Gerónimo wants to bend me to his will and make me fit in with his needs, his time and his plans.

HIM: – I don't want to lose her because I love her. She cries floods of tears every day for twenty days in a row. We see each other a couple of times. It's incredible, when we're screwing it's just love and tenderness, but outside of that it's hell. She suffers, doesn't eat, loses weight. I feel like a total shit. She was such a happy girl when I met her,

HER: – One day he comes and says to me.

HIM: – You've got to move on, I told her. Get away from this place of pain, sweetheart. Look for alternatives my love. See other people for example, I don't know...

HER: – Last year he nearly died from a fit of jealousy because I went out one night with a boy I liked. I had to cut the date short and run home to chat with him online. And now Gerónimo is telling me to sleep with other people. Perfect.

HIM: – She tells me a couple of days later that she's going to see an ex-lover.

HER: – Nacho

HIM: – Nacho had always been affectionate with her. They hadn't seen each other for nearly a year, ever since Maria Sol had fallen in love with me. The third or fourth time we fucked, more or less. I knew about the guy. Keen, she said. 'To screw her, Gerónimo', I thought.

HER: – I didn't want to go to bed with anyone else. I only wanted Gero. I wanted to be yours alone.

HIM: – Yes, I know, my love...

(They look at each other. Then they look out front for a few seconds, pensive, empty.)

HIM: – Maria Sol and Nacho agreed to have dinner at hers. I could hardly sleep that night, I imagined her in bed with a man who's probably bigger than me. I see her the next day. She needs to share with me some of the things she felt, she says.

HER: – It was so lovely to see him, we hugged for a long time when he arrived, I felt him close to me. We talked, I told him why I was so sad – I didn't tell him who you are, I kept your identity a secret – don't worry *(–)*

HIM: – That's good.

HER: We had a great time at dinner. He said the weight loss suited me. It was getting late by then. My evident distress obviously meant that he was unlikely to try it on with me and I wasn't about to seduce him either. I needed to say to him: 'I have to go to bed with you because the man that I love, thinks that if I do, it will help me cope better in my relationship with him *(–)*

HIM: – But I didn't ask you to *(–)*

HER: – Yes you did! I felt uncomfortable so I dithered but finally I suggested it. He looked at me so tenderly and said, of course, he would be there for me whenever I needed him.

HIM: – A friend indeed...

HER: – So we went to my room.

HIM: – And?

HER: – It was strange. Different.

HIM: – In what way *different?*

HER: – He started by kissing me for a long time on my neck and the nape of my neck as he undid the buttons of my blouse. He played with the lace edging on my panties. I really felt like crying at that point and then I saw you. Literally I mean. You were there, at my side, my love... It was as though what was happening formed part of you and me, rather than him and me, understand?

HIM;– ...

HER: – I got even sadder seeing you there, looking at me. At the same time, I could tell that he was getting really turned on and that turned me on too, a bit and *(–)*

HIM: – Did he lick your pussy *(–)*

HER: – No, I didn't want that.

HIM: – And did you give him *(–)*

HER: – Not that either,

HIM: – Did he finger you?

HER: – ...

HIM: – So, you didn't suck him off and he didn't finger you, you were saying…

HER: – Yes. He fingered me, and it was very nice.

HIM: – Look…

HER: – Then we screwed, me on top. And then instead of feeling you were at my side when I looked at him directly, I saw you. Your face appeared to me the entire time. I closed my eyes and the only thing I felt was that I was missing – desperately – was your way of grabbing me by the hips. I asked him to stop. I couldn't go on, by that time I was completely overcome with weeping.

HIM: And afterwards…? Will you see each other again or *(–)*?

HER: – Afterwards, nothing. Nacho is the perfect gentleman. He covered me with the sheet, he brought me a glass of water. He sat down by my side and stroked my hair until I stopped crying. Then he left.

HIM: – I look at her.

HER: – He looks at me.

HIM: – And I say. It's a half romantic, half adolescent tale; a little bit sad, a little bit sexy, rather pathetic, very human and above all it has, deep down, what seems to me a fundamental message: the other is a part of me.

HER: – That's what he said to me *(–)*

HIM: – I am part of her, and she is part of me.

HER: – As though he were giving me feedback on the theme of a play or something like that.

HIM: – Deep down I wanted to kill myself. To punch a hole in the wall. I had to hold the rage in and push it right back down. I don't want to share her with other people, that's obvious, but what the fuck can I do… Tell her to be faithful? *(–)*

HER: – As though he were my analyst or something…

HIM: – What right did I have to make demands… It hurts like a dagger to my heart, but I swallow my pain as I deserve to.

HER: – Completely indifferent.

HIM: – She accuses me of ordering her to fuck someone else as a way of distancing myself. She yells that she will not accept the scraps of just two hours a week with me. She insults me, she humiliates me, she threatens me. We stop seeing each other. Some weeks later, tired of missing me, she calls. I am happy. I had been suffering like crazy. In order that she knows she is important to me and that I adore her, I decide to ask her something.

HER: – He tells me that his wife and daughter will be away for the weekend and he asks me if I would like to see his house *(She looks at him.)* What, and you want me to sleep there?

HIM: – Of course, sweetheart. Or if not, come and see it and afterwards we'll go and find a hotel room nearby…

HER: – I told him that yes, I would go and yes, I would sleep there. I think that somewhere in my idiot brain I thought that when he saw me in the setting of his house the 'Christmas plan would re-materialise', if you like. That seeing his little mouse walking around the kitchen, the garden or the terrace would touch his heartstrings. Perhaps he would again realise that his world can't be complete without me, I thought, and then he would hasten to do the right thing, which is to be with me, because I am his love, his 'one true love', as he has said so many times.

HIM: – After my show was over, I went to collect her, and I took her home. Her kid was staying at his father's, so we had the night and the whole of the next day to ourselves.

HER: – He had told me that he was going to make me a roast dinner.

HIM: – We arrive at the house, I open the door, I am nervous. In you go, sweetheart, I say.

HER: – I regretted it the moment I entered.

HIM: – I switch on all the lights. I chose all the appliances myself and I want her to see how beautiful the house is when it's lit up. She is silent.

HER: – I felt breathless and I couldn't bring myself to look.

HIM: – She kept her head down, she was adjusting the bow of a ribbon on her dress. That seemed to be more important to her than looking round my house. It was a couple of minutes before she raised her head.

HER: – He was everywhere at once, running up and down stairs, arranging things. He moved rapidly around the house. Living-dining room, the bedrooms, spaces, wide passageways. It's modern and made of good quality materials. It's lovely, but that wasn't what got to me.

HIM: – I'm so pleased that you've come, my love, even though it might be difficult for you. Because my houses have always been well thought out by me – especially this one – and I think that by getting to know it you will know me better too.

HER:- To see the little domestic details, signs of his other life, the real one, the one that doesn't include me, was what tore my soul; dirty plates in one of the sinks, his daughter's toys scattered around the living-room, he and his wife's toiletries all around the basin in their en-suite bathroom. I managed to say 'your house is lovely' in a small voice.

HIM: – We have something to eat. Maria Sol is quiet. She drinks a lot of wine. Later I am waiting for her in the bed. She brushes her teeth and comes over. I watch her get undressed and leave her turquoise sundress on Laura's chair.

HER: – Her bedside table is crowded with the latest books and some horrible bracelets, so I don't take off my rings. I sit on the edge of the bed with my back to him. I imagine them doing this every night. One already in bed waiting for the other one to get in and go to sleep.

HIM: – She had her sky-blue panties and was naked. So fragile… She stayed sitting there a moment. I couldn't see her face but as her breathing was slow, I knew that she was sad. I caressed her.

HER: – He began to rub my back, as though consoling me. In a paternal tone, he said 'What's wrong, little one…' *(–)*

HIM: – What's wrong, little one, I said.

HER: 'What's wrong, baby girl. Would you like to live in a house like this with me, is that what you want, my love?'

HIM: – She burst into tears. Yes, she said. Yes. I want to live in a house like this with you. She repeated it over and over. I grabbed hold of her and put her into bed. She curled up and cried into my neck. I felt so sorry for her.

HER: – Later that night, as we were making love, she asked me to move a door with a full-length mirror on it so that she could see me.

HIM: – Her on top of me, climaxing, will be the sweetest sight that mirror has ever witnessed in its life.

HER: – That was very poetic, what you just said...

HIM: – Will you use it in your play as well?

HER: – Do you mind?

HIM: – I don't really like to see my most intimate moments on stage...

HER: – But I wrote it for you... It's the last thing that we have together. I made Gerónimo multi-faceted, which is what you wanted, not just one *(–)*

HIM: – I know. But I don't need your writing now.

HER: – But isn't that what you came to find in me? Didn't you tell me that you wanted to return to poetry, Gero?

HIM: – ...

HER: – *(Disillusioned.)* – With you I felt, for the first time, something very close to what I had always imagined love to be. But the cost is too high. Bringing me to your house, pushing me to go out with other people, wanting to hang on to me at all costs knowing full well that you will never *(–)*

HIM: – But, little mouse...Why aren't you more intelligent about life? Don't you realise that I did it for us as well? The passion will always be here, in its entirety, to fill us both. We will always miss each other, always find each other, always desire each other *(–)*

HER: – Always be adrift, you mean...

HIM: – But being adrift can be beautiful and truthful. Being adrift in the present can be our own eternity my darling. What does love need to stay alive: a roof, projects, lines that lead towards the future, plans?...

HER: – And when I miss you and need you. When I feel alone, and you are far away?

HIM: – You could wake up next to me every morning of your life and still feel that I am far away.

HER: – ...

HIM: – We're all alone, baby. There's no need to be scared.

HER: – No *(Cries.)* It can't end like this. I am too miserable like this.

HIM: – She was right. The dreams of a little mouse cannot end like this. So, I had to make it possible for her to leave. She shouted, cried, suffered and made me suffer for a while too – I went with her as far as I could – but in the end she left. Without Facebook, without messages, threats or songs.

HER: – *(Sitting in front of her laptop.)* I can't live my life crying in front of my son. Not even for a love like his.

HIM: – She left for good. As she had always known she would.

END OF PLAY

HER: *(Writes.)* Dreams and poetry do not end this way.

(She puts on a song. It is subtitled. It is 'After Hours' by Velvet Underground. She exits the two ACTOR-STAGEHANDS enter to do a final clean. A complete clean-up. They take all the scenery, the furniture and props. They vacuum up the tissues that are scattered around the stage. They sweep. They disconnect the lap-top and the screen suddenly turns itself off. An empty space. He has been watching them strip the stage and has had to move around awkwardly to let them do it. He is on his own. They have given him a black raincoat. He puts it on. The ACTOR-STAGEHANDS use two hoses to make a light rain shower on the stage.

HER: *(She enters wearing a beige raincoat and carrying a colourful umbrella.)* One day, some years later, I will walk right past you. You will be distracted, taking cover somewhere, waiting for the last drops of rain to stop falling. Standing beside the door of a cinema or coming out of a restaurant. Your family will be nearby, around and about. Our eyes meet,

HIM: – ...

HER: – My heart stops for an instant.

HIM: – And mine. Obeying an unstoppable impulse, I go towards her.

HER: – You stutter.

HIM: – Hi, Sol.

HER: – Hi, Gero. How are you?

HIM: – Good… I'm good. You?

HER: – Good.

HIM: – Your son?

HER: – Amazing, very tall, blue belt in karate, moving up to sixth grade already. And Carrie?

HIM: – Fine, fantastic. She's that young lady over there, splashing around with that brown dog on the corner.

HER: – She's so pretty. Is she already in secondary?… Beautiful.

HIM: – It's crazy that we haven't run into each other for so long isn't it?!

HER: – Yes, well. I never… Anyway, after putting on a couple more plays, I decided to return to Córdoba, I don't know if you knew that?

HIM: – Yes.

HER: – I'm in the mountains. I took up philosophy again. I'm peaceful and content, doing a doctorate.

HIM: – Well, that's great… *(He wants to say something but doesn't.)*

HER: – Yes. You well?

HIM: – …

HER: – They gave you that award. I saw it on the telly, best leading actor, about time. I'm happy that you got it, well deserved.

HIM: – Did you see the play?

HER: – No, no I couldn't. I'm so rarely in Buenos Aires these days. However, I say well deserved because you were always an excellent actor within your little bubble.

HIM: – Little bubble… Anyway, these things aren't important… Awards I mean. You look really lovely.

HER: – He smiled. Polite assent holding his gaze.

HIM: – I wanted to ask her if she was staying in the city for a few days, if perhaps she would like to meet for coffee, but *(–)*

HER: – I have to go…

HIM: – We said goodbye courteously and with good wishes.

HER: – I will walk away making sure my lungs are filled with air. I will quicken my step.

HIM: – She walks away. She goes.

HER: – I don't want to look back.

HIM: – I do. I will see that image of you leaving, over and over again. You leave. The sun comes out just as you turn the corner. You lower your umbrella and throw your head back slightly. You don't look at me again. It is she who is walking away, my darling, my baby, my Sunshine. It is she, the little mouse, that I loved. And this image of her lights up from time to time, it will insist on lighting itself up. And it is always fleeting, and it moves around a little and its visits are smooth and clean, but they don't linger. And time cannot reach her. And our naked bodies, her eyes and mine, her skin and my hands come back to me like an image of intense light, orange, green, golden and blue that wants to live on forever. And I keep on going. Each day I keep on going. Burning like the remains of a Wood Dragon, scorched by the intense heat of Dragon Fire.

(The words 'The End' from the Word file are projected onto the screen, just as they were in the first scene. Then, the asterisk that is inserted can be seen and the disclaimer below being written across the screen.)

THE END*

Other Anthologies by Oberon Books

**The Oberon Anthology of
Contemporary American Plays: Volume One**
9781849431538

**The Oberon Anthology of
Contemporary American Plays: Volume Two**
9781786823205

**The Oberon Anthology
of Contemporary French Plays**
9781786820723

**The Oberon Anthology
of Contemporary Greek Plays**
9781783197675

**The Oberon Anthology
of Contemporary Norwegian Plays**
9781786826978

**The Oberon Anthology
of Contemporary Spanish Plays**
9781786825827

**The Oberon Anthology
of Contemporary Irish Plays**
9781849433914

WWW.OBERONBOOKS.COM

Follow us on Twitter @oberonbooks
& Facebook @OberonBooksLondon

www.ingramcontent.com/pod-product-compliance
Ingram Content Group UK Ltd.
Pitfield, Milton Keynes, MK11 3LW, UK
UKHW020717280225
455688UK00012B/402